"Performance management," "organizational behavior," and "stakeholder management" are well established in the academic world as well as in business practice. Frank has integrated these principles into a comprehensive "Performance Leadership" approach. By doing so, he conveys a lively coverage of essential ideas and examples of ways to improve performance.

–Dr. Frank Jaenicke, Group Vice President MIS,
Group Planning and Controlling, ABB

Frank Buytendijk has written something important. Not only has he established the methodology for successful performance leadership, but he's established the measurements that are part and parcel of a truly authentic organization. Authenticity is the contemporary basis for customer trust, and building that kind of organization is a vital must-do in the 21st-century world of business. Frank Buytendijk has written the organizational blueprint for doing just that.

–Paul Greenberg, President of The 56 Group, Executive Vice President
for the CRM Association, Author of *CRM at the Speed of Light*

Performance management also has a "dark side." Insufficient attention to the behavioral aspects of measurement systems will create all sorts of unintended consequences, often actually damaging to the business, leaving well-meaning managers in confusion or frustration. Building on a comprehensive theoretical foundation, combined with illustrative real-life examples, Frank Buytendijk provides an innovative approach that combines the "numbers" and the "people" aspects into true "Performance Leadership."

–Torsten Ecke, Chief Information Officer, E.ON AG

We've all been subjected to leaders who forced the seemingly simple concept of performance management on an organization with some positive results and usually some unexpected negative outcomes. *Performance Leadership* adds in a human component not previously explored. Understanding how to measure and how to manage the human-social reaction yields the potential for real leadership and performance. Frank Buytendijk, through his own experiences and good research, brings together all the aspects in a book with real-world practical applications.

–Michael D. Fleisher, Executive Vice President and
Chief Financial Officer, Warner Music Group

This is not a book about the traditional top-down performance management. *Performance Leadership* takes a more horizontal, process-oriented approach. This really drives the improvement of the performance of companies. What you measure is what you get. Therefore, Frank proposes to measure collaboration between the silos in companies. I love it! From my point of view an unconventional approach and a must-read for business managers, CFOs, and CIOs!

–Gerben Otter, SVP and CIO of the Adidas Group

Unlike anyone else I know, Frank approaches performance management with a fresh and unique perspective. His genuine connection with people and his sincere desire to show them a "better way" make this book especially valuable. Unlike most books on the subject, Frank doesn't try to reaffirm all that came before. He's willing to speak the "truth" and challenge "conventional wisdom." He does all of this with a style that is readable, witty, and entertaining. I recommend reading Frank's book first—before all other books on the subject—to put them in the right context.

> –Howard Dresner, father of business intelligence, industry consultant, and author of *The Performance Management Revolution*

In order to succeed in the future there is one criterion that overshadows everything else: Understanding people! It is daring and challenging to thrust oneself into the jungle of human behavior in the modern organization. Frank shows us how to grow, from just knowing where to go to how to do the right thing. Through this approach Frank gives us the most fundamental quality, which a leader of today must possess: a vision for a new common sense of what the future will bring, the tools to find our shared mindset, and ability to build what the world demands the most today—a better and more meaningful tomorrow.

> –Anne Skare Nielsen, chief futurist and partner, Future Navigator

Early prospectors in the Wild West would say, "There's gold in them thar hills" and then had the pioneering courage to exploit and lay foundations for a new world. Frank Buytendijk has clearly done a lot of prospecting research. *Performance Leadership* provides business leaders with a map and compass to help us ensure we are in the right hills, with a strong chance of finding those essential nuggets.

> –Mandeep Hansra, Head of BI Strategy and Systems, BT Group Finance

Moving beyond performance management to performance leadership, Frank Buytendijk's book clearly articulates the role of and need for performance leadership. An incredibly useful guide to improving your organization's performance

> –Professor Andy Neely, Director of Research, Cranfield School of Management, author of *The Performance Prism*

PERFORMANCE

Leadership

*The Next Practices
to Motivate Your People,
Align Stakeholders, and
Lead Your Industry*

FRANK BUYTENDIJK

New York   Chicago   San Francisco   Lisbon   London   Madrid
Mexico City   Milan   Montreal   New Delhi   San Juan
Seoul   Singapore   Sydney   Toronto

The McGraw·Hill Companies

Copyright © 2009 by Frank Buytendijk. All rights reserved. Printed in the United States of America. Except as permitted under the United States Copyright Act of 1976, no part of this publication may be reproduced or distributed in any form or by any means, or stored in a data base or retrieval system, without prior written permission of the publisher.

1 2 3 4 5 6 7 8 9 0   DOC/DOC   0 1 0 9 8

ISBN: 978-0-07-159964-1
MHID: 0-07-159964-9

McGraw-Hill books are available at special quantity discounts to use as premiums and sales promotions, or for use in corporate training programs. To contact a representative, please visit the Contact Us pages at www.mhprofessional.com.

This book is printed on acid-free paper.

To my wife Alexandra, for her wisdom, faith, and support.

To my children, Casper and Rosaly, who taught me that often questions are more interesting than answers.

And to baby Emilie, for the potential she represents.

CONTENTS

ACKNOWLEDGMENTS

Writing a book that challenges conventional wisdom and tries to come up with original solutions and viewpoints is a lonely exercise. However, all of the content is deeply grounded in practice, and I have worked with many people: brainstorming, validating ideas, sharpening them. Many have been a true inspiration. This book's journey started with a conversation with Christa Hörchner, who introduced me to Stephen Covey's four dimensions of personal development. It occurred to me that these four dimensions could be applied to organizations as well, and this insight completely changed my idea of performance management, ultimately leading to much of the content of this book.

I also need to thank many of my colleagues. Particularly the years I spent with Gartner, lastly as Research Vice President, have had a massive influence on my own professional development. At Gartner, my managers, Regina Casonato, Joel Wecksell, and Alexander Drobik, always supported my out-of-the-box research projects that have taught me analytical and contrarian thinking. I have very much enjoyed the lively debates around these topics with many colleagues in the Gartner research community. However, I would like to highlight Andreas Bitterer, Ted Friedman, Lee Geishecker, and Nigel Rayner. Special thanks go to Howard Dresner, who has been a great mentor, first at Gartner, later at Hyperion Solutions. At Oracle, where I now hold the position of Vice President of Enterprise Performance Management Strategy, the support of John Kopcke, Senior Vice President, has been invaluable in making this book a reality. I would also like to thank my colleague and friend Thomas Oestreich, not only for his review and comments, but also for his contributions and passionate discussions.

I have had support from the academic side as well. In particular, Professor Ed Peelen of Nyenrode Universiteit helped me to find the right path multiple times. I would also like to thank Professor André de Waal of the Maastricht School of Management for the many times he encouraged me over the years, as well as Professors Thomas Malone (MIT) and Andy Neely (Cranfield University) for their few subtle but crucial advice and encouragement. Bernard Marr, the author of the book *Strategic Performance Management*, was an inspiration as a brainstorm partner.

Theory is only useful if it can be turned into practice. I am very thankful for the time that many have spent describing the success they've had in their companies and their willingness to discuss the ideas in the book. In particular, Wouter van Aerle, Leon van Bakel, and Egbert Dijkstra of Ahold, Eric van der Wolk of BCE Entrepreneurs, Mandeep Hansra of British Telecom, Wessel Berkman of Brown Paper Company, Sebastiaan Hooft of CentralPoint, George Steltman and Rutger van den Berg of Deloitte, Ulrich Coenen of E-Plus, Oliver Germer of Germer Consulting, Cok van Boheemen of Heineken, Martin Vonk of ING Direct, Jani Rautiainen of Metso Corporation, Rik Op den Brouw of Rabobank, as well as the people whose names I can't mention as their contributions were made on condition of anonymity. I've been broadly testing a lot of material in this book in workshops worldwide, from the United States to all over Europe and South Africa. I would like to thank all the participants in these workshops for their feedback and contributions. Many of their examples are now part of the book.

A big thank you to my editor Lauren Lynch of McGraw-Hill, who has been enthusiastic from the start. Lauren, you really know how to deal with the fragile souls of your authors!

But mostly, I would like to thank you, my reader. First, for picking up this book. I hope you will enjoy it. But thank you even more if you visit the Web site, www.performance-leadership-book.com, and leave your comments behind. Please share your experiences on how performance management has—or hasn't—been working in your organization.

Frank Buytendijk
The Netherlands, 2008
f.a.buytendijk@planet.nl
www.performance-leadership-book.com

INTRODUCTION

Why do so many balanced scorecard projects fail? Why are there are so many political budget games? Why are most performance management implementations tactical and fragmented of nature, and why do managers not see the big picture? How come managers treat information as a source of power to be protected, instead of an asset to be exploited? Why do managers still ask for better information when there are thousands of reports available?

As a systems implementation consultant, project manager, management consultant, manager, research analyst, and strategist, I have spent all of my working life asking myself those very same questions many times. For a long time, I thought the answer was "politics" and "bad people" displaying opportunistic behavior or simply not understanding what was good for them. It has only been in the past several years that I have come to understand that it's not bad people, but rather bad management information and bad management processes that drive the bad, or at least immature, behaviors. This leads to the next logical question, what is a better way of managing performance?

Most of the literature, papers, and field experiences describe "best practices" by stating how things are, rather than by asking how performance could be, or even should be. In my quest I have chosen to challenge these best practices by using a simple philosophy: Every best practice has a dominant disadvantage. If we turn the best practice around into the opposite approach, the opposite approach obviously has a dominant disadvantage as well. If this new, opposite disadvantage is less of a disadvantage, we win something—a better way of doing things. And it it turns out to be an even bigger disadvantage, we win again; we have confirmed the best practice. Let's use an example: One best practice states that every performance indicator should have a single owner who is accountable for the results. The dominant disadvantage is sub-optimal results. Managers optimize the resources at their disposal to maximize the output on their performance indicators only. Now let's examine what happens if some key performance indicators are owned by two owners. The advantage is that they are driven toward collaboration, as neither manager can make the goals without the help of the other. The disadvantage, however, is that shared responsibility is no responsibility. If we can address that problem (and I will show you we can), we have won something.

Writing a book, as the adage goes, is a journey. In my quest to identify and challenge the best practices in performance management, in order to come up with the "next practices," I have explored many territories. I've relied on my nearly 20 years of experience in a variety of roles, discussions with hundreds of organizations, and countless hours of study. The journey has taken me through various areas of strategy management, through transaction cost economics, corporate social responsibility, organizational behavior, intercultural management, service level management, corporate communication, social psychology, discussions around shareholder versus stakeholder orientation, practical problems around "one version of the truth," and various hypes, such as "real-time management information."

Many of these areas provided interesting viewpoints leading to answers—and more important—to new, more basic questions. Toward the end of the process of writing this book, I came to explore one of the most foundational questions: what's an organization? We discuss this question in business school, but only now did the full gravity of the question dawn on me. Choosing how to answer this question drives the complete business model. Most people I asked, and most sources I referred to, define an organization similarly as "a group of people that share the same goals and objectives."

I have come to think that this answer actually is the reason for many of the problems with performance management—the reason behind why so many initiatives fail; why there are so many political games; and why there are so many fragmented projects. Working with this definition of an organization, leads you to think that stakeholders all share a set of central goals and objectives, and can be aligned in this direction. In reality, nothing could be further from the truth. In fact, many of the goals and objectives live at odds with one another. Shareholders want the highest possible shareholder value; employees look for job security and a place to build their skills and make a career; customers want a good price and a decent product or service; and suppliers want to sell as much as they can. In the hierarchy, we don't really recognize that. There is vertical alignment, we all report up, and goals and objectives are cascaded down. We don't really know what our stakeholders require, nor does the hierarchy really invite us to care.

I have adopted what I think is a better definition of what constitutes an organization: An organization is a unique collaboration of stakeholders by which organizations each reach goals and objectives that none of them could have reached by themselves. The trick to performance management is not to align everyone to the same goals and objectives, but in finding ways to bridge conflicting goals and objectives. Taking this approach leads to subtly different and sometimes entirely different views on performance management. It has been my intention to make performance management work better. I have aimed to broaden the horizon of performance management and introduce new points of view. I hope that these new — and sometimes opposite — points of view make you think and challenge your assumptions. Best practices are a starting point; success starts when you try to apply them in your own world, in your own way, with your own original solutions. To get an overview on the established best practices, this book should be read in combination with books on the balanced scorecard, budgeting, strategy implementation, management control, business intelligence, and other related topics.

A REVIEW OF PERFORMANCE MANAGEMENT AND WHAT'S WRONG WITH IT

—

Part I sets the stage for the rest of the book by providing a straightforward but comprehensive view on one of the most important management challenges we face: creating organizational alignment. It offers an overview of current performance management best practices, and it elaborates on the most influential methodology of all—the balanced scorecard. This part of the book also uncovers what's wrong with performance management today: the lack of insight into how measurement drives behaviors of managers and employees on all levels in the organization. Part I ends with the introduction of the performance leadership framework.

Chapter | 1

SETTING THE SCENE

*Not everything that counts, can be counted. And not
everything that can be counted, counts.*
—Albert Einstein

Measurement Drives Behavior

Measurement impacts on our personal lives every single day. If we want
to lose some weight, we start by standing on the scale. Based on the outcome, we decide how much weight we need to lose, and every other day
we check our progress. If there is enough progress, we become encouraged to lose more, and if we are disappointed, we're driven to add even
more effort in order to achieve our goal. In short, measurement drives
our behavior. For many people, buying a house is an emotional decision
based on how comfortable and "at home" they feel. However, before you
sign a contract, you need to talk to the bank and do the calculations to
see whether the house is affordable for you. Measurement helps you act
with confidence.

Watching sports is no fun without keeping score. Imagine just
watching people playing tennis outside the frame of a game, set, and
match or watching a soccer game where two teams just kick the ball
around for 90 minutes without keeping score. Measurement is part of
our daily lives. It guides the decisions we make and the goals we set
for ourselves.

In the business world this is no different; measurement also drives
our professional behavior. Once your business starts measuring the

results of a certain process, your employees will start focusing on it. There are numerous examples: If the CFO starts tracking the days-sales-outstanding (DSO—i.e., the average number of days it takes customers to pay their bills) on a daily basis, instead of assuming that customers will pay within 14 days or so, the people in the accounts receivable departments are more likely to pay attention and exert greater effort to make collections. If hotel managers and their front desk staff are held accountable for the percentage of guests that fill out the customer satisfaction survey, they will be more likely to remind guests of the survey. The marketing manager of a professional services firm whose objective is to generate leads will structure the firm's Web site in such a way that it collects customer feedback.

Measurement helps us not only to focus on our goals and objectives, but also to balance our actions. If you measure production speed alone in a manufacturing process, it is likely that quality issues will arise. For balance, you also need to measure how many produced units need rework. If a procurement department is only measured on how much additional discount it can squeeze out of contract manufacturers, it becomes hard to avoid unethical practices, such as the use of child labor in low-wage countries and the use of cheaper and environmentally unfriendly materials and production processes. Procurement departments need to identify a balanced set of metrics[1] that includes ethical issues as well as price. When evaluating a management-level employee for promotion, human resources managers need to identify a set of metrics that evaluates candidates on more than just "accomplishments," such as how respected that person is within the organization.

In each of the functional disciplines within an organization—finance, sales, marketing, logistics, manufacturing, procurement, human resources (HR) or information technology (IT)—measurement is a key element of management, and ultimately of bottom-line performance.

I am not suggesting that measurement is the only driver of performance: Business processes are crucial in creating an efficient organization that makes few mistakes and makes optimal use of resources. Leadership is important in order to create a culture in which people feel motivated to give their best. And a good overall strategy is needed to distinguish a company from the competition.

However, measurement cannot be ignored, even if it is only to check if the other drivers for performance are doing the job.

PERFORMANCE MANAGEMENT, OR PERFORMANCE MEASUREMENT

Academics prefer the term *performance measurement* because its scope is clearer. Performance measurement may be defined as the process of quantifying past action, in which measurement is the process of quantification and past action determines current performance.[2] Another definition states that strategic performance measurement is the integrated set of management processes which link strategy to execution.[3] However, people in the business world seem to prefer the term *performance management,* perhaps because it sounds more actionable or broader in scope.

The analyst firm Gartner defines performance management as the combination of management methodologies, metrics, and IT (applications, tools, and infrastructure) that enable users to define, monitor, and optimize results and outcomes to achieve personal or departmental objectives while enabling alignment with strategic objectives across multiple organizational levels (personal, process, group, departmental, corporate, or business ecosystem).[4]

Performance management is deeply rooted in the domain of management accounting and control, typically the responsibility of finance. For instance, the balanced scorecard, the best-known performance management methodology, originates in management accounting.

From a management accounting and control point of view, performance management usually is a top-down process. Most "best practices" point out that it is important to start by understanding the corporate strategy and to translate that into objectives or goals.

Then, key performance indicators (KPIs) need to be put in place to track progress, and a program of improvement activities needs to be created to make sure the goals are achieved. Lastly, a process in which managers are made responsible for these goals, KPIs, and any improvement activities is set in place and linked to the managers' compensation plans.

Unfortunately, the top down way of implementation often does not take people's behaviors into account, in other words, how people will react when confronted with performance indicators. Measurement drives behavior, and if we don't understand how, it drives behaviors in mysterious ways.

The consequences of not understanding the behavioral effects of performance management can be witnessed in most organizations on a daily basis. One of the most common mistakes people make is focusing on what is easy to measure, not what is important.

For instance, salespeople in many businesses are compensated on the basis of the revenue that they bring in, instead of on their contribution (revenue minus the cost of sale). The reason for this is that it is harder to measure the cost of sales than it is to measure revenue alone. At the end of the quarter the revenue measurement may very easily lead to excessive discounting, undermining the company's margins.

Often managers care more about the numbers than about the business. Over the years, managers have created an endless collection of number games to play. Numbers are easy to manipulate. We can change definitions; we can decide to count certain things while ignoring others; we can make the numbers look perfect on paper. If you make your target early, it makes sense to push new business to the next quarter. If there's money left in the budget toward the end of the year, let's make sure we spend it; otherwise it's gone.

In short, our performance management practices themselves often lead to suboptimal performance. If people are made responsible for just a few targets and have available all the means and resources in order to make that target—as conventional wisdom suggests—they will care about those targets only. The question therefore arises of whether it is possible to redeploy resources somewhere else in the process to optimize the organization's overall performance and whether there is a way to do this easily.

We act surprised and shocked when we discover all the unwanted behaviors I have mentioned happening, although I am sure you have witnessed them time and again, just as I have. We blame it on the people and their opportunistic, political behavior. However, performance management should drive the right behaviors, and we should be able to predict the dysfunctional ones so that we can counter those behaviors. Performance management is there to support performance, not hinder it. The top-down approach to performance management, aimed at management, focuses on goals, objectives, and objective measures—it simply doesn't take human behavior into account. Performance management should draw from the experience in the social sciences, particularly organizational behavior. Organizational behavior is a field of study that investigates the impact that individuals, groups, and structure have on behavior within organizations, for the purpose of applying such knowledge toward improving an organization's effectiveness.[5] Organizational behavior discusses topics such as motivation, leadership, communication, and learning, but also structure, control, and measurement.

I heard one management coach put it very eloquently. He said it is time we let go of the "soft, intangible side" of performance management, with managers typing in numbers in spreadsheets that do not mean anything. Instead we should focus on the "hard and tangible side" of performance management: human behaviors. After all, people either do something or they don't.

Strategic Alignment

Alignment is crucial. Many organizations today are not sufficiently aligned. This is the result of many mergers and acquisitions, too much decentralization, and unbridled growth in the past. So there is some spring cleanup to do, but that is not enough. There are strong business pressures to increased alignment. Alignment is important for every single organization, in order to run an efficient operation and to make sure you do the right things. But today, alignment is more crucial than ever. Political factors, economic influences, social trends, and technology advancements[6]—the four aspects of what is called PEST analysis—make an overwhelming business case for increased alignment.

The political climate has changed business profoundly in the last few years. In the United States, the Sarbanes-Oxley Act was passed in July 2002 to address the business scandals of late 2001 and early 2002. Among other things, it aims to increase corporate transparency. It also has the specific goal of raising standards for corporate governance. The act makes CEOs and CFOs of publicly traded companies personally responsible and liable for the effectiveness of internal controls and the quality of external reporting. Furthermore, executive management is now required to immediately report to their stockholders any issues that they believe will materially affect the performance of the enterprise. But Sarbanes-Oxley is not the only set of rules. Many other countries or industries have introduced their own regulations. Business can no longer easily hide dysfunctional behaviors and lack of alignment.

The economics of business has changed too. Organizations are becoming more "virtual." Noncore activities, such as logistics, finance, human resources, information technology, or even production, are routinely outsourced. Operational excellence throughout complete value chains is improved by very tight value-chain integration. Many innovations today come from organizations combining forces and creating new and unique combinations of products and services. Think of Nike+, a collaboration between Nike and Apple, where a sensor in your running shoes sends real-time data to your iPod on your progress. Think of Senseo, a one-touch-of-a-button perfect espresso machine, developed by Douwe Egberts, a coffee maker, and Philips, the producer of home appliances. Or consider airline alliances such as OneWorld, SkyTeam, and Star Alliance, where competing airlines realize they can improve business performance by collaborating. In many different forms and shapes, organizations increase the level of collaboration with others. Business is not a rigid hierarchy anymore, but a looser network of organizations. Command and control is replaced by collaboration and communication. Trust through reliable behavior and strong intercompany alignment makes the difference.

Society doesn't accept immoral or amoral business behavior anymore. Organizations not only have an obligation to their shareholders, but a need to be socially and environmentally responsible as well. Institutional investors weigh management practices in their decision to invest in a certain company or not. Although "sustainability" and "corporate social responsibility" are still just lip service in many organizations, the profoundness of this change is slowly becoming recognizable. Organizations that pride themselves on their sustainability report and social programs are punished even more than their peers when the general public finds out about "incidents" caused by business processes that are still based on maximizing efficiency at the cost of social and environmental circumstances. Ask any manufacturing or oil company that didn't really drive down "clean" thinking into their operations. Only truly authentic and aligned behavior, where every single employee and stakeholder is motivated to do the right thing, can change deeply rooted business processes, behaviors, and beliefs. Sustainability has a deep impact on every organization's daily life.

Lastly, technology developments have increased the need for extreme alignment. Internet technology has dramatically increased consumer control over business processes. In many industries, mass customization is becoming the norm. Internet applications allow customers to configure and tailor their orders themselves and make changes until the last possible moment. The number of configurations for cars is endless. Consumers can visit the Web site of their insurance company and compile their general insurance policies in a very personal and detailed way. Sports companies have built Web sites where consumers can custom-design their own personal sport shoes in different colors, with a personalized text woven into the leather. The customized pairs are then produced and shipped to customers. Pharmaceutical companies are carefully starting to talk about personalized medication. When consumers control the business processes, there is no difference between front office and back office.

Information technology doesn't support the business, IT has become the business. Profitability and pricing is not a finance and marketing issue, it has become an operational management issue. In environments like this, alignment cannot come from a management hierarchy and weekly management meetings. Business processes and operational management need to be strongly aligned in order to manage this level of flexibility and speed.

Organizations that are successful with performance management use it to create focus and alignment. Bottom-line success comes from identifying a limited number of really important goals and going for them. We can't do everything because our actions would be fragmented or lacking in focus. We need to choose and focus. Alignment basically means that everyone agrees on what those goals are and understands his or her own contributions.

Best practices in performance management tell us that creating focus and alignment is a top-down process. Senior management defines the strategic objectives and cascades targets down the organization, making all managers commit to those targets. But, as I described in the introduction, an organization rarely exists where people all share the same goals. Senior managers need to satisfy shareholders, who ask for a financial return; middle managers try to build their career; specialists seek to perfect their skills—everyone has his or her own agenda.

Not taking people's objectives and their behaviors into account leads to dysfunctional results. In essence, people want to do a good job and want to do the right thing, but they are often driven in the wrong direction, playing number games and displaying political behavior. This is clearly not a good start for alignment in the organization.

Dysfunctional behavior causes misalignment, yet at the same time is caused by misalignment. Organizational misalignment starts at the personal level. Social psychologists talk about people being aligned, or authentic, or "in their middle." A person is considered aligned if the self, the person's perception of the self, and the external world's perception of the person match closely. In this verbiage, the person's "self" represents who he or she really is, with all the positive and negative behaviors he or she exhibits. An individual's self-perception may be quite different. Ego may stand in the way of an accurate view of the self, or a lack of reflection may inhibit the person's understanding of his or her behaviors, motivators, and values. A healthy person's self-perception improves over time, with that person becoming wiser, and more self-reflective throughout life. In other words, ideally you develop and mature as a balanced and authentic person when the perception you have of yourself closely matches your true self, and when ego doesn't stand in the way and you accept yourself the way you are, without false pretenses.

People's self-perception can be unrealistic, with a gap between an idealistic self-perception and one's true behaviors. This leads to what is called *cognitive dissonance,* which is what happens if one cognition does not match the other, self-observed behavior does not match idealistic self-perception. For instance, "I do not like being lazy" versus "I don't feel like cleaning up and would rather read the newspaper." This dissonance is an unpleasant experience, leading to negative emotions such as anger or frustration if the dissonance cannot be lifted.

There might also be a gap between external perception and self-perception. "External perception" means how others view a person, which impacts on people's behaviors again. For instance, you may have a senior position in business or society that calls for certain behavior that may not be your natural behavior. Not acting that way may lead to losing that position. As such, group pressure might lead to conformist behavior. You play a role, showing behavior that is not internalized. This is called *role distance*. Again, this is a form of cognitive dissonance,

Figure 1.1

Self, Self-Perception, and External Perception

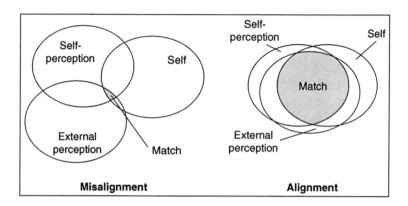

two cognitions ("I want to be liked and keep my position" and "what they want me to do, doesn't fit me").

Self, self-perception, and external perception are interrelated. When there is a big gap between self-perception and self and/or external perception, you are not balanced and do not display authentic behavior. Conversely, the more self, self-perception, and external perception match, the more a person will develop into a balanced human being (see Figure 1.1). We all recognize authentic people in our personal lives. They build bridges between others around them and demonstrate a natural authority.

Exactly the same can be said for organizations and their strategies. Organizations are living organisms. Like people, organizations are born; they grow up, mature, and in the end die. Some become old and wise, others never leave adolescence. Some organizations become popular, others don't. Some are dysfunctional, others are authentic. Authentic behavior and alignment within organizations should be seen as being the same as authentic behavior and alignment in people.

Many organizations show all the signs of dysfunctional behavior. Beautiful mission statements describe how important the customers are, but in reality the managers only think of their own goals. The Web site describes the values of the organization, but the employees do not recognize these in daily life at all. This obvious gap between self and self-perception leads to cynical reactions and a passive-aggressive attitude. In many cases there is a gap between external perception and self-perception as well. Sometimes the organization is able to keep up appearances. The organization's public relations is very effective. Customers see the organization as ethical and authentic, yet behind the scenes a completely different picture emerges. The longer this situation persists, the harder the fall once the public and the media find out. The opposite situation also occurs. Management believes it is doing a great job, but customers and stakeholders have an entirely different opinion. As a result they will take their contributions elsewhere as soon as there is a better alternative. In those organizations, there is a difference between external strategies that are communicated and "real" internal strategies. Much of the time spent by management on strategy consists of thinking how to "spin" internal strategies.

Conversely, an organization matures and develops as balanced and authentic if there are no false pretenses. The members of the organization are in touch with the positive and negative sides of the culture and the way things work. Self and self-perception match. Furthermore, the balance exists if the self-perception and true self of the organization closely match the perception of customers and other external stakeholders such as suppliers, shareholders, and regulators. The stakeholders see the organization as it truly is. The organization's customer value proposition is true and authentic. Self, self-perception, and external perception are in alignment.

This is less esoteric than it sounds. In the field of corporate communication, the self of an organization is called *corporate identity*, the external perception is called *corporate image*, and *corporate strategy* continuously links corporate identity and image.[7] As such, corporate strategy drives alignment or misalignment between identity and image.

An organization is aligned if the self, the self-perception, and the external perception of the organization closely match.

All stakeholders have their own angle in viewing the organization, and the only way to deal with these conflicting requirements is to be authentic. There needs to be alignment between what people do within the organization and what people tell the outside world, and between how the organization is perceived by the different stakeholders and how the organization perceives itself. It is then, when conflicting requirements become visible and the different stakeholders can view the complete picture, that we can understand the different trade-offs.

Performance Leadership—The "Next Practice"

As previously discussed, performance measurement and performance management are not clearly differentiated terms. Yet there is one important difference. Performance measurement focuses on what has happened; it quantifies past action. In a typical planning and control cycle, it is the step after executing a plan that helps to bring the realized results together so that an analysis of differences can be made. Performance measurement can be found in every business domain imaginable—from procurement to logistics, from finance to human resources, from information technology to marketing, and from sales to manufacturing. However, performance measures are seldom integrated. They typically describe line-of-business performance. Performance measurement leads to visibility of what happened.

The next step up from performance measurement is performance management. Performance management implies a more methodological approach using, for instance, the balanced scorecard, activity-based management, value-based management, or any other framework. The idea is that most of the performance management frameworks link business drivers to results. For instance, problems in the manufacturing department lead to product defects or insufficient production, leading to customer satisfaction problems, ultimately impacting on revenue and profitability. On a positive note, if a local government decides to invest in a new IT system, this may lead to less administrative work for police staff and allow them more time to focus on being on the streets, which drives down crime rates. Performance management tries to capture an organization's business model. As it becomes clear how various business domains affect the business results, performance management provides insight into who drives results and how results are driven.

But this book is not about what we today would call the best practices. This book is about the next practices, something I call *performance leadership*. Business performance is not just a process and not just a system, it is about people.

Chapter | 2

TRADITIONAL PERFORMANCE MANAGEMENT

We can do things quick, cheap, and well. Pick two.
— Sign in a shoemaker's shop

This sign posted in the window of a shoemaker's shop makes a lot of sense. If the shoemaker is asked to mend a pair of shoes quickly and well, it will not be cheap since he will have to drop everything else in order to repair that one pair of shoes. The shoemaker can then charge a premium. If the work needs to be done quickly and cheaply, the shoemaker will ask his apprentice to do the job, and thus the quality may suffer. The third option is for the shoes to be done well and cheap, which means it will have to wait. But you can't have all three at the same time. Strategic focus and the basics of performance management are as old as business itself.

Loops of Management

No matter what performance management methodology you are using, no matter what industry you are in, no matter the size of your company, you are fundamentally dealing with the same management paradigm—the two loops of management (see Figure 2.1).

Figure 2.1

The Two Loops of Management

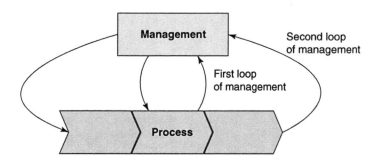

The first loop of management, or inner loop, concentrates on monitoring activities on the operational level, and comparing those against the targets. If measurements go in the direction of critical thresholds, adjustments need to take place. In the first loop of management, we generally let the decisions follow the facts; the decision-making process tends to be rational. We operate within the rules, and actions tend to be reactive and defensive. The first loop of management works with metrics that are all very close to the process, such as call queue length or average call duration in a call center; number of customers contacted, sales pipeline value or conversion rate in sales; or scrap percentage and machine downtime in manufacturing.

But discontinuities do occur, and although we may not be able to predict them, we need to be ready for them. The second loop of management, or outer loop, works more offline. In this loop, we seek improvement through change, not through control. The first loop of management focuses on measuring how the performance compares to the targets; the second loop of management focuses on whether the targets are set high or low enough, or attempts to assess whether we are measuring the right things. On a more strategic level, the processes themselves should be evaluated. How does a specific process relate to the other processes in the organization? Could it be structured so that it is more efficient or more aligned to other processes? How does the process support the customer value proposition? Some examples of metrics in the second loop of management are profitability or return on investment for finance, market share, brand value or customer lifetime value in marketing, absenteeism, and salary balance in human resources.

Every organization, large or small, operates under these loops of management. It is the most elementary management model. The double loops may not function well because the organization is not using them effectively, but they are there. Unfortunately the loops do not tell us what strategies are the right ones, or which performance indicators are needed to measure success; it is just the basic principle. More insight from other, more specific performance management methodologies is needed[1].

A Summary Guide to Performance Management Methodologies

The most powerful management process that is usually deeply embedded in an organization is the budgeting process. Almost every organization has adopted this process to translate strategy into action and determine a benchmark for performance. A budget is a fixed performance contract, expressed in financial terms, against which future results can be compared.[2] Furthermore, a budget is a means to allocate the scarce resources of an organization and to let managers commit themselves to predetermined financial results. The budgeting process is seldom appreciated in business. Budgeting tends to take a lot of time; three to five months is not exceptional at all. This often leads to somewhat disconnected results because budgeting processes are often negotiation-based. Jack Welch, the former CEO of General Electric, is often quoted as saying, "The budget is the bane of corporate America. It never should have existed. . . . Making a budget is an exercise in minimalization." The only thing I would add is that this statement holds true for companies around the world, not just for corporate America. Over the years various alternatives have been proposed, such as activity-based budgeting, zero-based budgeting, and rolling forecasts[3]. However, the beyond-budgeting model[4] offers the most radical alternative. Its proponents argue convincingly that the practice of budgeting may have worked in the industrial area where business was predictable, but that a modern business is much more decentralized and networked than the traditional hierarchical organization of the past. Table 2.1 lists the principles of the beyond-budgeting model.

Table 2.1

Beyond-Budgeting Model

Beyond-Budgeting Process Principles	Beyond-Budgeting Leadership Principles
Target setting. External benchmarks set aspirational medium-term goals.	*Governance framework.* Clear principles provide a framework for local decision making.
Motivation and rewards. Relative rewards based on external benchmarks and evaluated with hindsight reduce gaming.	*High-performance climate.* High expectations lead to sustainable competitive success.
Strategy process. A continuous process and more local involvement encourage ambition and fast response.	*Freedom to decide.* Empowered people with freedom and scope to make strategic decisions are more committed to success.
Resource management. Resource-on-demand approach reduces waste.	*Team-based responsibility.* Small teams have a sharper focus on creating value and reducing waste.
Coordination. One team approach encourages cooperation and excellent customer service.	*Customer accountability.* Frontline teams accountable for results are interested in satisfying customer needs profitably.
Measurement and control. Fast and open information focuses on learning and encourages ethical behavior.	*Open and ethical information culture.* Information on openness and "one truth" promotes ethical behavior.

Instead of an annual budget, beyond budgeting proposes a process of continuous updates, a so-called rolling forecast. If an initiative has a clear business case that realistically predicts a profitable outcome, a lack of budget may never be the reason for not doing it. "Blowing the budget," (a bad thing) is replaced by "blowing the forecast" (a good thing). The targets are set in aspirational terms, building a sense of urgency and a "can do" mentality. Of course, a benchmark for performance is needed. There is no fixed budget with which to compare performance, but rather a dynamic ranking of regions, offices, salespeople, projects, and so on. Also, a company peer group comparison is important to make sure your company not only did better than previously, but also better than the market. Hope and Fraser, who developed beyond budgeting, point out that fast and open information leads to more ethical behavior and empowers more people to make the right decisions. Also, fast information implies a high degree of automation and elimination of most manual steps in the process that can lead to "creative interpretations." Although adopting the beyond-budgeting model fully might be too radical an approach for many organizations, it is important to understand the basics and how they relate to your budgeting mechanism.

The beyond-budgeting process creates financial focus and alignment, but feedback—after completing operations—is needed too. In 1919, one of the financial executives at DuPont, founded in 1802 as a gun powder mill and now one of the largest science companies in the world, came up with the *DuPont ratio analysis* (see Figure 2.2). This analysis uses a financial performance indicator called *return on equity* (ROE).

Return on equity is one of the most important indicators of a firm's profitability and potential growth. Of course, two companies with the same return on equity may not have the same perspective in the market. That is where the DuPont analysis adds some clarity. It describes, through a tree of calculations, the drivers for return on equity. The profit margin is of course the element that drives profitability. Asset turnover describes how effectively a company converts its assets into sales; this has an impact on the potential growth of the company (how fast the engine is running).

Return on equity could be financed by taking on extra debt, and the financial leverage shows what portion of the ROE is based on debt. By aggregating data at the right level, all of a sudden the raw data turn into meaningful information. This ratio tells a story, usually based on trend information: where the ratio has been, and where it is now. Based on these trends, perhaps corrected for seasonal influences and other factors,

Figure 2.2

DuPont Ratio Analysis

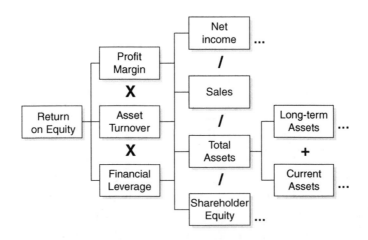

an extrapolation into the future is possible. Ratios on an aggregated level also make it possible to benchmark organizations against other organizations, if they are all using the same definition. Essentially, these ratios provide almost immediate insight for the skilled reader.

The more popular financially oriented performance indicator today is the *economic value added* (EVA) formula. This measure aims to capture the true economic profit of an enterprise and to describe creation of shareholder wealth over time. EVA formula equals net operating profit after taxes (NOPAT) minus the required return times capital invested.[5] EVA explains to business managers on all levels that capital is not for free and should be applied to activities that at least provide a higher return than the cost of capital. Managers are forced to focus on creating value. Business unit plans, investment proposals, and even some projects can be evaluated on their return in the EVA formula as to their contribution to the net operating profit and their expected return. But EVA doesn't describe your company strategy, nor does it give guidance on how to create the highest return. You would need a more operationally focused methodology to help you figure out how to get there.

Activity-based costing (ABC), popular in the 1980s but dating back to the 1930s in Germany, bridges finance and operations. On the operational level, it identifies the activities that are required by a company to deliver the goods or the services that it produces. It also defines which resources are needed to fuel these activities. On the financial level, activity-based costing provides managers with insight about the costs of business activities or processes by allocating direct and indirect costs to various steps for each activity or process, the so-called cost drivers. Examples of cost drivers include purchasing, warehousing, sales, invoicing, shipping, customer service, and so on.

Activity-based management (ABM) aligns activities, resources, and financial results.[6] Financial results are achieved by selling products and services that are produced through certain activities. Activities, in turn, are fueled by resources. If the products and services are not providing the right results, on the financial side you can either adjust the price (increasing the price for a higher margin or decreasing it for lower margins but higher turnover), or you can adjust the resource cost by renegotiating contracts or switching to a supplier that will deliver the same goods or services for a lower price. Organizations can also try to influence demand, to make better use of the available resources, or can influence how much resources (time, money, materials, labor) are consumed by the company's activities. The principles of ABC can be applied to areas broader than cost accounting. For instance, most organizations today are concerned with customer, product or channel profitability. In the case of customer profitability, we need to identify how much the customer-facing processes cost, how much they deliver, and how we can use customer segmentation to optimize different processes for different customer segments. And increasingly there is an interest in service pricing, where customers' requests generate products or services. ABC helps to set a profitable price on these one-off requests.

Six Sigma[7] is described as a rigorous and disciplined methodology that utilizes data and statistical analysis to measure and improve a company's operational performance, practices and systems. Six Sigma identifies and prevents defects in manufacturing and service-related processes. In many organizations, it simply means a measure of quality that strives for near perfection.[8] *Sigma* (the lower-case Greek letter σ) is used to represent the *standard deviation* (a measure of variation) of a statistical population. The phrase "six sigma process" means that if you measure six times the standard deviation between the mean outcome of the process and the nearest critical threshold, there is a minimal chance of failure. Six Sigma is rooted in quality management, based on, for instance, Deming's Plan-Do-Check-Act cycle. Six Sigma is not a project, but a process aimed at continuous improvement. Processes are continuously monitored, analyzed, improved, and controlled, to ensure that any deviations from target are corrected before they result in defects. But perhaps the term most connected with Six Sigma is "black belt," the name for Six Sigma experts who dedicate their time to continuous improvement.

In addition to methodologies originating from finance and operations, there are methodologies with a strategy management background. Perhaps the biggest step forward in performance management in the last century is the fundamental understanding of the concept of *critical success factors*[9] (CSFs), originating in the 1960s and widely popularized in the 1980s. Critical success factors are the limited number of areas in which satisfactory results will ensure successful competitive perform-ance for the individual, department, or organization. CSFs are the few key areas where "things must go right" for the business to flourish and for the manager's goals to be attained. Because these areas of activity are critical for the business to succeed, management should have the key performance indicators to monitor progress and determine whether the goals are realistic and will likely be met. A key performance indica-tor (KPI) is a metric that is deemed of strategic importance to an organ-ization. As a rule of thumb, an organization (or part of an organization) should have three to five critical success factors, each perhaps with three to five key performance indicators. CSFs make sure all managers are on the same page because they help focus on the overall strategy. They allow managers to discuss how to deploy the limited amount of resources an organization has, and allocate them to the activities that really make the difference between success and failure. Just as people's strategic insights and industry and environmental trends develop over time, CSFs are not cast in stone either. For instance, the CSFs in the automotive industry have changed dramatically over time.[9] First, styling, service, and cost control were the important factors. Then, meeting energy stan-dards became important too. Later, overall brand perception became a crucial addition. The CSF methodology provides a straight top-down definition process. The industry and environmental trends dictate the strategic themes, together with the strategy of the organization. Man-agers add their own domain specific and temporal CSFs to the mix. Then the combination of CSFs is being translated to KPIs to monitor progress. Lastly, improvement initiatives are then undertaken to step in where results are not satisfactory.

Another, less well-known strategic performance management method-ology comes from the European Foundation for Quality Management.[10] The *EFQM Excellence Model* is a framework based on nine criteria. Four of these criteria are outcomes, with respect to one's own performance, customers, people, and society. These are achieved by managing the five enabling criteria: leadership, strategy, partnerships and resources, people, and processes. The EFQM process largely consists of self-assessment. According to EFQM, self-assessment is a comprehensive, systematic and regular review of an organization's activities and results referenced against the EFQM Excellence Model. The self-assessment process allows the organization to discern its strengths and areas in which improvement can be made. Following this process of evaluation, improvement plans are launched, which are monitored for progress. Organizations carry out this cycle of evaluating and taking action repeatedly.

Balanced Scorecard

The balanced scorecard[11], developed by Kaplan and Norton, is a framework to describe an organization's strategy and to provide feedback as to its effectiveness. The key message of the balanced scorecard is that the performance of an organization should be structurally viewed from four perspectives: financial, customer, business process, and learning/ growth (see Figure 2.3).

- Financial perspective: How are we perceived by our shareholders? Without profits there is no supply of capital and no sustainable business models. Having sound insight in finance is important for every single economic entity.
- Customer perspective: How do our customers look at us? The customer perspective ensures we not only measure an internal

Figure 2.3

The Four Perspectives of the Balanced Scorecard

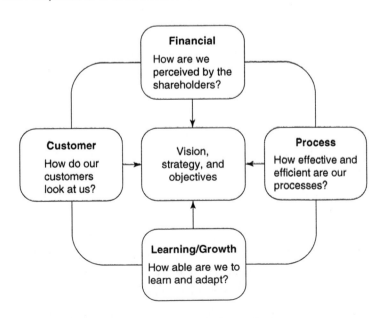

view, but that the metrics also show how the organization is viewed by the customers

- Business process perspective: How effective and efficient are our processes? Processes need to be efficient so that the costs can be managed. Equally important, processes need to be effective so that the customers' needs are served. Proper management of day-to-day operations ensure the short-term health of an organization.
- Learning/growth perspective: How able are we to learn and adapt? Investing in human capital (skills), information capital (insight) and organizational capital (ability to change) is necessary in order to be successful in the long-term.

It is widely estimated that more than 50 percent of large enterprises use a balanced scorecard in some shape or form. Several publications even mentioned the balanced scorecard as one of the most influential management concepts of the twentieth century. This may be a slight overstatement, but it is clear that the balanced scorecard is here to stay. One of the reasons why the balanced scorecard is such a recognizable tool is that it describes something fundamental, regardless of the industry or geographic location in which you are situated. In order to be successful and have a healthy bottom line, you need to have your shop in order and keep your customers happy. And to make sure it stays that way, you need to adapt to changes in your environment. These cause-and-effects are described with a strategy map. Figure 2.4 shows the strategy map of a U.S.-based retail company.

This retailer has one overall strategic objective: it wants to be the world's leading retailer at the $1 price point. In the area of learning and growth, the retailer believes that the key to sustainable success is to develop good information systems (LG1), to invest in employees by providing training so that they will stay with the company for a long period of time (LG2), and to cultivate the culture (LG3). With good information systems and people that are experienced in the business, the retailer believes that in the area of business process it will be able to know its customers and be able to predict what they want (BP5). Another effect of well-performing people and systems is that the retailer saves significant time and costs when opening new stores (BP4),

Figure 2.4

U.S.-Based Retailer's Strategy Map

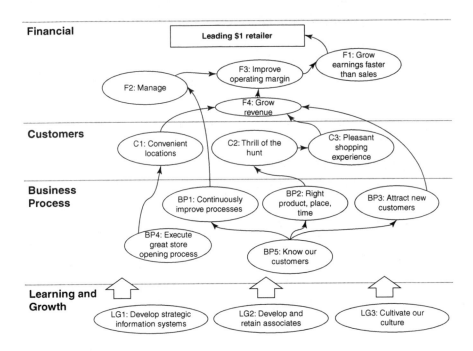

something the retailer is aggressively pursuing. Knowing your customers leads to new insights in improving internal processes (BP1). It
also leads to being able to put the right products at the right place at
the right time (BP2). From the perspective of customers, it also leads
to being able to attract new customers by addressing them with the right
products and promotions (BP3). Success in retail is all about location
(C1) and customers finding the right products (C2), which this retailer
calls the "thrill of the hunt," based on impulse-buying behavior. Entering the shop with no particular need in mind and finding something
attractive is the customer experience (C3) the retailer is looking for.
Convenient locations, the ability to attract new customers, and a pleasant shopping experience all lead to revenue growth (F4) in the financial segment. Continuous improvement in the company is aimed at
managing margins and costs (F2). Cost reductions and revenue growth
lead to improvement in operating margins (F3), which is the driver for
growing earnings, even more than growing the sales (F1). The retailer

sees earnings growth as the main metric to being the leading retailer in a particular market segment.

Strategy maps have significant strengths. In many organizations the real problem is not a shortage of reports, but an abundance of overlapping and contradictory reports. A strategy map helps determine which performance indicators and which reports are truly needed. If there are reports and metrics that do not fit in the strategy map, the metric most probably does not represent one of the business drivers. In that case the metric is not a key performance indicator. It also works the other way around. When creating a strategy map, most likely there will be places where, in order to make a connection, a leap of faith is needed, such as "innovation leads to revenue growth." Obviously something is missing in the middle, and one or more additional performance indicators, probably involving the customer perspective, need to be added, such as "adoption of new products by the market." Another strength of strategy maps is that they help create leading indicators instead of lagging indicators. At first thought, the term "leading indicator" may look strange, as you can only measure something once it has happened. But it is when performance indicators are linked together in a cause-and-effect relationship that they become predictive. For instance, if a customer process indicator such as speed of delivery shows there is a problem, the impact on the customer relationship indicators, such as customer satisfaction, will be affected later, which ultimately impacts on the financial bottom line of the organization. In this example speed of delivery is a leading indicator for customer satisfaction. Strategy maps also visualize how different parts of the organization contribute to the organization's overall performance. Not all activities of an organization are directly revenue driving. Many activities have a certain revenue distance and are rather intangible, such as brand marketing and large portions of supporting functions such as HR, finance, or IT. Strategy maps align these activities with the bottom line and show their contribution to the overall performance of the organization.

As with any methodology, strategy maps have limitations too. A strategy map is an abstraction from reality. Various researchers have criticized the cause-and-effect relationships in particular.[12] The strategy map suggests a one-way linear approach, starting with the learning/growth perspective and culminating in financial results. However, it is equally easy to link relationships between the perspectives in the opposite direction. For instance, revenue growth may lead to a positive press, which will in turn have a positive effect on corporate image, and as a result part of that increased revenue could lead to more investments on research and development (R&D). Or let's assume there is a problem with customer service. The organization is not responsive enough in e-mail communication. Yet e-mail communication increases and the number of letters that customers send is only going down. This issue is addressed with an improvement initiative and a project is started. Given the importance of the project, it is manned with key staff. The unwanted result is time away from customer service because of the time spent by the key staff on the project. The effort to fix the problem is temporarily focused inward instead of outward. This may lead to a drop in customer satisfaction and revenue at first before it improves.

The process of implementing the balanced scorecard is perhaps even more important, than the actual result. The alignment between people comes from discussing what drives their business, how they see their strategy map, what performance indicators they share, and which performance indicators are unique to their domain. In this process it is perfectly fine to adapt the framework, to cater to the criticism of some that the balanced scorecard does not address all stakeholders.[13] Some organizations have chosen to add a fifth perspective, such as "environment," "supplier," or "society." Perhaps it is to highlight specifics from an organization's strategy that otherwise would not get enough attention. In some cases, managers think their organization is unique—whether true or not—and adapting the four perspectives would not do justice to their specifics.

Sometimes, in the case of departmental scorecards, the four perspectives need to be reorganized. For some departments, such as finance, HR, or IT, the customers are the other departments. Obviously, there is no goal to maximize the profits of such departments, since these departments are required to support the other parts of the business. Or consider the public sector, which is not profit-driven but budget-driven. In cases like this, you can switch the customer and financial perspective around.[14] Finance then becomes a contributing perspective, leading to (internal) customer service as the bottom line. Another common misconception is that scorecards need to reflect the organizational structure. Simply stacking scorecards following the corporate hierarchy may not reveal the value drivers behind the complete value chain. A retailer might for instance determine that the best way is not to organize its scorecard by department and business unit, but rather by customer contact channel. Another example of a nondepartmental balanced scorecard is the project balanced scorecard. Others have implemented supplier scorecards or even personal scorecards.

Although the balanced scorecard is a very generic business concept, figuring out how to actually implement it is harder than you might imagine. People sometimes ask if it is "allowed" to move a few metrics from the process perspective to the learning/growth perspective, as there are "too many" metrics in the process perspective, and people sometimes find it hard to create adequate metrics to assess growth and learning. This of course is not the right approach. Others have done the opposite of doing a checkbox exercise and have taken an extremely analytical approach. In one case, the project team performed a broad and deep investigation and came up with an ultimate set of metrics that proved to be stable for over two years. According to this team, the metrics showed how fundamental their analysis was. However, the sad truth was that, in reality, the metrics weren't actually being used and no change requests came in. Scorecards should be living systems.

Organizational Learning

Throughout this chapter, I have discussed a number of performance management methodologies, as summarized in Table 2.2.

With this overview of methodologies and approaches, the question quickly arises of what the best methodology would be. The most *popular* methodology is the balanced scorecard; the most *ubiquitous* is budgeting (although you cannot compare the two, as they are complementary). But empirical evidence that explores the performance impact of the balanced scorecard is extremely rare and much that is available is anecdotal at best.[15] For every success story, there are multiple examples of projects that have failed or did not deliver to the desired extent. However, this holds true across all performance management methodologies, not only the balanced scorecard.

The conclusion is obvious: There is no direct link between bottom-line performance and implementation of a specific performance

Table 2.2

Types of Performance Management Methodologies

Origin	Example Methodologies
Finance	• DuPont • Economic value added • Budgeting • Beyond-budgeting
Operations	• Activity-based management • Six Sigma
Strategy	• Critical success factors • Balanced scorecard • European Foundation for Quality Management (EFQM) Excellence model

management methodology. The balanced scorecard is not better than EVA or activity-based costing. It is not a specific methodology that improves performance, but people's actions and their behaviors. Any methodology can work, as long as it is the single methodology that collaborating people work with . . . as long as you stick with it. I have heard many times remarks like this: "Yes, we tried to implement the balanced scorecard, but we dropped it after three months. It didn't work." And indeed it didn't work, nor would any other methodology. It takes time to learn how to use a framework.

All performance management methodologies have one thing in common. They are based on the concept of "double loop learning."[16] In single-loop learning, people and organizations take action according to the difference between expected and obtained outcomes; in other words, it is a simple variance analysis. In double-loop learning, you question the values, assumptions, and policies that led to your actions in the first place. If you are able to view and modify those, then double-loop learning is taking place. In more compact terms, double-loop learning is learning how you learn. The most important goal of the various methodologies is to spark a discussion. Once a cost price is calculated, ABC tells a story on how the costs were accumulated and provides a way to verify the assumptions that managers have when driving costs down or pricing the products and services. That insight is invaluable. EVA should be used to clarify assumptions and discussions among the management team and other stakeholders. It should not be used merely to justify these assumptions as part of a generic formula. Even the "objective" financial numbers are based on assumptions. Depreciation is a guess, the weights of the cost of capital are subjective, and the various reserves on the balance sheet used to calculate the total invested capital are likewise based on subjective decision making. Beyond budgeting is totally structured around discussing the right investment proposals, as it is a zero-based plan approach. The balanced scorecard forces us to discuss how to align our business and create a strategy map with cause-and-effect relationships. Links in a strategy map are not a tool for command and control, but an instrument for communication and collaboration. It drives management toward collaborative behavior. Although statistical techniques are valuable to establish cause-and-effect relationships, the strategy map is not a statistical forecasting tool that predicts what the financial outcome is when someone "turns a dial" in one of the operational processes. Strategy maps are not an exact science but they do provide an agenda for discussion in management team meetings.

We can only build an aligned company if we understand our and each other's assumptions, to make sure our perception matches reality and to build authenticity. Only when we discuss our assumptions and the things we value, can we understand each other's behavior. Behaviors are the link between plans and results.[17] Seeing the financial results of actual change may take weeks or months, while we can work on our behaviors from the beginning. Next to measuring results, we need to use performance management to drive and reward the right behaviors.

Chapter | 3

MEASUREMENT DRIVES BEHAVIOR

I recently gained a few pounds. "More Frank to love," I tried to justify to my wife. Her reply came almost immediately. "Yes, but the love per pound decreases."

Why Measure?

There are three objectives of measurement.[1] First it is important to track results for compliance and reporting reasons, as a means of control, and to justify your actions to stakeholders. These stakeholders include regulators and shareholders that have very specific reporting requirements. Increasingly, organizations also justify their actions to society at large, with what is often called a sustainability report. The need for increased transparency (discussed in Chapter 1) largely drives advances in performance management from this perspective. The second objective of measurement is to enable strategic decision making and learning (as discussed in Chapter 2), providing feedback from an operational to a strategic level, to see the extent to which strategies are successful. The third objective of measurement is to drive people's behaviors, the focus of this chapter.

In parts of the organization, this is usually already well understood. Most human resource departments use performance review systems with specific quantitative performance indicators. Sales departments have very direct experience with driving certain behaviors, using sales targets on particular revenue and a certain mix of revenue, to make sure salespeople do not sell only the products or services that are easy to sell. In other parts of the organization, in finance, manufacturing, and information technology, for example, performance measurement is rarely a means to drive people's behavior. Usually performance management initiatives in these areas focus on compliance and reporting, as well as strategic decision making and learning.

The impact of measurement on the behaviors of people runs quite deep. In fact, the process of measurement alone, regardless of what is being measured, has an impact. In the social sciences this is referred to as the Hawthorne effect.[2]

The Hawthorne effect refers to experiments between 1924 and 1933 conducted in the Hawthorne works of the Western Electric Company in Chicago.[3] One of the experiments dealt with the relationship between the illumination in the factories and worker productivity. When the illumination levels were increased, it was no surprise to see that productivity went up. However, when the illumination levels were decreased, productivity went up again. That was unanticipated. Even stranger, productivity went up in the control group as well, where there was no change in the illumination levels. This was puzzling. It was Professor Elton Mayo from Harvard Business School who came up with a widely accepted explanation. It wasn't the illumination process that improved productivity; it was the fact that productivity was being measured. One can speculate about the reasons—perhaps people felt a positive impact because the company paid attention to working conditions. Or it could be a negative driver—the people on the work floor were afraid the experiments would lead to further rationalization and layoffs, and therefore they worked harder. Whatever the reason, measurement affected performance.

The Hawthorne effect is obviously a curse for the social sciences because these sciences study subjects in their natural environment. The Hawthorne effect shows that the fact that you study the subject already alters the natural environment. But for performance management, the Hawthorne effect is a blessing. In fact, just putting measurements in place already impacts on behavior, even before you think about what to measure.

Measurement Drives Behavior . . . in Mysterious Ways

Measurement affects behavior regardless of what is being measured. Even where performance measures are instituted purely for purposes of information, they are probably interpreted as important aspects of that job or activity and hence have implications for the motivation of behavior.[4] Unfortunately, even in the academic world little empirically based research exists that has attempted to understand the relationship between performance management and, for instance, management styles.[5] In daily practice even less attention is paid to the subject.

It would be important to know up front which behaviors can be expected when introducing performance management. We know, for example, that introducing metrics is a very political exercise. Not everyone is interested in having deep insight into their own performance, and being open about it. This is particularly the sentiment felt in middle management. The position of middle management in many large organizations is not easy, being squeezed between the workforce and senior management. Middle management uses the lack of transparency to protect its position. So when we introduce new targets and performance indicators, we can expect elegant evasive behaviors, strong passive-aggressive reactions, and sometimes even sabotage.

The problem is that the behavioral consequences of performance management are usually not taken into account when designing, implementing, and using performance indicators. Typically, it is a top-down process.

From the top down you make sure everyone understands the corporate objectives. What are the short- and long-term targets the organization needs to meet? The next step, based on that knowledge, is a long list of performance indicators. Which indicators can be defined that describe to which extent the objective is met or is in the process of being met? Then, based on what data are available, you are able to define what is relatively easy to measure versus what best describes the objectives, and a short list of performance indicators is selected. This short list is finally implemented. The way people will behave when these indicators are implemented is typically not discussed, nor part of the design and implementation process. It will remain a surprise, although we all know that measurement drives behavior.

Let the Games Begin!

Metrics can tell you anything you want. For every event, metrics can be found that present different, even opposing, conclusions. My personal experience, which I shared when opening this chapter, is a good example. "More pounds to love" indicated adding weight was a good thing. "Less love per pound" on the contrary, stated that adding weight was a bad thing. Managers have an interest in finding and presenting the metrics that make their performance look good. It is hardly debated that many companies suffer from "gaming the numbers" and "cheating the system." But it would be too easy to blame middle management or divide-and-conquer and other forms of opportunistic behavior.

The problem is not bad people. The real problem is bad performance management that makes people behave in opportunistic and political ways. This, in its turn, increases the gap between how people want to behave and how they are driven to behave. All these dysfunctional behaviors tend to be hidden. So to understand them, and be able to predict and perhaps prevent the unintended consequences, we need to know where to look for these behaviors. Research on unintended consequences of performance management dates back more than 50 years.[6] We can distinguish two basic types of consequences:

- *People impacting on measurement.* People trying to play the numbers so that they don't have to alter their actions.
- *Measurement impacting on people.* The metrics put in place drive dysfunctional behavior.

Table 3.1 shows the unintended consequences of performance management.[7] Perhaps the most well-known example of dysfunctional behavior is *measure fixation*. It happens when running the numbers becomes more important for managers than running a successful business. An example of this is the railway organization that saw its accuracy deteriorate. Accuracy here is defined as the percentage of trains that leave the station on time and arrive at their destination on time. Confronted with the performance problems on this metric, the operations manager decides to widen the margin of the definition. Previously, "on time" was defined with a margin of two minutes, one minute before the listed time until one minute after. Now the metric is redefined and trains are considered to ride on time within a margin of four minutes. To prevent this type of unintended consequence from happening, make sure that not only the performance indicators are published but also their definitions.

When measure fixation grows out of control, it can lead to *misrepresentation*. This usually looks like a minor means of cheating the system.

Table 3.1

Unintended Consequences of Performance Management

People Impacting on Measurement	Measurement Impacting on People
• Tunnel vision—focusing on what is easy to measure instead of what is important	• Gaming—underachieving once targets have been made
• Measure fixation—trying to change definitions to make the numbers look better	• Misinterpretation—incorrect or incomplete interpretation of the metrics
• Misrepresentation—cheating the system, forging numbers	• Suboptimization—using corporate resources to optimize one's own targets, instead of corporate objectives
• Ossification—presenting outdated information	• Myopia—focusing on the short-term quick wins, instead of longer-term strategic objectives

For instance, a group in a back office asks one member to work late, but to punch the time clock for all. In the end this is the most serious of all dysfunctional behaviors, because it can easily become fraud. Many of the recent bookkeeping scandals were caused by pure misrepresentation. For instance, consider a large multinational that operates many different off-balance entities that buy products and services at the end of the quarter so that the main entity makes the numbers it forecasted to the shareholders and financial analysts. This is a form of "stuffing the channel." Another example plays on a more operational level. In many consumer goods industries a salesperson sells the products to retail, such as shops and chains. In one case the salesperson promised the customer an additional discount if he would order more products than were needed. Secretly the salesperson advised the customer to ship back the surplus of goods the day after receiving the order. Returns were not part of the compensation plans of the salesperson, and returns were not correlated to the revenues. Obviously, a more balanced set of metrics is needed.

Gaming is the opposite of measure fixation and misrepresentation. It means manipulating the business to make the numbers look good (instead of manipulation of the numbers to make the business look good). Both transgressions are equally serious. Gaming occurs when managers start to underachieve once the target has been reached. The next period's targets therefore are forced not to be higher any more than absolutely necessary. Another variant is overspending at the end of the year to make sure all the budget is used and thus secure an equally high or higher cost budget for the next round.

Due to compliance and shareholder pressures, there is an increased focus on short-term objectives instead of the longer-term strategy. *Myopia* is the result. For instance, a professional services firm found out it had a problem with its DSO (days-sales-outstanding). On average it took customers about 60 days to pay the invoices, whereas the chief financial officer calculated that there would be a significant financial performance improvement if customers would pay on average within 45 days. All the account managers were urged to work with their clients to have the invoices paid sooner. One particular account manager was extremely successful—all the outstanding invoices were paid immediately. Unfortunately, these were the last invoices the firm could send. The account manager had pushed his client to such an extent that the client paid the bills and terminated the relationship. The actual performance indicator was considered more important than the overall customer relationship. Again, a more balanced set of metrics is needed to avoid this type of measurement fixation.

Another common behavior can be observed when managers focus not on the important targets and the key performance indicators, but on the targets and indicators that are easy to measure. This phenomenon is called *tunnel vision*. A widespread example is the use of "revenue" as a target for salespeople. This often leads to high discounting by the salesperson who needs to reach his or her target at the end of the quarter or year. At the same time, the CFO will complain about margin pressures. This sales behavior is a logical consequence of measurement on revenue because it is the easiest metric to track. Measuring salespeople's performance based on contribution margin is much more worthwhile. This metric takes not only the revenue into account but also the cost of goods sold and, to a certain extent, the cost of sales. With that information, the salesperson will check the profitability of the deal when a customer asks for a discount, instead of making the revenue target at the expense of the margin.

A common best practice states that performance indicators should have a single owner and that management should provide this person with all the means to make the target on the performance indicator. Although this sounds good as a plan, in practice it can lead to *suboptimization*. Managers look at maximizing their own targets, even at the expense of the overall strategic objectives. Many small suboptimal results then lead to one big negative result. Having co-ownership for performance indicators will lead to more collaboration.

Misinterpretation happens when people base their decisions on faulty data. Often this happens if the measurements and systems are old and full of forgotten exceptions and modifications. A typical example would be the accuracy of the number of customers the organization has. If the faulty measures are the result of a programming error that repeats itself every time the report is run, the consequences may be limited. At one point managers become used to a certain number and track the positive or negative change. Given the stability of the error, the reported changes may trigger the right interpretation anyway. Sometimes misinterpretation may not be the result of an honest error, but deliberate. A good set of metrics triangulates the business drivers and performance indicators, so that there are multiple ways to calculate the correct results. Of course, the results should match.

Another form of misinterpretation happens when a metric is out-of-date but still available in the management reports. This phenomenon is called *ossification*. As the metric has lost its relevance, it may very well lead to users ignoring the information because they cannot apply it in their decision making. The danger is that the sentiment spreads and the overall set of information is being seen as outdated. Ossification may even be a political instrument. Middle management might choose not to update the management information. This allows the lower levels of management to shield their operations and not provide current insight. This is dealt with best by creating a schedule for reevaluating the validity of the metrics, like a "best before" date.

Before putting metrics in place, it is important to determine the ways in which to play the numbers. It is equally important to realize that no matter how many ways you come up with, there is always someone who finds another way. The way people use the numbers needs to be reevaluated once in a while. Then there needs to be a brainstorming exercise on how people would possibly react and behave in their daily work when confronted with the new metrics, and which actions need to be put in place to prevent dysfunctional behavior from happening.

In short, you need to understand the behavioral context of metrics. Current best practices do not do that. In different organizational cultures, people have different ways of dealing with performance management. In very contract-oriented cultures, the numbers speak for themselves. Failing to make targets may impact on variable salaries or even lead to dismissal. In more relationship-oriented cultures, numbers are there to track the progress of people and to direct contributions of the group to places where these are most needed. Failure to understand different organizational cultures will lead to unexpected behaviors and very likely to dysfunctional behaviors.

Not understanding the behavioral aspects of performance management also has a negative impact on the business case for performance management. Business cases are often based on a desired return on investment, and they are usually quantitative in nature. However, although a return on investment may be significant in terms of reduced cost or increased revenue, if the organization does not accept the way in which an initiative is rolled out, it will not be a success.

Driving the Right Behaviors

In every organization, one of the most important success factors is collaborative behavior—a synergy that makes the contributions of individuals into more than just the sum of its parts. However, it is remarkable that cooperation within an organization generally remains underexposed in management reports. One of the reasons for this is that cooperation is generally considered not quantifiable and therefore cannot be measured. However, the results of collaboration are easy to measure.[8] Think about the following examples:

- First-time-right percentage of "triple play" installations in a telecom company that offers telephony, high-speed internet, and television through its various divisions
- Tracking the use of an expertise location system that helps engineers find colleagues who may be able to answer difficult questions in a photocopier service company
- Cross-sell percentage of products in a large bank

We can expand on this concept to create metrics that *drive* the right behavior, in this case collaboration. One of the adverse effects we have seen is suboptimization, which is what happens when we follow conventional wisdom. But conventional wisdom is not always right. Therefore, some key metrics should not be assigned to a single performance owner, but to two performance owners who need to collaborate to achieve the target, because both own an essential part of the means and resources. In this case, the targets are not defined for a single business domain, but for crossovers between the business interfaces.

A CIO had a problem with the business interface between IT development and IT operations. Development was responsible for implementing systems, and operations was responsible for running them, after extensive acceptance testing. A new performance indicator was introduced: time used to take new development into production. Both managers complained, as they did not have the means by themselves to achieve the target. The CIO rightfully pointed out that they hit the nail on the head. The metrics drove the behavior to collaborate.

Understanding the Impact of Feedback

Every person needs and likes feedback, even when it is negative feedback. It is important to hear how we are doing and how we are perceived. When feedback is positive, it will spur the displayed behavior. If the feedback is negative (but constructive), there is a good chance it will alter behavior. However, the way feedback is delivered is crucial for how you will choose to either accept it or not. Let's have a look at two case studies to show how organizational culture affected the impact of feedback.

Case Study 1: Positive Impact of Measurement due to Understanding Company Culture

A claims department of an insurance company has four groups in one wing of the building—North, South, East, and West. Each day, the claims are sorted by postal (zip) code and distributed to the right group. One of the most important performance indicators for the department is average process time. The sooner a claim is processed and the client is notified, the higher the customer satisfaction, even if the claim is not always awarded. It fits the customer value proposition of the company: clear and fast results. When the average processing time lapsed, the claims manager decided to publish a weekly graph of claims processing production for each group on the message board near the coffee machine. It was a very straightforward initiative, no speeches about targets, no full-balanced scorecard implementations or cultural change programs, massaging of the data by middle management, just feedback through the graph. After a few weeks, the effect became visible. Operational staff typically strive for harmony, not competition (like most management groups). Group East offered Group West help, taking over some of its claims because two staff members in Group West were absent due to illness. Group East relied on the help of Group West over the following two weeks while a few employees were on holiday. The workload began to balance itself automatically and the average processing time decreased. This was all done through straightforward feedback.

Case Study 2: Negative Impact of Measurement due to Misunderstanding Company Culture

A waste management company, a privatized organization that was previously owned by the city, decided to implement performance indicators. The CFO had a difficult time achieving this, as the various districts felt this was violating the "privacy" of the district and its employees. The CFO pushed the initiative through. He proceeded in the way best practices suggest. If you share performance data throughout the organization, you are providing feedback. By sharing that feedback openly, you allow different parts of the organization to rank one another in a competitive culture or to ask other units for best practices in a collaborative culture. Unfortunately, contrary to theory, the performance of the highest-scoring districts went down after a few months. Upon investigation, the CFO found that the worse-scoring districts were accusing the best-scoring districts of being "traitors" because they made them look bad. This led to conformist behavior of the better-scoring districts to create equal, or even lower, performance.

The two examples, although playing out in different industries, are very alike. Both organizations have cultures based on harmony, and both examples deal with direct feedback to the people at the operational level. Perhaps a defining difference is that the waste management company was in a process of cultural change. It is interesting to see how both groups reacted differently. Could this have been predicted? It could certainly not be predicted if the behavioral outcome is not considered. It could've been predicted if, before providing the feedback, the management team had considered the behavioral options. What could go right, and more important, what could go wrong.

The key to predict behaviors is in understanding organizational values. In our example both cultures are based on harmony. However, a value in the insurance company was "helping each other," while in the waste management company "taking it easy" was a key driver. Not all organizational values are noble and positive.

Balancing the Metrics

The basis of every set of balanced metrics consists of three different elements: cost or revenue, quality, and speed. There needs to be a balance, if quality is the only aim, then the speed of processes will decrease, and the costs will increase. Perfectionism comes at a price. If cost saving is the only factor, then quality will almost immediately suffer, and often speed will deteriorate too. You get what you pay for. If speed is of utmost importance, then quality may suffer, and cost will most definitely be an issue. It is not possible to optimize all three of the elements. Speed and cost will require quality trade-offs, speed and quality will come at a premium, and low cost and quality will take time.

There are additional balances when implementing performance management.[9] There needs to be a balance between short-term and long-term issues. Reaching strategic goals usually takes a while, up to a number of years. Step by step, you manage to get closer to the goals until you reach them and it is time to stretch those goals again. In order to reach those goals in the long term, today's action is needed. Short-term focus and long-term focus go hand in hand. Focusing on just the long-term leads to a lack of sense of urgency. Focusing on just the short-term leads to myopia.

A balance between financial and nonfinancial performance indicators is also needed. Financial results do not tell the whole story. Accountants learn that management consists of controlling multiple flows: the flow of goods (operations), the flow of money (finance), and the flow of information. Although the financial bottom line is important, the value drivers of the organization reside in the operations. A too-strong focus on finance easily leads to misinterpretation, even misrepresentation. A too-strong focus on operations may lead to nonaccountable behavior. The balance between financial and operational information leads to a higher predictability of financial results as well as a better understanding of financial consequences of operational decisions.

Organizations should also balance leading and lagging metrics. Lagging metrics are put in place in order to be able to report and to justify. Leading metrics support decision-making processes. Both should drive the right behaviors. Internal and external focus should be balanced as well. Our definition of alignment is that the self, self-perception, and external perception of the organization should closely match. Organizations should realize that the market and the environment at large have a huge impact on the organization. These influences should be weighed in internal decision making. Competitive intelligence is a crucial discipline in an organization's performance management. Another reason for external focus is the added value of benchmarking on an organization's behavior. Many operational issues are not unique, and it makes sense to face the truth and compare your organization with the best. It leads to a more realistic self-perception. At the same time, organizations shouldn't be led by the outside world. Strategies should not be copied from the competition, they should be authentic. Strategic differentiation comes from having a unique strategy. And the best way to predict the future is to shape it yourself. A good internal focus on your own strength is fundamentally healthy.

However, another balance is emerging. In most organizations, performance management and risk management are seen as separate disciplines. This is mostly because both disciplines have not reached full maturity within the average organization. The focus within performance management and risk management is more on establishing themselves than on reaching out to each other. Yet, the two disciplines are very much related. Key performance indicators complement key risk indicators. The balanced scorecard speaks of the financial, customer, process, and learning/growth perspective; risk management distinguishes financial, customer, and operational risk. There are multiple advantages to combining the two disciplines. First of all, risk management allows the organization to establish improvement projects before the performance metrics show that a problem is looming, which leads to preventive action. Secondly, risk management challenges the intuitive belief of performance measurement that everything will proceed as planned. When there are discontinuities that threaten corporate objectives, having gone through a risk management exercise prepares the organization better for dealing with them. Last, if identifying business risks leads to mitigating them already, why wait until performance indicators light up in red?

Dare to Break the Rules

Performance indicators should not be used just to judge performance but also to spark discussion. Current processes aimed at evaluating performance are very aimed at control and are restricted to evaluating the metrics themselves. The numbers come into the management information system, are compared against target, and are color-coded. Superior performance leads to green numbers, performance on target is shown by black numbers, and underperformance is shown by red numbers. The management information systems apply a filter to manage by exception and produce a list of indicators where people have underperformed. They are then warned and, at year's end, are evaluated to decide if they get a bonus or not. The results are predictable: people try to "game" the numbers, coming up with better scores that look good on paper, but actually damage the business. A more communicative process is needed. Color coding should not be automatically added the moment the new data comes into the management information system. By comparing results with the target, the responsible manager assigns the color coding. Perhaps a target is met, but the manager still assigns the color red to the metric as it could have been done even better. Or a target has not been met, but is assigned a green color, because external circumstances significantly changed. With the analysis at hand, the managers go into the management meeting where each manager explains the color coding. The manager then is queried about choices made and in the end receives a sign-off (or not) by senior management.

This process may come across as peculiar. "Writing your own report card" is something we instinctively reject. All managers would immediately score themselves a "green" on all metrics. But in the new process there is still a sign-off. Senior management approves or modifies the end evaluation. When managers score their own performance, evaluation is needed, leading to the right discussion. Setting the right example helps reduce the tendency to game the numbers, perhaps even carefully planning this example up front.

People who show that they do the right thing should be publicly recognized. Consider the example of a consulting firm. Every month, the firm held a sales meeting. In one meeting, not even halfway through the year, one of the salespeople spoke up and said that, most likely, he would not make his target if his sales didn't improve. The other salespeople at the firm believed that he had ruined his chance of receiving a bonus, because there was more than half a year to try to make the target. Senior management, however, praised that salesperson for having the courage to step forward and ask for help. Immediately, two pre-sales consultants were assigned to this salesperson, the chief operating officer promised to tour the sales manager's region, and the sales manager was awarded a special incentive for loyalty. All other sales managers stood corrected. They had learned a valuable lesson.

The new process increases the alignment of the organization and reduces gaming of the numbers, helping to lessen the gap between the organization's self and self-perception. Stepping forward and explaining one's performance evaluation leads to understanding ways of thinking within the management team, and may even reconcile differences.

Aligning Personal and Corporate Objectives

"On the Folly of Rewarding A, While Hoping for B,"[10] originally published in 1975, is a management classic. This article describes numerous examples of dysfunctional reward systems that drive dysfunctional behavior. Management is fascinated with "objective criteria," so it seeks simple, quantifiable metrics against which to reward performance. In many organizations this can be observed particularly in the sales department, where the compensation of salespeople usually consists of a very large variable component. In good years, salespeople make a lot of money (perhaps even more than their managers), but in bad years they have to do with their base salary only. Most salespeople are measured on revenue, as well as on some other indicators such as customer retention or customer satisfaction. Although revenue is an important corporate objective, it is profitability that often matters most. Many CFOs complain that margins are under pressure because salespeople give away too large a discount. However, this is caused by personal objectives (sales targets and on-target earnings) that are not aligned with corporate objectives. There is an overemphasis on visible behaviors. It is assumed that it is easier to measure revenue, or cost savings, than collaboration. It is also assumed that it is easier to measure day-to-day operations than creativity. Yet many organizations stress collaboration and welcome creativity.

Managers need to understand which behaviors are triggered by the reward systems. Not all behavior is explained by a reward system, but when the reward system creates misalignment between personal and corporate objectives, undesired behaviors will appear. Alter the reward system to drive more aligned behavior. For instance, a much better sales target would be profitability or, if profitability analysis on a per transaction basis is too complicated, contribution margin. *Contribution margin* consists of revenue minus direct costs, such as cost of goods sold or of sales. When a customer asks for a discount, the salesperson then has a different mindset, one more aligned with the overall objectives, contributing more directly to overall business performance.

When trying to recognize and reward positive behaviors, again it is crucial to understand the cultural context. Let's look at another example. In a consultancy firm there was unexpected resistance to adopt a knowledge management system, in which the company had invested millions. The company realized that, for the system to be successful, the contributions of its consultants were critical. The company created an incentive program for people who contributed actively. But the incentive program failed. Actively contributing consultants who received management recognition were viewed by their colleagues as "losers" who "obviously had nothing better to do" than to fill in a system. The consultants believed that "really important, busy consultants" wouldn't have time for that.

It is not only important to align personal and corporate objectives. This should also happen between an organization and its stakeholders. Stakeholders, such as shareholders, employees, regulators, society, business partners, suppliers, customers, and even competitors, each have an interest in organization. Mostly (with perhaps the exception of the competition) they would like the organization to succeed. However, they seldom have the same objectives. Everyone is interested in the organization obeying the law. Regulators focus on the organization's strictly following processes; whereas shareholders may worry about the cost of these processes. Customers like the organization to be trustworthy, but they are also asking for a certain speed and flexibility. Both customers and suppliers would like a high stock turnover, for fast business. However, customers want a good deal from the organization, and suppliers want a large margin. An understanding of stakeholder requirements (and their contributions) starts with an understanding of the type of relationship the organization has with its stakeholders.

Consider the example of a telecom company, seeking a good relationship with its regulator. It would like to have clear and reasonable rules to obey and advice and guidance on how to follow the rules. The telecom company works under the assumption that the regulator wants the telecom company to be successful, realizing joint value in the market. The telecom company supports the economy; the blessing of the regulator adds to the trustworthiness of the organization. However, the telecom regulator has a different view. It sees itself more as a police officer, critically watching the telecom's behaviors. The regulator is not looking to give guidance and advice beforehand; it is only interested in judging the results afterward. It treats the telecom company in a transactional way. Nothing will change until both stakeholders have the same understanding of their mutual relationship.

Every type of relationship needs to be managed, and the key in doing so is to create transparency. Without sharing information, organizations cannot collaborate and build a functional relationship. In transactional relationships transparency usually consists of operational information, such as status information on processes and perhaps financial results. In richer and deeper relationships, organizations share information on what impact they have on each other's operations, or they even build integrated balanced scorecards. The performance indicators in such relationships should be reciprocal of nature. They should focus on understanding what the stakeholders require from each other and what they contribute to each other.

For instance, the success of product sales to customers should be measured in terms of cost savings, better business opportunities, or contribution to a customer's life, instead of product or service profitability.

Or consider a healthy relationship between a hotel chain and the employee union. They do not have to be adversaries. They could measure results in terms of benefits achieved for their employees or members. The employer provides salaries, the opportunity to round out skills, and, more intangibly, a certain purpose for employees. Unions should make sure their members are skilled and efficient employees, and they could even be a preferred source for new employees.

Relations between stakeholders are ultimately based on trust and shared values. Consider the example of a private bank outsourcing its information technology operations. If the outsourcing company has a very contract-oriented culture, and prides itself on a highly process-driven approach to business, while the bank's culture is based on flexibility and an extreme customer focus, both parties will unlikely build the trust that is needed to really work with each other.

Again, stakeholder relationships are characterized by having different objectives. These objectives can be aligned to focus on the bottom-line financial results between stakeholders. These objectives can also be aligned based on power, by making the objectives of the most powerful stakeholder everyone's objectives. But by understanding the type of relationship, building the right level of transparency based on reciprocity and trust, the different stakeholders seek reconciliation of these different objectives, which is the strongest form of alignment.

Call to Action

Performance management has predominantly been a top-down exercise for most organizations. The behavioral aspect has been missing. There has been too much focus on reporting, justification, and support for decision making. Management focuses on planning and budgeting, controlling, problem solving and producing predictability, and order. Performance management so far has focused too little on establishing a common direction, aligning the different objectives of people, and making sure this is still the case tomorrow and the day after. That's where the behavioral aspects come in. That's where you need to understand the cultural context as well as the positive and negative values in your organization. That's where you use metrics to drive the right behaviors. This is how you grow from performance *management* to performance *leadership*. Although this sounds like a long-term goal, change can be surprisingly easy. Behaviors improve long before financial results do. Ask yourself the following questions:

- Which dysfunctional behaviors do I recognize in my organization, and which performance indicators drive them?
- How can I put in performance indicators that trigger positive behaviors? How can I recognize and reward these behaviors?
- Do I understand the values of my organization that drive behaviors, and are my performance indicators in line with them?
- Is my set of performance indicators truly balanced, or am I driving results in a suboptimal direction?
- Are the goals for my employees, on which their recognition and compensation is based, the same goals I have on the corporate level?

Performance management professionals, in areas such as finance and control, claim the "cultural aspects of performance management" are the hardest. The opposite is true: Behavioral change is the most concrete of all performance improvement. If you push the right buttons, meaningful and sustainable change of behavior is a matter of weeks.

Chapter | 4

PERFORMANCE LEADERSHIP FRAMEWORK

A friend of my grandmother is a medical doctor, a therapist, and a wise lady. Whenever I speak with her, we have the most wonderful discussions: for instance, about personal development. She explained that in order for people to fully develop their potential they need to mind four dimensions: the physical dimension (health, to have energy to spend on the other dimensions); the mental dimension (to intelligently set goals and know how to achieve them); the emotional and social dimension (to understand our ties to the environment in which we live); and lastly, the spiritual dimension (what we stand for in life). Only a full understanding of these dimensions unlocks a person's optimal potential. This prompted me to think about the development and performance of organizations. What happens if we apply these four dimensions to performance management? It opened my eyes and gave me a much broader view and a deeper understanding of everything I had seen so far. Later I found out the four dimensions were described by Dr. Stephen Covey.

The Organization as a Living Organism

There was a time that organizations were compared with machines. In the industrial time perhaps this was a fair comparison. Raw materials went into the factory and products were produced and distributed, very much like a machine. People, in that sense, represented little gears in the overall machinery that need some oiling once in a while or need to be replaced when they are not running smoothly anymore. Today it is more popular to compare organizations with living organisms or even human beings.[1] We place people at the heart of our performance, not machines. At least, we believe we should.

Like people, an organization has values, a character and behaviors as well. This makes a lot of sense. Like people, organizations are born, grow up, and die. Some hardly grow up, they die young and irresponsible. Other organizations mature and grow old and wise. Over time organizations expand and sometimes contract, like people who gain weight and diet when necessary. Organizations, like people, create children in the shape of new activities and business units that sometimes spin off into other activities and units.

People can only understand who they are by understanding their place in society. Equally, organizations do not operate as an island; they interact with their stakeholder environment all the time. They affect their environment and their environment affects their behavior. Organizations have a responsibility toward their environment. Organizations build partnerships and alliances, just as people have friends. Some of these relations last a long time and cross various phases in the organization's existence; some belong specifically to a particular phase in time, as friendships do. Partnerships and alliances are based on certain compatible behaviors or on an organization's values. Every organization has these values; they drive the organizational behaviors, positive and negative.

Like a human being, an organization also has a dark side; this consists of the characteristics and behaviors that are dysfunctional and of which the organization is not so proud. In order to grow and mature, these need to be understood and embraced as part of the overall package. Organizations have a will and the capability to change their mind over time, and, like people, organizations have an immune system. When new employees with incompatible values and behaviors enter the organization, they will not be accepted and will be forced out.

Some organizations even picture themselves as a human being, by defining a fictitious persona. For instance, Iceland Telecom has taken to doing this. Iceland Telecomm personifies itself as Siminn: "Siminn is a trustworthy and reliable family-oriented person around 35 years old, modern, quite fit and healthy, cheerful and pleasant to be around. He/she is respected in the community and is looked upon as a role model. He/she is international, travels a lot, and keeps up with the world and new innovations. Furthermore, Siminn is trendy, exciting, and cares about other people." Iceland Telecom uses Siminn to put a face on their values and to portray the organization as a person.

However, our approach to performance management is still very mechanistic. We try to command and control; we impose rules and regulations, external as well as internal. We align people with a common goal; we provide them with targets that we expect them to meet, instead of allowing them to be inventive and resourceful. The assets on the balance sheet include capital, raw materials, produced goods, and the valuation of the machinery and buildings. But the general ledger doesn't detail the human capital, other than the goodwill to valuate an acquired company or salary costs. As it is with managing a machine, we set up systems of control, when in reality we should set up a system of encouragement, improvement, and innovation.

The Four Dimensions of Performance Leadership

The performance management methodologies that I described in earlier chapters provide feedback on how you are doing, but they don't provide much guidance for why you are doing what you are doing or what you *should be* doing. So how do you know you have the right strategy, let alone the best strategy?

Strategic questions on which strategies to pursue tend to be quite difficult. Performance improvements can be reached in multiple ways. Should costs be saved by outsourcing to another country? Or, should it be done by innovating processes so productivity becomes higher? Should the organization focus on product innovation that leads to customer demand? Or, should it be done by listening carefully to requirements and offering what customers ask for today? The answers to these choices do not lie within the performance indicators, but within an organization's character, values, culture, or mission.

Current performance management methodologies do not provide the right encouragement. They are instruments of the mind, not of the heart. Take for instance strategy maps, DuPont schemas, or EVA. These methodologies aim to align people toward improving the bottom line—profitability and maximizing shareholder value. But to which extent does that capture what motivates people to go the extra mile, to put in the extra effort every day, to excel in what they are doing? How many people get up in the morning and as a first thought think, "Today is the day when, yet again, I am going to maximize shareholder value"? Unless you have a controlling share in your business—and even then, chances are your motivation comes from elsewhere. Bottom-line results such as profits and market share are merely the oxygen for an organization, a means to live instead of the purpose.[2]

Yet motivation is a key driver for success. A motivated person displays positive behaviors, has an eye on the business, and gives to the organization an important emotion: a passion to perform. Napoleon already acknowledged this when he said, "The moral is to the physical as three is to one." Meaning, a well-motivated force could achieve more than a larger (three times larger) less motivated one.

It's when you start to use the four dimensions of personal development, as described by Stephen Covey in *The Seven Habits of Highly Effective People,*[3] and translate them to performance management, that the questions on what the right strategies are and what truly motivates people pop up. And the answers, for that matter, as well.

In *The Seven Habits of Highly Effective People,* Covey describes the four dimensions of how to "sharpen the saw" by reflecting, taking the time to be ready, instead of being too busy sawing the tree with a blunt saw. To reflect and to develop, you need to:

• Mind the physical dimension (the body): leading a healthy life that provides the energy for development.

• Make smart decisions about yourself and understand where you stand in your life and environment: the mental dimension (the mind).

• See the importance of the emotional/social dimension (the heart), building meaningful social relationships and making decisions because they are right.

• Pay attention to the spiritual dimension (the spirit), figuring out what we want to be remembered for, and have added to the world or at least our environment.

In *The Seven Habits of Highly Effective People*, Covey writes as follows:

In an organization, the physical dimension is expressed in economic terms. The mental or psychological dimension deals with the recognition, development, and use of talent. The social/emotional dimension has to do with human relations, with how people are treated. And the spiritual dimension deals with finding meaning through purpose or contribution and through organizational integrity. When an organization neglects any one or more of these areas, it negatively impacts the entire organization. The creative energies that could result in tremendous positive synergy are instead used to fight against the organization and become restraining forces to growth and productivity.

In his later book, *The 8th Habit*, Covey expands his lessons to organizational development.[4] He describes the four needs of an organization as follows:

1. Survival—financial health (body)

2. Growth and development—economic growth, customer growth, innovation of new products and services, increasing professional and institutional competency (mind)

3. Relationships—strong synergy, strong external networks and partnering, teamwork, trust, caring, valuing differences (heart)

4. Meaning, integrity, and contribution—serving and lifting all stakeholders: customers, suppliers, employees and their families, communities, society—making a difference in the world (spirit)

According to Covey, organizations whose only driving force is economic, show negative behaviors, such as interdepartmental rivalries and protective communication. He also warns against the opposite: organizations that almost exclusively focus on the social or emotional dimension. This is not good either; profit and good management practices are needed for a sustainable business model.

In the words of Covey, the four dimensions of personal development are about "preserving and enhancing the greatest asset you have—you." Performance management is exactly the same thing, preserving and enhancing the organization. Analogous to Covey's dimensions for personal development and his application of those to the business world, I have identified four dimensions of performance management: the operational; the analytical; the social; and the value dimensions.

Operational Dimension

Organizations need to be healthy and to have energy for development. Day-to-day operations need to be in good shape, and ambitious goals need to be set in order to reach and stretch and become faster and more agile and have more capacity. But we also need to give the organization some rest so as not to overstress. We allocate enough time for our people and our processes to recuperate and do the necessary maintenance, or we provide feedback to reflect and innovate. The operational dimension matches the "first loop of management," monitoring how we are doing against established goals. Performance indicators in the operational dimension are by definition very transactional in nature and measure the effectiveness and efficiency of the daily work of various business domains. In physical terms, it's important to keep the body healthy so it can function, and there are general rules about healthy living. There are many best practices for operational management, and it makes sense to put a benchmarking program in place to compare parts of the organization with other parts or other organizations. Even the performance indicators can largely be standardized.

If we have swift and agile management processes, we can quickly detect changes in our environment and our own performance. We can act immediately and prevent or correct before any potential issues become a wildfire. There is a need for integration points between the first loop and the second loop of management, and some real-time management information. Managing the day-to-day operation never stops. We can never take our eyes off the ball. In Covey's words, "This dimension is about discipline."

Analytical Dimension

You need to answer a set of three questions for the development of your organization. The three questions are:

- Where do we want to be?
- Where are we now?
- How are we going to get there?

In large part, the journey is the destination. Strategy is a continuous learning experience instead of a five-year plan. In Covey's terms, strategy requires us "to see the end from the beginning and to see the entire journey, at least in principle," and to fill in the details as we go. The analytical dimension represents the second loop of management, asking yourself if the targets are ambitious enough or if you are managing the right process.

In order to be successful, you need a strategy that sets you apart. Best practices only bring you so far. High performers don't benchmark themselves with others, but with their aspirational goals. On this level, strategies, processes, and performance indicators cannot be standardized, as every organization has some unique characteristics. First of all, different organizations, even in the same market, have different strategies. Some organizations excel in being lean and mean; they have clear cost leadership and deliver their service with unrivaled speed and operational excellence. Others are completely original in their approach to service, product development, and speed to market; they excel in innovation. Lastly, there are companies that may not be the cheapest or most advanced; they are simply there for when the customer needs them, and they excel in customer service. Each of these strategies leads to a different set of business drivers and therefore business metrics. Further, even two organizations in the same market with the same strategy have key differences, because of different levels of maturity and skill sets of the key staff. Lastly, every organization has strategic projects that need to be monitored and issues that need to be resolved that require specific metrics, but only for a certain period of time.

The analytical dimension represents the mental state: is it clear and organized? Or is the mind of the organization less focused, distracted, and ineffective? In order to make the continuous learning exercise a mutual process, all involved parties need to have a common understanding, "speak the same language," or in business jargon "have one version of the truth." Defining a single language and a single way of working is crucial for an organization's alignment, but—like everything worthwhile—a difficult exercise. As in day-to-day operations, working on the analytical dimension never stops. We need to be agile and respond to changing circumstances—or, even better, drive changing circumstances. This dimension is about learning and strategy as a continuous process.

Social Dimension

People perform best as part of a group. It brings out our social behavior; we can be challenged to achieve goals we wouldn't dream of achieving alone. We take pride in what we contribute to the group, and value the appreciation that is returned. This doesn't mean we are only defined through our position in the group. That would be called *dependence*, where one person cannot function without the other or others. In cases where this is a mutual condition, it is called *codependence*. Dependent or codependent relationships run a high risk of collapsing, or being lost completely in the relationship. The opposite would be *independence*, where a person relies on himself or herself totally. However, people usually need to be part of a group to be most effective. The best relationships are based on *interdependence*, combining the best of both worlds. Based on our own, intrinsic security we choose to depend on others. We choose mutual responsibility because we want to, not because we need to. As a result, we rely on and, if needed, fall back on ourselves. We have sustainable relationships on which we can build in good and in bad times.

Having organizations dependent on each other would be an economically unfavorable position. Most organizations believe in independence, describing their environment as "dog eat dog" or "lunch or be lunch." But, just as it does on the personal level, *interdependence* creates the most sustainable business model. The organization understands very well that its existence is based on business granted by the customers, support capital from the shareholders, and infrastructure supplied by society. The social dimension shows that good management is based on a sound business model that bridges the needs of the various stakeholders. Like every other strategy, the effect of social business models on innovation, customer perception, and (future) bottom line can and should be measured.

Values Dimension

Covey connects the spiritual dimension to leadership. He states that values are the "leadership center of our lives, what life is ultimately about, it spreads like an umbrella over anything else."

Again, this is no different in organizations. Like a person, organizations have beliefs and values too. Organizational values can be defined as an organization's principal behavior on the highest level. These values are an aggregation of the personal values of people who work for the organization, and they attract people with the same values to the organization. Values help us understand the behaviors of people; they provide the necessary context. Next to positive values, organizations have negative values as well. It is important not to dismiss them; they have the same power the positive values have on an organization's culture. This organizational culture can be defined as an organization's practical behavior that can be observed over and over again in similar situations. Culture is an important driver for the success of performance management. If you don't align your performance management, feedback, and reward system to the organizational culture, dysfunctional behaviors will result.

A good mission statement helps. Most organizations have them, but few actually live by them. Bad mission statements state the obvious. Great mission statements pinpoint organizational values that are recognized internally (self-perception) as well as externally (external perception), leading to strategic alignment. A great mission statement guides which performance indicators and initiatives are needed in the other dimensions, in order to make the mission statement tangible.

In comparison, the social dimension of performance leadership teaches us that strategies need to be aligned with how we serve our stakeholders. We look to the outside world to see where we can add value and respond accordingly. The values dimension then balances this with an inside-out view. It tells us who we are and what we are really good at, to make sure we keep adding value over the longer term.

Performance Leadership Framework

Management and leadership are not the same.[5] Management is about planning and budgeting, organizing and staffing, controlling and problem solving, as well as producing predictability and order. And this is exactly what traditional performance management supports in the operational and analytical dimensions. Leadership is something else; it entails establishing direction, aligning, motivating, and inspiring people, as well as producing change. Leadership is often simply defined as "achieving results through other people." And this is exactly what the performance leadership framework helps you do.

Performance leadership doesn't neglect the traditional objectives of performance management. Planning and controlling are still clear goals. But performance leadership requires more. Establishing direction and producing change requires organizational commitment. Aligning, motivating, and inspiring people requires pushing the right buttons so that people take the right actions. That's where the behavioral aspects come in. These are needed to create strategic alignment—all people taking the right actions, not only within the organization but across all stakeholders.

PERFORMANCE LEADERSHIP

Performance leadership achieves results through all stakeholders (within and outside the organization) by building a common purpose and bridging the different and sometimes conflicting objectives of the various stakeholders.

An organization is a unique collaboration of stakeholders for the purpose of realizing goals they could not achieve by themselves. Stakeholders all make unique contributions to the success of the organization, but they also have specific requirements. Often these requirements are conflicting. The performance leadership framework shows how to identify these requirements and how to align the various stakeholder contributions. The performance leadership framework also clearly shows that optimizing one's own performance is only a small piece of the pie. Performance leadership is about eating the whole pie.

The performance leadership framework (outlined in Figure 4.1) aims to improve our understanding of performance management and

Figure 4.1

The Performance Leadership Framework

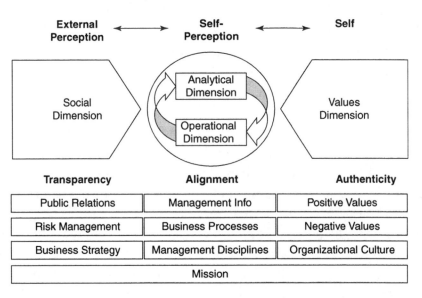

to raise the bar. The operational dimension and the analytical dimension represent business-as-usual performance management, the two loops of management. The operational and analytical dimensions provide an organization's self-perception. Management reports show how we are doing against targets. Reports are analyzed, interpreted, and then discussed by the management team; results are perceived as good or bad. The key to better self-perception is alignment, making sure the management reports have a "single version of the truth," instead of different stories. Business processes need to be aligned for managers to understand their contribution to the overall results. And management disciplines, such as performance management and risk management, should be aligned for complete and balanced decision making.

The social dimension and values dimension are new to performance management. They provide the *guidance* that is needed to come to the right strategies and decisions. The social dimension provides the "outside-in view." It guides organizations in determining how the actions and reactions of the organization's environment affects the business. This is important, at least for public relations and risk management purposes, but on a more strategic level it also helps define a better business model. The values dimension does the opposite from the social dimension. It presents the "inside-out view." Different organizations have different cultures, values, and missions. Things that make business initiatives successful in one organization can be a complete failure in another organization. The traditional business case, based on the operational and analytical dimension, will not reveal that.

The social and values dimensions are often at odds with each other. The market may ask for a different approach to the products and services the organization sells than the values prescribe. The organization may value quality, while the market is asking for low prices. Organizational cultures may contain elements that you would be less proud of, such as a touch of opportunism or greed, that you wouldn't like to share with the outside world. An organization's mission may be noble, but it may not always be recognized by the outside world in daily behaviors. This can lead to dysfunctional behaviors such as "tricking the system" to do "the right thing" (or the wrong thing for that matter) despite what procedures and processes state. It could also lead to wrong decisions, where — despite a glowing business case — a new business initiative that looked good on paper fails. In any event, failure to understand the context of the social and values dimension, leads to unanticipated or badly understood behaviors. The performance leadership framework improves organizational behavior.

What becomes clear, when going through the four dimensions, is that our current performance management processes only take two of the four dimensions into account: the operational and analytical dimensions. We run the day-to-day processes in our organization, and once in a while take a step back and see if we are still doing the right things — that is, if we can agree on what the right things are. What is missing in traditional performance management methodologies is guidance on what the right things are. The performance leadership framework does not replace other methodologies, such as the balanced scorecard, value-based management, or beyond budgeting. In fact, these methodologies are perfect to manage the operational and analytical dimensions of the business. However, traditional performance management needs the overlay of the social and values dimensions of the business. Usually these are missing, or at best, they're assumed to be known to the organization. This may be true, but practice shows that as a result there is no alignment. The mission statement is either catching dust on the Web site, or it is viewed in a cynical way. Social aspects are reduced to "corporate philanthropy" and are part of the public relations program of the organization.

The performance leadership framework helps to make sure other people, beyond your direct span of control, care as much about the business as you do and that they do the right thing. They need to be on the same path, the same mission, and intuitively make the same decisions as you would. They need to be driven by the same guiding values and have a common purpose. In this we need to realize different people have different agenda's. True leaders define a common purpose between the various stakeholders and build bridges instead of favoring a single stakeholder.

PRACTICAL IMPROVEMENTS FOR THE OPERATIONAL AND ANALYTICAL DIMENSIONS

—

Part II discusses the traditional operational and analytical dimensions of performance management, and it introduces a different view on alignment of management information, business processes, and business disciplines.

- The horizontal alignment of management information provides a fresh perspective and a surprisingly simple solution for creating the "one version of the truth," a big issue in performance management.
- The management hierarchy has introduced business domains. These various domains interact or interface with each other, but current methodologies do not take these business interfaces into account.
- No performance is without risk. Strategic risk management and performance management need to be aligned; they are not separate disciplines.

Chapter | 5

OPERATIONAL
AND ANALYTICAL
ALIGNMENT

Most of us have—deep in our minds—models of management
based on the classic, centralized philosophy of command and control.
To be successful in the world we're entering, we will need a new set
of mental models.[1]
—Thomas W. Malone, Professor,
MIT Sloan School of Management, Boston

The operational and analytical dimensions form the basis of the performance leadership framework. The operational dimension focuses on how to manage day-to-day operations, or the first loop of management. The first loop of management concentrates on monitoring the current state of business processes. The operational dimension is by definition transactional: it manages the effectiveness and efficiency of the daily work of various business domains. Activities on the operational level are monitored and the results are measured against targets. The moment the targets are not met, or the measurements go in the direction of critical thresholds, adjustments need to take place. Managing the day-to-day operation never stops. We can never take our eyes off the ball. In Covey's words, "This dimension is about discipline."

The analytical dimension focuses on the second loop of management. The second loop of management works offline to study information and to aid in planning. Where the first loop of management focuses on measuring how the performance compares to the targets, the second loop of management looks to see if the targets are set too high or perhaps even too low. In the second loop of management the managers should, from time to time, also discuss if the right things are being measured or if better metrics are available. Lastly, on a more strategic level, the processes themselves should be evaluated. How does a specific process relate to the other processes in the organization? Could it be structured more efficiently or be more aligned to other processes? How does the process support the customer value proposition?

There's an incredible amount of research on operational excellence, strategy implementation, business intelligence, performance management, and other topics related to the operational and analytical dimension. In this book, I will not attempt to summarize or synthesize; instead, I will focus on a number of key improvements organizations can make by looking at the operational and analytical dimensions in a different way. See Figure 5.1.

Figure 5.1

The Operational and Analytical Dimensions of the Performance
Leadership Framework

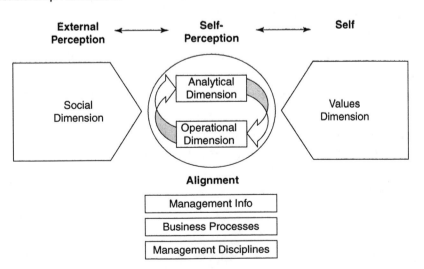

Aligning Operational and Analytical Dimensions

If implemented well, the two loops of management allow for double-loop learning, as well as for management control. However, this can only happen if the loops are integrated. In many organizations, there are countless processes, systems, and reports on the operational dimension, and even more presentations, studies, systems, and money spent on the analytical dimension. But these dimensions are often disconnected. This makes it hard to implement new strategies or apply quick course changes from the analytical dimension to the operational dimension. It makes it equally hard to escalate operational issues to the analytical dimension in a structured and reliable way. I refer to disconnected loops as the "donut model" and to the connected loops as the "pretzel model" (see Figure 5.2).

The donut model represents the classical approach to strategic management and strategy implementation. A new strategy is implemented,

Figure 5.2

The Unaligned (Donut-Shaped) Loops of Management versus the Aligned (Pretzel-Shaped) Loops of Management

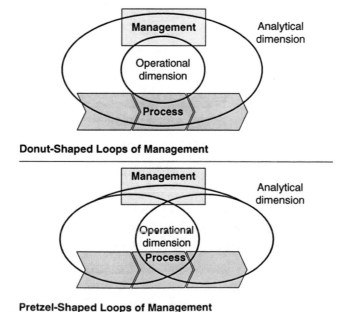

Donut-Shaped Loops of Management

Pretzel-Shaped Loops of Management

typically in the form of a project, and it starts to run. In the first loop of management, feedback is collected and the processes that are managed are fine-tuned within the confines of the specifics of that particular strategy. An offline feedback loop may report the performance of the overall process on a monthly basis or may be triggered when an external discontinuity (such as changes in the market) occurs. Typically, there are multiple donuts, as organizations tend to optimize just a certain domain, such as in supply chain management, customer relationship management, or back office management (enterprise resource planning).

To achieve operational and analytical alignment, the two loops of management should be shaped like a pretzel, a continuous cycle of not only the first loop but also the second loop of management. Within the pretzel model, the first loop and second loop of management invoke each other. Early warning signals from first loop monitoring can immediately trigger a strategic review. It is not necessary to wait for a trend to appear. Previous experience or an early warning signal in related connected cycles can be observed and acted on. For instance, decreased performance in the supply chain may affect the performance in customer-facing loops a little while later. Bottom-up input, collected from a larger group of people, either triggers new strategic thinking or contributes to an existing exercise. At the same time, improvements and changes in the strategy are carefully implemented in an incremental manner and tested; instead of necessitating heroic decisions, dramatic strategy shifts, and radical process redesigns. There are multiple reasons why the pretzel model design is important for operational and analytical alignment.

Escalation of Major Operational Problems

Organizations do not live in a closed system. Hiding information from the outside world is a losing strategy, if it were even possible. But for transparency to be successful, it is crucial to have the processes on which you share information under control. This is important all the time, but it is vital when there are operational issues so that problems can be corrected quickly before the problem escalates. A well-known example from the field of crisis management comes from the reaction from a baby food company when glass fragments were found in baby food jars. A well-defined process was in place to prevent the escalation of the problem; a full set of details were shared with the public, which helped address a major public image risk.

External Triggers

Being in touch with your stakeholder environment is of vital importance in decision-making processes. The higher up the ladder, the more external events affect management. Increasingly, real-time information on competitive initiatives, major events in the market, or legal threats needs an immediate response. The sooner the response comes, through an aligned management decision-making process, the better the external world will perceive the organization.

Strategic Initiatives

Every organization has a few strategic projects or activities that have to be watched closely for a certain amount of time. These special initiatives always need extra attention. Although new products, services, joint ventures, and special marketing campaigns may not have a substantial impact on today's bottom line, they are of strategic importance and will affect the future performance of the enterprise. Typically, these special business activities need more short-term attention than established activities. This warrants executive attention and much more frequent monitoring than other day-to-day activities. The same goes for special business events, such as quarterly closings. Where in other weeks perhaps a weekly overview of the sales pipeline is sufficient, in the last week of the quarter a daily update may be needed; in the last two or three days perhaps an update every hour is required.

Comfort Information

Senior management, like everyone else in the organization, needs "comfort information." Comfort information can be defined as those performance indicators that most likely will be under control, usually do not need specific attention, and make the manager feel in control. Real-time management information is not always about exceptions that need to be corrected. An executive of a mobile telecom operator, for example, may want daily reports on the availability of the network or the number of subscriptions sold. A sales manager may want daily overviews of sales from the point-of-sale system.

Economies of Scale

Increasingly, organizations are centralizing back-office operations across more than one line of business. Sometimes these are outsourced, or they form shared service centers. This can be seen in typical support functions, such as HR, finance, and IT. Although a large part of the work may be transactional of nature, the sheer size of such a combined operation affects the whole business, particularly when the processes do not run smoothly. A small problem may immediately have a large cost consequence. It is vital to monitor centralized operations closely. This must be done on an executive level, as these centralized operations transcend a single line of business.

Alignment, by building the pretzel model, is one of the most important goals of performance management. If management has a shared insight, it bridges the gap between the self and the self-perception of the organization. But there is also an external side to alignment: understanding how external trends affect our business, so that we can align external events with swift and adequate internal reaction.

Increased alignment and use of the pretzel model are driven by the need for increased transparency and agility. Performance management uses scenario analysis (top-down implementation of the pretzel model), rolling forecasts (bottom-up implementation of the pretzel model), and real-time information (speeding up the overall pretzel model).

Scenario Analysis

Scenario analysis is a way of exploring multiple potential future realities as part of a strategy formulation process. One practical way of creating a scenario analysis is by first listing the most important assumptions in the business model, both internal and external. External assumptions can be economic in nature, such as the growth of the economy, the cost of capital, and the cost of labor. There are also social assumptions, around demographics or fashion trends, for instance, or what constitutes attractive product design or effective messaging. There may also be political or legal assumptions, around tax pressure, labor laws, ecological practices, subsidies, compliance, or accepted business practices. Many assumptions are based on technology restrictions: What is possible today is being extrapolated into the future. Internal assumptions may be based on the company's typical business processes, for instance, from order to cash, or decision-making processes around, for instance, financing projects. The next step after listing these business assumptions is imagining the opposite. What happens if what we hold as true, doesn't work anymore? How would the business model change if there is no market growth, or if the cost of labor is going up (or down, for that matter)? Or what happens if an important technological restriction is lifted because of new research?

Scenario analysis is also a behavioral tool for structuring one's perceptions about alternative future environments in which one's decisions might be played out.[2] A set of stories may be built around a few major "plots" about how the world may turn out to be. Others have taken a more quantitative approach, by applying probabilities on scenarios and calculating expected returns. Scenarios don't help predict the future, but they do help organizations to be ready, no matter which of the scenarios becomes a reality. The often-recited and most well-known example of the enormous business impact of scenario analysis comes from Shell. When the 1970s oil crisis hit, Shell had the scenario ready. As a lot of the thinking had been done, it was easier for Shell to drastically change strategy while still being in control. Shell came out as a strong market leader.

Even if reality is different than any of the plotted scenarios, there is a huge advantage of having gone through a scenario analysis exercise. Thinking in terms of flexible outcomes and alternative strategies unfreezes the mind. People experienced in thinking in terms of scenarios will be less likely to stick to an established strategy even if reality is moving in a different direction. Scenario analysis contributes to alignment between the first and second loop of management, from a top-down direction. Continuously considering different courses of action asks for an agile strategy implementation process. Strategies are not cast in stone and are implemented to last a number of years.

Scenario analysis helps managing external perception versus self-perception. A large part of scenario building has to do with external factors, what happens in our political, economic, social, and technological environment. Change in our environment may lead to changes in how the organization is being perceived and what is expected of the organization. Structurally thinking about the consequences of these changes demonstrates that the organization doesn't close its eyes to the environment. Just as with people who act effectively within their environment, external perception influences self-perception.

Rolling Forecasts

The management process with the greatest impact in most organizations is the budget. It is also the most rigid process, leading to significant frustration. Budgeting processes are expensive, take a long time, are often based on negotiation and power; but they fail to optimize the use of corporate resources. As a result, many budgeting processes lead to dysfunctional behaviors, such as gaming and measure fixation. Budgeting is often structured as the donut model. Every year a new budget cycle is started. Discontinuities, during the year, may lead to a new forecast, but they do not change the budget. When it is time for the final variance analysis, chances are that the new situation cannot really be compared with the old situation, and all games begin again.

Many organizations are already adopting rolling forecasts. A rolling forecast is typically a monthly or quarterly process that evaluates the last period and updates the forecast for the next periods—four or five quarters, or twelve to fifteen months.

In the beginning of the first quarter of the year, the fourth quarter is evaluated and based on what is learned, the forecast for the first to the fourth quarter is updated, and becomes the new target. In that first quarter of the year, there should be some progress toward the forecast; and in the beginning of the second quarter, based on the feedback, the forecast is updated again. This updating process never stops regardless of which period of the year it is. The artificial event of a new year does not affect the process.

However, for public companies a new quarter or a new year still has a significant business impact. Perhaps during the last month of a quarter, there is even a weekly rolling forecast and during the last week of the quarter perhaps even a daily process. Moreover, the concept of a rolling forecast doesn't prescribe it should be a periodic process to start with. Periodic attention makes sense to keep the right focus on the forecast, but external events may trigger a new rolling forecast as well. External events can be new regulations or laws, sudden economic turns such as increases in the price of oil, changes in the social environment such as public opinion, the availability of new technology, or strategic moves or failures of the competition that require an immediate response. Including a continuous external analysis in a rolling forecast encourages the organization to benchmark itself, creating a relative view on performance.

Rolling forecasts bring alignment between the first and second loop of management, connecting operational resources with financial outcomes. At any moment, the first loop of management can invoke a second loop, to create a new forecast and implement measures to work against that updated forecast. In other words, rolling forecasts provide an upward trigger. By using a rolling forecast, there is a continuous check to see whether business reality changes and how that affects the bottom line. Where budgets only trigger discussion on having "made the numbers" or not, rolling forecasts invite a different discussion: assessing internal and external changes and what to do about it. Rolling forecasts, because of their higher frequency, also lead to a mindset of continuous improvement, instead of hitting that single number.

Real-Time Information

The pretzel model, where the first and second loops of management are aligned and invoke each other when necessary, can only be effective if the periodicity of information as a feedback mechanism matches the speed of the decision-making processes. The needed periodicity of information is changing, and this highly affects the pretzel model of aligning the operational and analytical dimensions of performance leadership. It is clear that the pace of business is increasing. The time-to-market for many products has dramatically decreased, as well as overall product life cycles. Where traditionally the fashion industry had a collection per season, today Spanish fashion retail chain Zara has 26 collections per year. Because of the increasing pace of business and the huge variety of demand, businesses need to be continuously monitoring their performance. Last, but not least, continuous focus on monitoring is needed because of price competition in many industries. With tiny margins there is no room or time for error. Organizations use the pretzel model so that they can be on top of the game all the time.

However, caution is warranted. For years, managers claimed they needed comprehensive and immediate information in order to make optimal decisions. Others have countered that, pointing out the dangers of "analysis paralysis," where too much information leads to stifled organizations. Immediacy of information has been a hot topic for years, but mostly a theoretical discussion because it wasn't possible on a technical level. With IT innovations, it becomes possible to create and supply more real-time information. This means that considering where real-time information makes sense, and where it doesn't, becomes a crucial question. Sometimes daily is more than enough, and sometimes an immediate response is necessary.

There is much "hype" surrounding the subject. In many cases, real-time simply doesn't make sense. Consider the example of "real-time customer satisfaction." How should that be monitored? And if customer satisfaction is decreasing during the day, what can be done about it? It is much more important to have a solid understanding of what drives customer satisfaction. For instance, in a logistics organization it makes sense to have control of overnight delivery, predicting workload in the various activities of the process. Managing these drivers of customer satisfaction in real time should lead to overall customer satisfaction.

To know where real-time management information is needed, it is important to understand how decision-making processes work. Decisions at an operational level, such as those concerning inventory management or workload analysis, are usually based on quantifiable data, singular facts, and clear events, all of which usually come from a single process or system. Based on a clear set of data and a clearly defined scope, decisions can be made. Decisions follow facts.

For more senior managers the decision-making process is different. Often, decisions are based on market insight, various, seemingly unrelated and certainly unintegrated qualitative and quantitative sources. These decisions are more future-oriented, often based on uncertain scenarios, and not always as quantifiable. However, senior management needs to justify these decisions to shareholders, employees, and other constituents; their decisions should be based on facts too. On a more strategic level, facts follow decisions. Running the numbers and putting together a business plan is done after the topic has been discussed in the senior leadership team meeting.

Not by complete coincidence do these two ways of making decisions mimic the two loops of management. The obvious conclusion is that making all management information real time does not make sense; not all decisions are of the "decisions follow facts" kind. Senior managers, who often complain they are drawn into operational issues too much, should be careful in asking for more real-time information, as most likely this will involve them even more in operational issues.

In reality, it can be a good thing to have a short time delay between an alert and a response. Like with a thermostat, continuously increasing and decreasing the temperature level will make the temperature in the room less than stable; in fact, the amplitudes will become bigger and bigger. An example from the business environment that most of us have experienced is dealing with e-mail. How many times has it happened that you return to the office after a day having been offline, to find an e-mail urgently asking for your help, and another e-mail a short while later stating "never mind, it has been fixed already."

There should be a well-defined path down the management chain and a clear escalation path up. Senior management should not drill down to the operational level. Most alerts should be dealt with by lower and middle managers. Those alerts that reach senior managers should concern more complex, far-reaching problems and only the most acute of all others. In this way, managers are not overburdened with alerts, and problems can be dealt with by the people best suited to handle them.

A flood of alerts could lead to inertia. Managers will start to ignore alerts if there are simply too many. How about that one alert that actually was important? Even worse, a flood of alerts could lead senior management to micromanage their staff. Executives typically deal with escalated problems. If problems are escalated to a senior level too fast, it is assumed to be an example of a frequent problem, and the manager takes strong action. When a small issue is unnecessarily escalated, the reaction may be out of proportion.

The most important consideration in selecting what information needs to be in real time is the type of follow-up. If there are no processes and systems to follow up on a real time alert, it makes no sense to supply the information faster. In a way, information should be "right time" instead of real time. The required periodicity of information as a feedback mechanism depends on the speed of the other parts of the management process. Sometimes this means that processes to take action should be redesigned to speed up, and sometimes this will mean feedback simply shouldn't be that fast.

Right-time information makes the alignment between self and self-perception and the alignment between external perception and self actionable. The window of opportunity to take corrective or preventive action is an important consideration in establishing right-time information needs.

Horizontal and Vertical Alignment

The biggest problem with performance management is that everything, including the pretzel model, is structured in a hierarchical way. Strategy implementation is a top-down process, in which we need to identify everyone's contribution to the central, corporate goals. We say that we "cascade" scorecards down into the organization. We "roll up" budget numbers. We "drill down" to see where deviations from the plan occur. And we "work our way up" the corporate hierarchy. Each business domain only "reports up" strategic objectives; and most of the reporting is "self-reporting," that is, reporting based on a business unit's own data. Typically, managers are not aware of what their peers report and neither are senior managers—two levels higher—intimately aware of the subtle detail either. Alignment is a vertical exercise, our managers only get "the big picture" (if they get a fair picture at all).

Vertical alignment makes sense, at least in part. People need hierarchy. This has been the case since the dawn of society. Families are hierarchic, the church has a hierarchy, the military has a very strong sense of hierarchy. Then business came along as a new societal structure, again hierarchic. Hierarchies are very effective for managing people. People rise in the hierarchy through seniority based on a long career path. Leadership, which we earlier defined as the ability to achieve results through other people, is best served by a hierarchy, as it allows leaders to hand down instructions and collect and compile feedback.

After a scenario analysis, a management hierarchy translates clear strategic objectives into operational plans and makes sure there is an effective organization. Swift feedback to the strategic level comes from rolling forecasts and right-time information. At the same time, the hierarchy provides focus for the people on the various lower levels.

But work doesn't flow like a hierarchy, it flows from outside the organization into the organization, and out again, passing multiple nodes in a network of activities. Work needs to be managed as a network, with flows, interfaces, inputs, and outputs. There is feed forward information, that shows what is coming through the value chain, and there is feedback information, that captures the performance of the past steps in the value chain. As argued in methodologies such as zero-based budgeting, beyond budgeting, and activity-based management, planning and monitoring is best managed through the network of activities, and not a top-down hierarchic approach. Horizontal alignment is needed as well.

VERTICAL VERSUS HORIZONTAL ALIGNMENT

Vertical alignment uses the corporate hierarchy to implement strategy and to provide feedback. It is a top-down and bottom-up approach. The higher up in the organization, the more aggregated the data become, the more strategic impact management decisions have, and the more external the organization view becomes.

Horizontal alignment uses the value chain to create an efficient and an effective business. On the strategic level it tries to reconcile different (even conflicting) objectives of the different stakeholders. Next to feedback to previous steps in activities, processes, departments or organizations, to optimize collaboration, there is feed forward information to next steps.

When the need for both vertical and horizontal alignment is not well understood, performance management adds to misalignment in an organization. It will lead to unwanted isolated behaviors and not to collaboration and "doing the right thing." For instance, why is budgeting such a mess in many organizations? Why does the process take so long (four to six months is not an exception), and why does it result in a disconnect (artificial numbers)? The answer is that it is using a hierarchy where a network approach should be used. In a hierarchy, budgets are for the business domains and for protecting the hierarchy. The process leads to games and disconnected results. Usually the various domains are not intimately aware of the business of adjacent business domains or of how operational decisions affect the other business domains. Also, management that is two or more levels removed from a certain business activity looses insight into the finer details. The question whether to take away a part of the resources in department B and reapply them elsewhere in the value chain, in department A, to get a multiple of the output overall, including in department B, will not likely come up. And if it comes up, it will be fought by management, as loss of budget equals loss of power.

Budgeting, planning, and rolling forecasts should be an exercise focused on the cost and revenue drivers, and how resources and activities in the end translate as financial results, in other words, a value chain. The financial results, in the end, can then be allocated to—which is the opposite to cascaded down from—the various units in the organization, to support the hierarchy for the necessary people management. The process should be overseen and managed by the hierarchy, but not be structured hierarchically. Real-time information should not only benefit senior management, but it should be a tool to create feedback to previous steps in the value chain, to show them the result of their work, and as feed forward information to next steps in the value chain, as an early warning signal. Scenario analysis should not be an ivory tower exercise, focused at the organization alone; it should consist of continuous conversations with selected and trusted stakeholders, such as employees, long-time customers, strategic partners, and society representatives.

But not everything can be managed as a network, as a flow of activities. In the 1990s we saw many network organizations aiming to be completely work-managed. People were networked around business initiatives, bottom-up entrepreneurial initiatives were supported and departmental structures were dissolved. When economic times became hard, many of these organizations collapsed as they lost a sense of direction. There was a lack of leadership and structure to change course and pull everyone together. Or perhaps there was too much leadership from all employees, who all had their own ideas about the way to go. Lack of focus and coordination all of a sudden led to an ineffective response to changing market circumstances. In most situations, a strong hierarchy would have been needed to set a new course in time.

With the distinction between vertical alignment and horizontal alignment, we understand that success is not in minding your own business only, but in being collaborative. As measurement drives behavior, performance should not only be defined and measured in what you *achieve* in your business domain, but also what you *enable* for the rest of the organization or the stakeholders around it.

Scenario analysis, rolling forecasts, and more real-time information represent today's best practices. Applying horizontal alignment in performance management leads to new insights—to "next practices."

Chapter | 6

ONE VERSION
OF THE TRUTH

The more a business term is connected to the core business, the more definitions of it will be around.

In the Kingdom of Truth, Context Is King

Since the advent of MIS (management information systems), the "Holy Grail" has been to create a single version of the truth: a single set of reports and definitions for all business terms to make sure every manager has a common understanding of accurate corporate information. In the last 20 to 30 years, countless projects have been started to identify all these different versions of the truth. These projects then try to collapse these different versions into a single definition so that all business departments can align themselves with the crucial business term. In other words, these projects are trying to apply vertical alignment to the problem.

Rarely have these exercises been successful. It's no wonder as they have been misguided. The reason why all these versions of the truth, often under the same name, exist in isolation is the vertically aligned setup of the management structure. Each business domain only reports up, and most of the reporting is "self-reporting," the domain reporting is based on its own data. At the same time, apart from political reasons of not wanting to align, there is a reason there are multiple definitions of common business terms such as revenue, number of employees, and number of customers. There are also industry-specific terms that have many different definitions, such as *flight* for an airline, *mile*, or *kilometer*, for a taxi company, *student* for a university, *transaction* for a bank, and *hour* for a consultancy company. Using a process-oriented approach to create horizontal alignment, multiple versions of the truth actually make sense. To put it bluntly, if a business department does not have a unique view, what value is it adding to the organization? In short, there is an important rule here:

The more a business term is connected to the core business, the more definitions of it will be around.

This doesn't mean that every single definition is valid and should be preserved—in fact, many definitions may be redundant. The real question is how does an organization decide which definitions are valid and which are not. Valid definitions, placed in the right order, constitute "one context of the truth."[1] I will discuss a few examples from the following industries:

- A software company dealing with revenue definitions
- A European railway company managing multiple definitions of the term *train*
- E-plus, a mobile telecom operator, dealing with average revenue per user (ARPU)
- A retail bank counting the number of money transfers

Case Study 1: Software Company

In contrast to the manufacturing industry, the price of the product—a software license—is only indirectly linked to the development cost. This usually leaves a good amount of negotiation room between the company and prospective customers. Usually the amount of discount allowed is connected to the seniority and management position of the sales executives in the company. For instance, account managers are allowed to discount up to 10 percent, senior account managers up to 15 percent, sales managers up to 25 percent, and the regional vice president above 25 percent. In most software companies, on the other hand,

Table 6.1

Definitions of "Revenue"

Gross revenue	Total sales before software discounts, customer bonuses, and lead incentives for partners
Net revenue	Total sales after software discounts, customer bonuses, and lead incentives for partners
Net own revenue	Net revenue, minus royalties to third parties
Recognized revenue	Accepted bookings in the finance system
Revenue U.S. GAAP	Revenue according to U.S. accounting rules
Revenue local GAAP	Revenue according to country-specific accounting rules
Management revenue	Total revenue for a region including revenue coming from other regions or countries for local customers, and excluding local revenue for customers belonging to other regions or countries
Commission revenue	Total revenue matched against a salesperson's targets
Invoiced amount	The amount that is invoiced in the current period. This amount may not all be revenue for the current period. For instance, multiple years of maintenance revenue can be invoiced up front
Statutory revenue	Revenue as reported to the outside world
Fiscal revenue	Revenue as reported to the tax office
Cash inflow	Technically not revenue, but the last metric in the process

the steps taken before a quote is on the table are very well managed. Most software companies have a strong focus on building a "pipeline" of prospective deals to be closed that particular quarter, that provide "coverage" to make the "forecast" and the "budget." The realized revenue is the result. Or is realized revenue the end result?

Table 6.1 has a few examples of the many versions of the truth. In this somewhat simplified listing, there are 12 variants of revenue. Management reports will refer to "revenue" for many of the variants and which revenue actually is meant often depends on the context of the report and largely for which manager and which business domain it is created. The performance of that particular manager in that particular business domain is reviewed by top management. Horizontal alignment occurs when managers and their superiors see not only what they achieve within their own business domain, but also what they enable for their peers in other business domains, as displayed in Table 6.2.

Table 6.2

Alignment of Revenue

	Actual	Plus or Minus	Description
Gross revenue	10,000		
Net revenue	7,500	–2.500	Discounts
Net own revenue	6,000	–1.500	Royalties
Recognized revenue	5,500	–500	Not recognized this period
Management revenue	6,200	+1.000/–300	From/to other countries
Total commission revenue	6,800	+600	Double commission (overlay)
Invoiced amount	8,000	+500	Future revenue
Cash inflow	8,800		Paid from previous periods
Statutory revenue	6,300		
CIT/VAT revenue	6,600		

The country manager may see that the difference between gross revenue and net revenue is about average, and thus discounting has been kept within the normal range. However, if we also subtract royalties, the manager may consider net own revenue to be rather small. The software sold contains components for which royalties are paid to a partner. By itself, this is neither good nor bad. It decreases margin, but may indirectly improve the value of the relationship, potentially leading to acquisition of the partner, and therefore increasing overall revenue and profitability in the longer term.

The gap between net revenue and recognized revenue can mean different things. Usually, it is caused by revenue being recognized in future periods, such as maintenance or consulting services. This is perfectly normal. But, it may also tell the manager to what extent internal processes are in order. Errors in the sales negotiation process could cause this revenue not to be recognized immediately.

There is also an interesting gap between management revenue and commission revenue. Ideally, commission revenue adds up to management revenue. This ensures that the sales compensation structure (which is located on the cost side of the equation) is aligned with management revenue. However, there might be overlay revenue, where two salespeople (such as an account manager and a product specialist) each receive 100 percent commission based on the same sales transaction. Alternatively, there may be revenue for which no one receives commission. Too much overlay revenue will lead to a margin problem.

Lastly of course, there is cash inflow. If customers pay late, certain crucial financial obligations become difficult to maintain, such as paying suppliers and employee salaries. Why is this happening? It could be symptomatic of issues with credit control, customer satisfaction, lack of implementation resources, or customer solvency.

These insights can help the country manager to make partner management more successful, by focusing on sales where royalties are included. Or conversely, the country manager will see that he or she is potentially jeopardizing an important partner relationship by staying away from those sales. The country manager also sees statutory revenue and taxable revenue. This insight is valuable for the country manager in his or her relationship with the financial director or CFO, who needs to deal with the tax office, the regulators, and shareholders. Insight into patterns of these types of revenue is important, so that operational managers can see the impact of their decisions on external stakeholders, and how these ultimately impact on the market capitalization of the company. Feedback of this kind adds another type of alignment over and above horizontal and vertical. It helps align external stakeholder perception of the company with the company's own internal perception of its performance.

By organizing the different definitions of the term *revenue* in a flow, we can see the existing definitions that make sense and lead to alignment. And those that add to confusion. The former definitions should be kept and the latter eliminated. This revenue report, with its different definitions of revenue, has created the long-awaited single version of the truth . . . or rather, "one context of the truth." There are no synonyms possible anymore, as all terms appear in the same report, and the combination of these represents a single flow of revenue. Perhaps even more important, this style of reporting has a positive influence on the behavior of the account manager. Instead of revenue, the account manager is enticed to think in terms of contribution; which revenue will actually contribute to the company in the right period and how to avoid having delinquent customers.

Case Study 2: European Railway Company

The key term in the railway business is *train*, and many different definitions exist. High regulation adds to complexity and many stakeholders have a role to play. Typically, a train company has a government license to operate a train schedule. The rail infrastructure is often managed by a separate organization. Perhaps one or both are government owned or privately held. A reason to split the train operator and infrastructure company is to increase competition and create more efficiency, with multiple suppliers using the same infrastructure. The same can be seen in, for instance, telecom and the utilities industries. Each stakeholder, internal or external, will have a slightly different view of the core business. Let's explore a number of different views of what constitutes a train using the example of a major European country railway system (see Table 6.3).

For passengers, a train consists of a set of carriages, pulled by a locomotive. This "train" takes passengers from one train station to another. One might think this definition equates "train" with a journey. However, a train passenger may have to "change trains," and thus take multiple trains to get to a particular final destination. Already differences in term definitions emerge; that is, this isn't the same information that is held on the train ticket. So, for every 1,000 completed journeys the rail operator sells, travelers may utilize 2,500 trains.

Table 6.3

Definitions of "Train"

Stakeholder	Core Business
Passenger	Journey between the passenger's departure and destination train station, potentially changing trains one or multiple times
Regulator	A timetabled train which runs between a line's departure and destination station, running multiple times per day
Operations planners	Scheduled trains plus maintenance movements and empty trains traveling to reach a new scheduled departure station
Staff planning	Scheduled number of trains per shift
Operators	Actual, including unplanned, train movements
Infrastructure	Slots, a time window in which a train is supposed to travel

At the political level (since many train companies are regulated by their respective governments), a train is a physical entity (a set of carriages pulled by a locomotive) that takes passengers from departure to destination station and stops at a number of intermediate stations on the way. It does this frequently during a single day. So for every 1,000 passenger train journeys, 100 physical trains may be needed. While 90 of these might be supplied by the national railway company, the other 10 could be managed by an international operator.

Operations planners have their own unique view of the situation. Even though they may well define "train" in a similar fashion as outlined above, they may require 120 physical trains to provide the 90 trains needed to meet journey requirements. This is because some train movements are needed to transport an empty train to its next departure station. Or, in addition, a train will need to go for maintenance at certain times. Planners may not necessarily recognize all movements—for instance, those within a maintenance facility. In these cases, an official train driver is not always needed—a certified maintenance technician will do just as well. Then there is the staff planning process. The 120 trains required by operations planning can be broken down and combined into driver shifts. A driver needs a number of trains per shift to meet work requirement. From the point of view of personnel, 200 of these driver shifts may be needed—for instance, when two drivers are required to operate each train. Within these shifts, a driver may potentially have access to 400 possible trains for operation. Thus the driver's definition of a train is similar to, but not exactly the same as, that of a passenger.

Operators monitor train movements to make sure the overall train timetable is fulfilled. If there are problems, operators are responsible for coordinating extra trains and staff. For instance, 130 trains may be needed to meet the demand for 120 operational trains. Railway operators must closely collaborate with infrastructure companies. The infrastructure planning department oversees all railway companies and tries to optimize the use of the network (as opposed to the efficient running of the published timetable).

Traffic control monitors all train movements from all railway companies, but may also manage a few maintenance trains for scheduled maintenance on some tracks. Where the railway company may see

130 trains, traffic control sees 230 trains (including maintenance trains). There is also a financial relationship between the infrastructure company and the railway operators (who need to pay for use of the infrastructure). However, this is not based on trains, but "slots." The number of trains and the number of slots may not always be the same—instead of 130 trains, there may be 140 slots. Undoubtedly, within each viewpoint such as infrastructure, scheduling, operations, and so on, there are additional multiple definitions catering for specific exceptions—namely historical factors, lack of alignment, and other causes. See Table 6.4.

Working with this single context of the truth has a number of immediate advantages. It eliminates a great deal of overlapping reports, each with slightly different definitions without broader context. In reducing the number of reports, the horizontal alignment approach provides a benchmark of which definitions ought to be unique and recognized and which ones can be eliminated. For each step in the value chain, there is logic in having a specific definition, if that is needed. However, within steps of the value chain it doesn't make much sense having multiple definitions, and redundant ones can be eliminated. Definitions that do not fit in the value chain probably need to be eliminated as well.

Moreover, through a horizontal alignment approach, the definitions have become more transparent and comparable. There is value in analyzing the differences. It is important to minimize the difference between the demand plan and the operations. The difference is in planning efficiencies and the number of incidents and accidents. The closer the number, the more optimized the plan is. Then the difference

Table 6.4

Stakeholder	Number of Trains
Passenger	1,000 trips or 2,500 trains
Demand	100 trains, of which 90 are for the railway company
Railway company planning	120 trains
Staff planning	200 shifts with 400 trains
Railway operations	130 trains
Infrastructure planning	200 trains of which 120 are for the one railway company
Slots	220 slots of which 140 are for the one railway company

between operations and the staffing plan needs to be minimized, allocating scarce human resources as efficiently as possible.

With the single context of the truth, with all relevant definitions in a single report, the problem of making it all add up is solved. But horizontal alignment also achieved something even more important, there is more insight in the operational efficiency.

Case Study 3: E-plus

In the previous two examples, the software industry and the railways sector, the one version of the truth started to make sense when it was sorted as a value chain. This is very typical for straight metrics such as revenue and trains. However, if the performance indicator is a ratio and a composite of nature, usually it makes more sense to shape the versions of the truth as a matrix.

Let's look at another example, mobile telephony. One of the most important performance indicators in the telecom world is ARPU, which stands for average revenue per user. This is no different at E-plus, which is the third-largest mobile telecom operator in Germany. It has been in business since 1994, has close to 12 million customers, and around three billion euros in revenue. The E-plus value proposition is to make mobile telephony uncomplicated, straightforward, and easy to understand. E-plus's ARPU per month is around 20 euros.

As with any business term highly connected with the core of the business, there are many different definitions of ARPU around. E-plus now distinguishes between AIPU (average invoice per user), business ARPU, reported ARPU, and analytical ARPU. These definitions have a clear relationship. The AIPU is part of the "business ARPU" and the business ARPU in its turn is part of the "reported ARPU." Then, lastly, there is also the "analytical ARPU," based on various corrections after the reported ARPU. See Figure 6.1.

There are various revenue categories that contribute to the AIPU. These are based on the type of contract. For subscription users these are the basic subscription fee, the bundle fee, the fees for the various special options, such as text messaging, the roaming fees (revenues generated by the subscribers on other networks), the realized revenue based on the minutes spent calling, revenue coming from "value added

Figure 6.1

Visualization of ARPU Definitions at E-plus

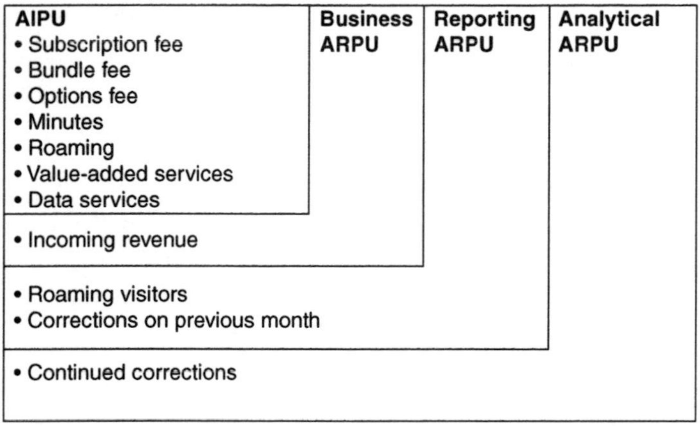

AIPU	Business ARPU	Reporting ARPU	Analytical ARPU
• Subscription fee • Bundle fee • Options fee • Minutes • Roaming • Value-added services • Data services			
• Incoming revenue			
• Roaming visitors • Corrections on previous month			
• Continued corrections			

services," such as paid 0900 numbers, and data services. The income from prepaid phones mainly comes from the actual minutes spent from the prepaid credit.

There is another revenue stream, coming from other telecom operators. Every time an E-plus customer is called by a non-E-plus customer, a part of the revenue generated for the other telecom operator goes to E-plus ("interconnection revenue"). This amount can be as high as 20 to 30 percent of all revenue per user. As it is not shown on the invoice to the customer, it is not part of AIPU. The combination of AIPU and incoming revenue is called business ARPU.

Subscribers of foreign telecom operators generate traffic within the E-plus network while using the E-plus network in Germany. The resulting revenue stream is "in-roaming revenue." These revenues are equally split over the E-plus users and contribute to their ARPU. As of this moment, the ARPU ratio is not "clean" anymore as the ARPU contains elements from different users. Furthermore, every month there are corrections. Not every telecom operator that E-plus works with is able to send a daily update of call detail records of the roaming or interconnection revenues for E-plus users. Every month these revenues are estimated and later corrected with the actual numbers. As these estimations are aggregated and not calculated on the subscriber level, the ARPU number reported at monthly closing is not precise. The business ARPU including in-roaming and including corrections is the reporting ARPU. This is the ARPU that E-plus's parent company wants reported. Lastly, there may be more corrections coming in more than a month later. Although these are not material of nature, they need to be processed and allocated to the month they are related to (and not the month they came in). This updated number is the "analytical ARPU."

There are also multiple user types. In the E-plus definition, a user basically equates to a phone number. A customer can be multiple users, and business customers can consist of multiple individual customers. The biggest impact on ARPU, however, is the definition if a user as "active" or "inactive," as the ARPU ratio is sometimes based on active users. When does a user start being active? The moment the phone number is activated, or the moment the first call is made or the first text message is sent? Or, in the case of prepaid users, the moment when credits are bought? And when does a user stop being active and become inactive? At the end of a contract? This may sound logical, but given the warranty on phones, for instance, there is still a legal relationship. Or in the case of prepaid, does a user become inactive when no calls are being made anymore? What about just receiving calls or "spam" text messages? What about the credit that is still left? Or how to count users that are temporarily shut off because the invoice has not been paid? And how long should the period of no activity be before a user is considered inactive?

Different parts of E-plus will have a different view on what the number of active users is. The operations department will look at call detail records and come to a determination. The finance department will look at the invoices and credit levels. The legal department will look at the contracts and warranties. The moment we would try to create one version of the truth, the result would be less insight, instead of more. First, we wouldn't be able to analyze the differences anymore between the operational, financial, and legal view on active users. These differences are important indicators for the health of the company. Second, in the current list of harmonized ARPU definitions, at the reporting ARPU the ratio is not clean anymore because of allocations. Revenue generated by non-E-plus customers roaming on the E-plus network is allocated to the ARPU of E-plus customers. The more you would try to align the business ARPU and reporting ARPU, the more these allocations would be needed to catch all facets of revenue. ARPU then becomes a complete black box.

Now we come to the one context of the truth. It starts with the assumption that there are different definitions for a reason. In the case of E-plus, because there are different revenue streams and different user types, it makes sense to list the various forms of ARPU as E-plus does in some of its reports as it builds up to the overall ARPU that is reported to the parent company. Let's try to take it to the next level. At the highest level, there are four different revenue components: fees (including various roaming fees), discounts, incoming revenues, and the corrections. There are also three different user types: active users, total users, and non-E-plus users. The full context unravels when we plot the revenue items and user types in a matrix (see Table 6.5).

The ARPU matrix doesn't mean there is no ARPU performance indicator anymore; it is still an important indicator. But now we have a single context of the truth, and we can analyze the various components for deeper insight. The higher the percentage of total revenue and ARPU for fees and incoming revenues from active users, the better it is; this is revenue you can influence with customers you engage with. This is called *controlled revenue*. The higher the roaming revenues from non-E-plus customers and the higher the incoming revenues, the more you depend on others, *uncontrolled revenue*. Although uncontrolled revenue is part of the business model, that revenue needs to be

Table 6.5

E-plus User Matrix

	Active Users (in millions)	Total Customers (in millions)	Non-E-plus Users (in millions)
Fees	1,900	+60	+250
Discounts	−170	−90	N/A
Incoming Revenue	480	NA	+30
Corrections	20	+15	+5
Total	2,230	2,215	2,500

AIPU = 1,900 million divided by the number of active users

Clean ARPU = 2,215 million divided by the total number of users

ARPU including allocations = 2,500 million divided by the total number of users managed differently. It shows that there is some revenue coming from inactive users but that the discounts given are higher than this revenue. The business case of making inactive users active again, or finding out how to minimize discounts to inactive users, becomes very clear. The matrix serves as a risk management model as well. The higher the percentage of revenue is toward the bottom right part of the matrix, the higher the risk, particularly if the amount of corrections increases.

With the matrix in mind, within the same context of the truth, we can expand our insight. For instance, we could start aggregating users to the "single customer" level. Or we can use the matrix to include other relevant information, particularly *contribution* per user, by adding direct cost categories, such as the interconnection fees that E-plus pays to the other telecom operators and promotion categories, to understand the cost of marketing and the impact on the user contribution.

Case Study 4: Retail Banking

Retail banks basically have two main sources of income: interest payments and fees. Banks attract short-term money by paying interest, such as the money that customers place on savings accounts. On the other side, banks supply loans, mortgages, life insurance, and other financial services for the longer term, charging interest that is higher than what they pay to attract short-term money. The difference is the margin for the bank. Second, retail banks charge fees (provision) for services, such as cashing a check, credit card fees, stock trading fees (as well as margin interest), mortgage fees, and so forth.

One of the most used terms in all parts of the operations of a retail bank is *transaction*. In this example we will concentrate on one process only: money transfer. People draw money from ATMs, use Internet banking to transfer amounts, both national and international, shift money between their current account and savings accounts or stock accounts, and use a wide range of other financial services. Every retail bank generates a vast array of reports about the number of these transactions and their monetary value, broken down by business unit, product, and most probably geography. But very few reports combine those definitions to closely align the various steps in the money transfer process.

The first benchmark for gaining insight into transaction streams is to know the number of customer contacts throughout all channels. This would include people at the tellers' windows at the bank branch, at the ATMs, at the call center, on the Internet, and for the more complex transactions, with the account managers. Not every customer contact would lead to the next step, which would be a transaction. A transaction would be every transfer-related activity. It would probably exclude sending brochures, but may very well include opening up a savings account, or changing an address or other personal information. It is not uncommon that a single customer contact leads to multiple transactions.

The vast majority of transactions would involve some kind of actual money transfer, which would be the basic business process in this example. However, there is a difference between the number of transactions taking place within the bank and between different banks. For instance, money transfers between customers of the bank could be done internally, and it doesn't require a clearing house, although this could differ by country and bank. This means the number of transactions between banks, net transactions, is much smaller than the total number of transactions triggered by customers.

Not every transaction may be accepted; some will be rejected. This could be the case with accounts or credit cards being overdrawn, missing collateral, mistakes in the bank account (some bank account systems use an internal algorithm to validate bank account numbers), or internal warning systems that flag a transaction that matches signs of money laundering.

When counting transactions over a period of time, like a week or a month, there might be differences as well. In many cases there is a clearing time for processing checks. This means a transaction has a transaction date and a clearing date. There is an interest date, where the transaction starts to affect interest. This can be interest that is charged for loans or for being overdrawn or interest that is paid on savings accounts, particularly for transactions during the weekend where there might be differences. Not only can these differences lead to differences in management reports, they ultimately also affect compliance regulations on operational and financial risk management.

Although the difference most likely is not material over time, counting transactions in any of these ways will lead to different results. For instance, counting transactions per week using the clearing date will include all transactions with a transaction date of the previous week, but a clearing date within this week. However, it will not include all transactions with a transaction date of this week, but a clearing date of next week. The definition of the interest date further complicates this issue.

Not all transactions may be accepted by the bank on the receiving end. Perhaps an account is blocked, or it doesn't exist anymore. This will again lead to a lower number of transactions.

Although from an operational point the story ends here, the impact of transactions goes beyond the core business process. Transactions need to be stored in various information systems, leading to a number of new records for each transaction. And in the end there is an impact on the bank's financial department, where the collection of transactions leads to journals in the general ledger. All definitions and shapes of a transaction, between the first customer contact and the general ledger of the bank, are connected (see Figure 6.2).

In the previous cases, we pointed out that connecting these definitions within a single report helps in separating valid and invalid definitions, brings new insight in the efficiency of core business processes by analyzing the differences, and helps operational managers see the financial impact of their decisions. The example of bank transactions shows another advantage: it provides a predictive view on the business. Sudden changes in the number of customer contact moments will predict the workload in the later steps in the value chain.

Call to Action

Adopting a horizontal alignment approach can bring about real insight and greatly enhanced business performance. But how can this approach be implemented?

A key barrier to implementing a horizontal approach to alignment lies in the current vertical structure of management reporting and performance management processes and systems, leading to information that cannot be reconciled or compared. The cases described here have demonstrated how management processes and business scenarios structured horizontally can provide greatly improved insight into an organization:

Figure 6.2

Money Transfers in a Retail Bank

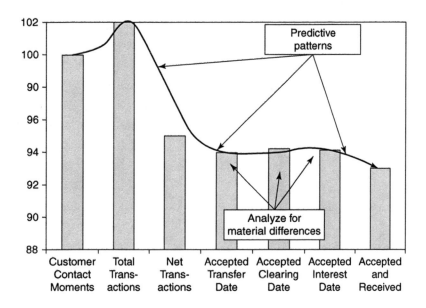

- In the software company example, understanding how to define revenue, which allows account managers to understand the financial consequences of their operational sales decisions, can lead to changed behaviors that are more fully aligned with strategic objectives.
- In the railway company example, gaining deeper insight into operations is possible through a horizontal value chain and a methodology that provides an understanding of what drives operational efficiency.
- In the mobile telephony company example, breaking out average revenue per user, helps us evaluate the quality of revenue and gain deeper insight into what average revenue per user actually means.
- In the retail banking example, transaction volumes can be predicted by understanding existing patterns and using forecasting algorithms.

You can start the alignment process by asking the following questions:

- Which business terms are most closely related to our core activities?
- What are our definitions?
- How can these definitions be organized in various steps or in various dimensions?

Once these three questions are answered, you can start separating the wheat from the chaff. In other words, this knowledge helps reduce the number of reports and definitions dramatically. Many different definitions have been created for historical reasons, or because people were not aware of any other relevant definitions, or perhaps for political reasons. With the "one context of the truth," every business department will see where it adds value in the chain and each can concentrate on the definitions that make most sense.

The results are combined in a single report, aimed at multiple business constituents. In this way, the different versions provide additional insight instead of more confusion.

Chapter | 7

BUSINESS INTERFACES DRIVE COLLABORATION

Coming together is a beginning. Keeping together is progress.
Working together is success.
—Henry Ford

Business Domains

Managers are usually responsible for a certain business domain. Business domains can be strategic business units, each selling a product line or serving a special market. They can also be business functions, such as marketing, sales, logistics, manufacturing, finance, human resources, and information technology. And they can be regions, such as Americas, EMEA (Europe, Middle East, and Africa), and Asia Pacific.

Performance management is structured in the same way. When confronted with establishing performance indicators and setting targets, the first thing you learn is to assign a manager to that metric who owns it. That owner then should have all the means and resources to make sure it is realistic to make that target. Assigning a single person to each metric creates a feeling of ownership and accountability. As the maxim goes, "Shared responsibility is no responsibility." Assigning the means and the resources to that person so that the targets can be made makes perfect sense.

As a consequence, the performance indicators in the organization very closely resemble the organization's structure. The problem with the common wisdom of assigning ownership to metrics is that it easily leads to suboptimization of business performance. If target owners can apply the means and resources to make their targets, most likely they will do exactly that—measurement drives behavior. They will optimize the use of the resources for their particular business domain, or a specific process or activity, but potentially at the expense of overall performance optimization. It could very well be that by reallocating resources by taking them away in business domain A and applying them in business domain B, the overall output of the process crossing these multiple domains increases dramatically. But due to the ownership of the performance indicators, the various managers in the organization are not encouraged to explore solutions like this. The current structure of ownership for targets doesn't drive collaborative behavior; more probable, it does the opposite. For instance, managers may even overspend in their business domain to secure future budgets.

One of the goals of performance management is to create discussion and a common understanding. As valuable as it is to visualize the contribution of each domain to the overall results, horizontal alignment shows it is equally valuable to visualize the contribution of each business domain to the other business domains. Managers are responsible for the performance of their own domain, but together they are responsible for the overall performance of the organization.

Many organizations have tried to solve this problem and increase business performance by reorganizing the business. They change the focus of the organization, typically from a divisional focus to a process-driven or a customer segment-driven focus, putting a complete process or customer segment under the management of a single business domain. This then, according to the single ownership structure, drives a new optimization. The sad truth is that once the organization has changed its focus, a lack of optimization between the new business domains appears: the different process managers or customer segment managers start to create suboptimization. As a consequence, complex matrix structures are built, having team leaders as well as process or customer segment managers and lower management report into divisional management, leading to excessive overhead.

If we let go of conventional wisdom and take a fresh approach, the answer is obvious. Changing an organizational structure, but within the same paradigm of ownership of targets, will always lead to a situation where the only thing that counts is what you achieve yourself. But what about what you enable for others? Doesn't that add to business performance as well? Or, sometimes even more. The answer is not in how the target ownership is translated in an organizational structure, but the structure of target ownership itself. We need an alternative.

Business Interfaces

There is an alternative approach. As measurement drives behavior, we can design specific metrics designed to drive optimization and collaboration. If we apply the idea of horizontal alignment, we should not create only metrics and targets that describe the performance of the various business domains, but also metrics that measure the effectiveness of *business interfaces.*

A business interface is the point where one business domain's activities and processes interact, bordering with activities and processes in another business domain. A business interface is where work gets handed over from one activity to another, from one process to another, from one department to another, or even from one organization to another. It is where managers need to collaborate with each other as peers and where, in practice, most of the efficiency and effectiveness of work is lost.

Most of the quality problems in a process are caused by a handover. If this is an administrative process, there may be different interpretations of the information that is part of the document or transaction that is handed over. Or due to unintegrated processes and/or systems, data needs to be reentered into a different system, which is an important cause of data quality issues. It also leads to rework, meaning processing the transaction or the document again until it is right. That is only the case if the mistake is detected. Quality problems cost time, as they require fixing. But the handover of the activity itself costs time as well: passing on the document or transaction to the next step and receiving it. And that doesn't even include the waiting time between two activities, which delays the overall process. Loss of time and quality introduce additional cost. If there is rework, there is cost of labor. The later in the process that the issue is detected and fixed, the more steps need to be redone. Delays in time introduce capital costs, as the revenue associated with the activity can only be invoiced and received later.

The answer is not in reorganizing the process and eliminating all interfaces or creating a single process step or transaction. Business domains exist for a reason: they consist of unique and specific processes and activities. They may require specialist skills and training. There most likely will be economies of scale in grouping process steps in a separate activity, to be processed in one go or in a highly optimized manner. Furthermore, the need for controls dictates separation of tasks; for instance, in an insurance company a person who approves claims cannot also pay out claims. Handover moments are crucial, and *business interface metrics* are needed to manage them. See Figure 7.1.

A business interface metric shows the performance of a process or set of activities across multiple business domains. Such a metric measures the efficiency or effectiveness of a handover point between people in an organization. A business interface metric has multiple owners, and their performance (and the evaluation thereof) depends on their collaboration to make these joint targets.

This poses an interesting question. If there are two people responsible for a business interface metric, does it drive collaborative behavior or does it violate the "shared responsibility is no responsibility" rule? On the other hand, as we have seen, creating a single responsibility

Figure 7.1

Business Domain and Business Interface Metrics

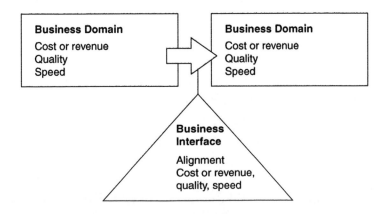

creates suboptimization. This dilemma needs to be solved. Through the concept of business interface metrics it is not hard to build the bridge between optimization and responsibility. Organizations have hierarchies in place, and the two business domains in our example report into the same manager. Performance accountability and responsibility is not something that can be delegated to lower management in this model. Next to target setting, performance monitoring, and allocating resources, fostering collaboration is the most important senior management task. It is not the job of senior management to be the best financial expert, sales professional, or IT guru; it is their job to make their team run successfully. In other words, the collaboration of their direct reports in the business interface is their responsibility. See Figure 7.2.

Obviously, business interfaces cross multiple domains, and therefore multiple levels of management that oversee the various business domains. The traditional management structure, with its various levels of management takes care of managing the business interfaces in exactly the same way. Where a middle manager manages the business interfaces within his or her span of control, the business interfaces crossing that span of control are then being managed by the manager of that

Figure 7.2

Collaboration Is a Management Responsibility

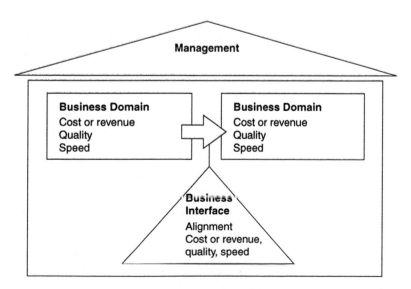

Figure 7.3

Multitiered Model of Business Domains and Business Interfaces

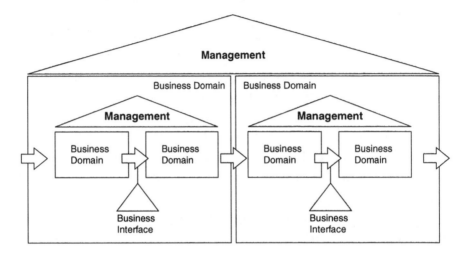

manager. Figure 7.3 depicts a multitiered model of business domains and business interfaces, showing the various levels of responsibility.

Although the idea of business interface metrics based on co-ownership is new *within* organizations, it already exists *between* organizations: managing customers. Many organizations have sales representatives or account managers that are responsible for developing and sustaining the relationship with their accounts. If the account purchases many products or services, the account manager gets paid more. If the customer decides to shop somewhere else, the account manager gets paid less. The account manager does not control the behaviors of his or her clients; yet making the sales targets depends on them. This also violates the principle that every target should have a clear owner and the owner should have the necessary means and resources to make that target. Most organizations have built a certain expertise with activities crossing multiple business domains and have designed controls called *service level agreements* (SLAs). A service level agreement is a contract between a supplier and consumer of services. This differs from a typical contract in the sense that the services usually are continuous of nature and not related to a single delivery, such as a product or a project. Particularly IT departments have a long history in creating and managing SLAs. It is typically the IT department that has business critical partnerships with external companies, which, for instance, run the communications networks between the various offices of the company and with the outside world or which run business critical transactional systems that are needed to perform transactions on a continuous basis. These SLAs contain very detailed performance indicators on availability of the systems, performance, scalability, and many other aspects that need to be managed. A good SLA also specifies escalation processes when the service levels are not met or may not be met without immediate action.

However, SLAs are not the answer to business interfaces. The most important objective of business interface metrics is to drive collaborative behaviors between the owners of the various business domains in order to optimize the complete value chain. Service level agreements can easily lead to further suboptimization of performance because they make managers behave more entrepreneurial. As desirable as that sounds, it leads to a further focus on one's business domain, not the overall organization. Although the philosophy of entrepreneurial behavior may help eliminate bureaucracy and bring about market conformity, it will also increase transaction costs. Managers will be less likely to buy into stretch targets, as there are contractual repercussions if those targets are not met. Margins will be built in to cover for risk, as there is no shared responsibility for that. It will be necessary to create internal offers that are compared to external offers, leading to loss of time and increased cost. There will be no overall resource optimization. Also, tightly managed SLAs may inhibit innovation. The performance indicators that are monitored and the service that is promised are managed best when aiming for a status quo. Current processes can be optimized and change is seen as a risk factor. However, we should not only support the current business practices, but also enable the business to respond to changes in an agile way.

The problem with SLAs is that they still have the same business domain focus as the original business domain metrics. They provide a dashboard measuring success for the supplier of services, and a mechanism of control for the customer. As a result, SLAs make relationships more transactional, turning colleagues into customers and suppliers, instead of co-owners of performance. Every business function should be focused on and aligned with overall business performance. As measurement drives behavior, it is collaboration that should be measured. Crucial metrics should be placed on the spot where cost, quality, and speed suffer most: the business interface. Let's explore a number of examples:

- Campaign management and the call center
- Manufacturing and logistics
- IT development and IT operations

Campaign Management and the Call Center

Almost every company that has a call center has been in the following situation: On Monday morning the available call center agents are flooded with calls because marketing launched a new campaign but did not advise the call center adequately as to expectations. As a result, the call center cannot handle campaign follow-up very well. The queue time in the call center increases and people calling hang up. The campaign manager is responsible for designing campaigns and for rolling them out by means of advertising, direct marketing, activities in outlets, the Internet, or other customer contact channels (including the outbound call center). The call center manager is responsible for follow-up on incoming calls.

But next to the responsibilities for their own activities, the campaign manager and the call center manager have a business interface to manage: The campaign manager needs to involve the call center in the roll-out plan of the campaign because the campaign follow-up is the next step in the value chain. As measurement drives behavior, creating the right metrics that track such involvement and communication will improve collaboration between campaign management and the call center. Figure 7.4 shows a few examples of the business domain metrics for campaign management and the call center.

Usually a campaign plan will contain expected response rate, converted into additional revenue, and a campaign cost estimate. But costs go beyond the campaign itself. As the campaign will create additional work for the call center, the campaign plan should take into account the costs of planning extra call center agents. If these costs are large,

Figure 7.4

Business Interface between Campaign Management and Call Center

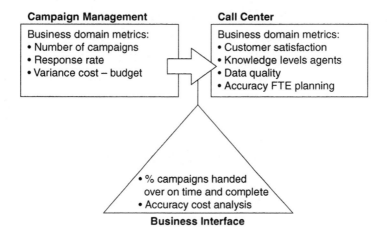

Campaign Management	Call Center
Business domain metrics: • Number of campaigns • Response rate • Variance cost – budget	Business domain metrics: • Customer satisfaction • Knowledge levels agents • Data quality • Accuracy FTE planning

• % campaigns handed
over on time and complete
• Accuracy cost analysis
Business Interface

perhaps a different follow-up strategy needs to be devised involving other channels, such as the Internet. If the call center doesn't have the resources to drive follow-up, another channel should become part of the campaign design, or the follow-up should be outsourced to an external call center taking care of the overflow. One of the performance indicators that defines the success of the overall campaign is a cost analysis of the follow-up. Overall there should be a metric for the campaign manager that measures for which percentage of all campaigns (with a target of 100 percent) the quality and speed of the handover to the call center was sufficient. The call center needs a few days to plan capacity, scheduling additional call center agents for the duration of the campaigns. The handover document should also be of high quality and contain all necessary elements, such as follow-up scripts and expected response rates over the days the campaign is running. Also, the call center manager should be part of the cost analysis for the campaign follow-up activities.

It looks like the business interface metrics all concern the campaign manager only, making sure he or she collaborates with the call center manager. However, it is also in the best interest of the call center manager to be actively involved. The call center manager is responsible for his or her own business domain, and the results will show in his or her own performance indicators. For instance, conversations are monitored and scored on how professional and knowledgeable call center agents handle the questions of the caller. Not knowing the details of a campaign will negatively affect that. Also, data quality is a metric important for the output of the call center. Not having enough time to fill in all fields in the system will negatively affect that. At the same time, the call center is a relatively expensive customer interaction channel, which means precision planning is important. There cannot be a surplus of agents manning the call center if the workload does not match. The cost analysis for the campaign will reveal the additional workload in addition to the tightly planned daily operations. Both the call center manager and campaign manager have equal responsibility for the business interface metrics.

Manufacturing and Logistics

In manufacturing firms, most manufacturing departments and logistics departments have a long history of optimizing their activities. Given the capital intensive nature of manufacturing, optimizing the production plan significantly contributes to the cost of goods. The manufacturing equipment often is extremely expensive and needs to be used as efficiently as possible. Maintenance is carefully planned to make sure the uptime and the capacity are used to maximum levels as well.

The logistics manager is dealing with the same issues. Distribution of goods is a very resource-driven business. Mail, cars, trains, ships, airplanes, and other modes for shipping goods requires complex optimizations to make sure that there is only one shipment at a time to a single customer and that shipments to the same region are bundled, as well as making sure that the transportation space the company owns or uses is utilized to the maximum capacity. On the other hand, capacity planning cannot be too tight; hiring additional capacity brings additional cost.

Each of these functions has a whole array of optimizing techniques and best practices at its disposal. They are often very mathematical of nature, with many software products performing these calculations; often times multiple departments are in charge of planning. However, a problem arises if both the production and logistics plan are not optimized with one another. If production and logistics are not aligned, a warehouse will be needed. The goods produced would be stored in this warehouse until these goods are picked up by logistics. From a purely logistical point of view, a large warehouse with many products would make it easier to combine different orders for different products for a single customer, geography, or transportation means. Although the optimization of both the production and the logistics plans may save costs for each, the additional cost of such a warehouse most likely will outweigh the saved costs in the optimized plans. First, the warehouse itself costs money to build and maintain, including the staffing. Second, the goods that are waiting to be transported, delivered, and paid for are not considered to be sold and are considered capital of the organization. And some goods may be perishable. We tend to think of perishable goods in terms of fruits or vegetables, but in many markets consumer preferences and product specifications evolve so fast that the warehousing of products almost immediately makes the sales window of opportunity shorter. Think for instance of consumer electronics that are only up-to-date for a few months until a new version emerges on the market. As a result, every day that these products are on stock in a warehouse the quality and associated value deteriorate.

The cost of goods sold (COGS), an important part of the organization's margin, is not only determined by the cost, speed, and quality of the processes in the manufacturing and logistics department, but also—and perhaps even particularly—in the business interface. See Figure 7.5.

The business interface here is defined as the handover point between manufacturing and logistics. The manufacturing and logistics manager should be jointly responsible for an optimized joint production and logistics plan. Inclusion of distribution criteria may create a better balance between the yield of the production lines and the yield of the distribution capacity. A lower yield in production may be overcompensated by a better distribution yield. Some metrics that would measure the success of that collaboration are the average storing time of the produced units, before they get distributed, and the number of units in storage during a certain time frame.

Figure 7.5

Business Interface between Manufacturing and Logistics

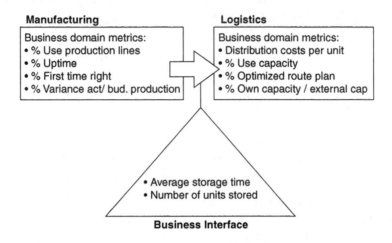

IT Development and IT Operations

Most IT departments consist largely of two parts. There is an IT development organization that implements IT applications, either packaged or customized, and there is an IT operations department that runs the systems on a daily basis. Both departments tend to have a different business model, a different culture, and a different set of best practices. It is the task of the chief information officer (CIO) to manage these two departments and the supporting staff.

The business model of the IT development department is project-based. The staff, made up of either internal employees or external consultants, go from assignment to assignment, implementing different systems or updating existing ones. On a project-by-project basis, the IT development organization uses various metrics to monitor productivity, quality, and control costs. Productivity can be measured by calculating the *function points* (FPs) per developer. (A function point is a unit of size in IT that helps in estimating the scale and complexity of an implementation project: the more function points, the bigger and more complex the project.) Quality can be measured by tracking the number of bugs discovered during testing, or the amount of rework during development, testing, and postimplementation. Cost control can be managed by continuously mapping the detailed project plan to the completed implementation activities.

The IT operations department typically works differently. The daily activities are less structured than projects, and they are managed through the hierarchy of the IT operations department. A certain amount of rigidity is needed, as the transactions of an organization often have contractual value and need to be protected. One of the main control mechanisms for the IT operations department is the service level agreement, which specifies the needed performance and capacity (speed and number of transactions) of systems, stability of systems (planning and unplanned downtime), or the quality of support. In order to make sure the service levels are reached, there are many internal performance indicators, such as tracking surplus capacity in terms of computer memory; processor cycles, and network bandwidth; and, with certain regularity, exercises in disaster recovery are conducted and monitored. From a financial point of view, the majority of system costs are usually incurred during the operational phase, not the implementation phase. Managing the total cost of ownership (TCO) is an important overall objective for IT operations.

The business interface between IT development and operations mostly consists of taking new developments into production. Those can be new systems or modifications to existing systems. There is typically a strict process that needs to be followed for development, testing, acceptance, and production (DTAP). In a classic situation this is a process where the IT operations department has rules about acceptance, informs IT development about those rules, and tests compliance of those rules ex post. The process often leads to frustrating, long, and difficult implementation processes. A more collaborative approach is needed. See Figure 7.6.

Business interface metrics for this process could include the monitoring of handover time per function points and the number of full-time employees (FTEs) involved in the handover process and establishing a risk factor for acceptance. The larger and more complex a system is, the more function points it will have and the longer handover will take. It might be a good idea to also introduce a risk factor for acceptance. Acceptance here means the success of taking new developments into production. At the beginning of the implementation project and at all

Figure 7.6

Business Interface between IT Development and IT Operations

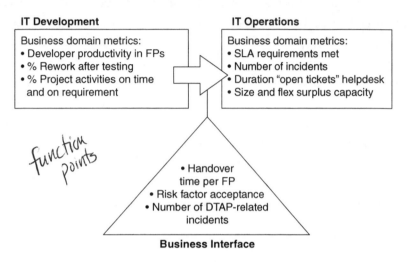

Business Interface

checkpoints both IT development and IT operations should jointly estimate the risks to production. The moment this risk estimate increases, a correction process can start (instead of waiting for acceptance testing). Lastly, there might be a need for a feedback loop, tracking how many incidents are happening over the first weeks or months of taking an application into production, related to the handover procedure. This metric will show negative results if the handover process was rushed through. In all three cases IT development and IT operations share the responsibility for hitting the targets on these business interface metrics.

The Basis for Business Interfaces Is in the Domains

Business interface metrics describe the handover process between two business domains. However, the seeds of the performance of the business interface are sown long before it is time to hand over work.

- The quality of a knowledgeable follow-up in the call center is based on the scripts that are created by campaign management with the involvement of expert call center agents as part of the handover process, as well as an accurate estimate of the response rate.

- Avoiding storing products in a warehouse depends on manufacturing and logistics closely aligning their overall plans and putting systems in place that on a real-time or daily basis synchronize the output of the manufacturing process with the input for the logistics process.
- The majority of the total cost of ownership (TCO) of systems is in IT operations, but it's the decisions made in IT development that heavily influence the future TCO.

Business interface metrics encourage involvement of business domains in each other's processes so that it becomes a natural thought process. Let's have a look at our IT example again. The IT development manager and the IT operations manager co-own the business interface metrics that measure the efficiency and effectiveness of taking new developments into production. At first, when the CIO introduces these metrics, both managers may even complain that they cannot make their targets without the help of the other manager. The reaction of the CIO should be affirmative; the metrics and targets were put in place to drive collaboration. However, it does not end there for the CIO. Where the two managers have co-ownership of the business interface, it is the responsibility of the CIO to manage the collaboration. In the end, the adage "shared responsibility is no responsibility" still makes sense.

The metrics that intuitively invite the two managers to actively seek cross-domain involvement are very carefully crafted. See Figure 7.7.

Risk estimation, which describes how much risk there is if the new development is not taken into production in time, is a leading indicator. A leading indicator predicts future performance; it works exactly in the same way as the strategy maps of the balanced scorecard. In this particular case it drives the collaboration between development and operations before the actual handover moment. It provides feed-forward information. The higher the risk, the more joint work both teams need to do to mitigate that risk and manage problems before they become visible. The handover time per function point is a very classical metric; it simply describes the efficiency of the business interface itself.

Figure 7.7

Business Interface Metrics in IT

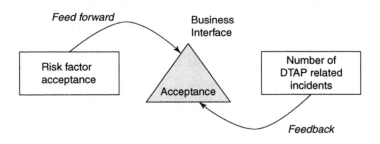

Another metric, the lagging metric reports on the quality after the handover.

In the event the handover was pushed through at the expense of quality and the overall TCO, it will show bad results and reflect badly on the collaboration. It provides feedback information. There are two loops of learning in these business interface metrics. If a certain project was not planned well and the handover is not effective and incidents are reported, the feedback loop triggers the rework that is needed for making the project successful after all. This first loop, aimed at correcting issues that are at hand does not differ from a traditional process. Both the IT development manager and the IT operations manager report to the CIO and have vertical alignment. They know about the IT strategy and adhere to the standards that IT has. But the business interface metrics also create horizontal alignment with co-ownership. As a consequence, both managers are interested in integrating their processes as much as they can.

Business Interfaces in Management Processes

Management processes have business interfaces too, and the same principles can be applied. One of the most important set of management processes is to manage budgeting, planning, and forecasting. Financial budgets are preferably aligned with the operational plans. New forecasts can be made in case of internal or external changes throughout the budget period. This is not a trivial exercise. In classic budget-driven organizations this process can take several months. The proof is usually the variance between the results at the end of the period and the original plan, budget, or subsequent forecasts. This way of working can easily lead to the wrong behavior. It becomes important not to over-shoot the target by too much, because it will negatively affect next period's target. When a cost budget is not fully used, it becomes impor-tant that it be spent as soon as possible; otherwise next year's budget will be smaller. Rolling forecasts, aimed at continuous improvements help, but these are usually vertical of nature as well. The finance department collects and aligns all plans from each individual depart-ment, and cascades down a new financial translation.

Measuring the efficiency of the business interface between finance and operations here is pretty straightforward: Are all deadlines in the workflow made? Bringing in the horizontal alignment approach adds precision and more meaning to the process. Operational plans from managers are interdependent. Sales can only sell what manufacturing has produced, or the other way around. Likewise, investments in logis-tics need to be aligned with production and sales too. Cost-saving tar-gets in procurement also depend on the same value chain. Supporting functions operate under the same principle. IT capacity is linked to the demand of the business functions. The HR targets for hiring people are connected with the FTE budgets of the various departments. A more horizontal approach for budgeting, planning, and forecasting leads to managers aligning their plans with their peers before submit-ting them. This makes the process more complicated, but also more realistic and aligned. The feed-forward indicator in this approach would be the variance between the estimates the various departments make. If there are multiple rounds of planning, variances in the first round of the process are bound to exist, and they should be eliminated in the last round of planning. Figure 7.8 shows the feed-forward and feedback indicators, as well as an indicator for the business interface itself.

Case Study: La Réunion

Brasseries de Bourbon, an operating company of beer brewer Heineken on Ile de la Réunion in the Indian Ocean, has been pio-neering the concept of business interface metrics.[1] La Réunion's work

Figure 7.8

Business Interfaces in the Management Process

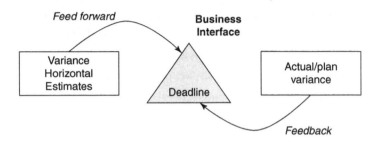

is the result of its ISO 9001 certification process and its strong process orientation. One of the major challenges in this effort was to formalize the interactions between the processes, in other words, the business interfaces. It took La Réunion almost three years to accomplish this task. First, because of the elaborate process descriptions that needed to be made, and also in part to the undertaking that went into changing people's perception on how to deal with targets, objectives, and performance indicators. La Réunion quickly found out that the traditional ways of target setting and ownership led to organizational silos and suboptimal results. For instance, it is in the best interest of the production department to have as large as possible production batches. The marketing department, in the meantime, would prefer as many production variants as possible. The solution has been to introduce a shared objective and target between both departments called "time to market." Another example is the shared objective between HR and production, each being equally responsible for an efficient workforce planning.

Throughout the process, La Réunion has developed some interesting insights into successful management of business interfaces, including its measurement. To show the concept of shared responsibility (part of the concept of business interface metrics) in a nonconfrontational way, the controlling department decided to measure its degree of health with an official performance indicator "total weight." The weight of the three people within the department was not to exceed 250 kg. Every month, in the management report, the team would have to comment on whether the team target was achieved.

Brewery-wide, Brasseries de Bourbon organized a meeting for all process owners twice a year. At this meeting, all participants would have to explain their processes, how they contributed to overall objectives, as well as to other processes, and what they needed from other process owners in order to be successful. Each process owner would build a little stand and show what it was doing. In this way, the different process owners would not only consider the needs of their process but also the needs of other process owners.

Board members would have their own performance indicators for the specific area they would be responsible for. They would also co-own a few performance indicators. In order to achieve those targets, collaboration and coaching by the other board members became a necessity. This was done particularly to connect core processes such as sales, purchasing, production, and logistics, with support process such as finance, IT, and HR. For instance, the CFO owns "working capital" as a performance indicator, but co-owns "stock levels," which was the direct responsibility of the operations manager. This process was cascaded down into the organization.

Brasseries de Bourbon concludes that there are a few essential preconditions that make for successful implementation of business interface metrics. First, it requires a strong process orientation. Second, there needs to be strong commitment of every director to focus not only on the business domain but also on the interfaces, in order to optimize the performance of the organization as a whole. The targets on the business interfaces also need to be connected to the bonus plan, so that there is a strong incentive for collaboration. Lastly, there needs to be an adaptive culture, in which the managers allow themselves to be coached by one another and are willing to change their plans if certain performance indicators show failing targets, regardless if this happens within one's own domain or someone else's. Perhaps the most important precondition of all is that information should not be proprietary and shared on a need-to-know basis. Successful collaboration hinges strongly on transparency, which means that an open sharing of information between the various stakeholders is paramount.

Call to Action

The concept of assigning performance indicators to a single person who commands all the means and resources necessary to make the targets for those indicators is so pervasive that it is nearly impossible to change it, or even question it. Therefore, implementing business interface metrics may be harder than anticipated. The Brasseries de Bourbon case highlighted the right order of steps.

Although business interface metrics are largely transactional, as a top manager, you need to lead by example and create your own business interface metrics first. On this level it is also easier to distinguish the business interfaces because the executive team together is responsible for the organization's overall performance. On the middle management level, on the other hand, managers need help with the concept.

This is done best by taking one business interface first and showing how it works. This business interface can be a "burning platform," where there are major quality, speed, or cost issues. Or it could be "low hanging fruit," where management is very receptive to trying something new. When you share the results of the improved business interface with other business domains and extensively praise the results from the first implementation, others will be enticed to adopt the principles as well. But most important, it is necessary to realize that by implementing business interface metrics for your direct reports, you have a great responsibility too: managing collaboration.

Chapter | 8

BALANCING PERFORMANCE AND RISK

Risk management is proactive performance management. Why wait until performance indicators show business is not going well? Performance management is proactive risk management: the best defense is a good offense.

Two Sides of the Same Coin

Through methodologies, measurement, management processes, and systems performance, management monitors and manages all domains in an organization; it ensures that these domains align for optimal business performance. This means performance management is related to almost every management discipline. Performance management is related to human resource management inasmuch as performance is ultimately tied to having the right people in the right place. Performance management is related to operational management because strategies need to be implemented and need to work. Performance management is related to knowledge management because much of the decision-making process is based on tacit knowledge. Performance management is also related to risk management; in fact, they are two sides of the same coin.

Performance management focuses on strategic objectives and how to reach them. Performance leadership recognizes the differences in stakeholder objectives and tries to bridge them, to create a win-win situation. However, it would be short-sighted to assume that every part of the strategy goes according to plan. There will always be things that go wrong, and it would not be good if every deviation from the original plan were to come as a surprise. Up-front planning, involving scenario analysis of what could go wrong and how to deal with it, improves the speed of reaction if indeed something does go wrong. As the famous axiom states, "You cannot predict the future, but you can be ready for it."

Strategy maps actually recognize that idea by putting together cause-and-effect relationships between performance indicators. Early warning signals at the bottom of the strategy map indicate that strategic goals at the top of the strategy map might not be reached. However, strategy maps can never be exhaustive. In reality, it will always be an unanticipated factor that causes the surprise. Going through risk management exercises creates knowledge of the various business scenarios that could play out. And even if changes in reality are not the ones you predicted or identified as a risk, the experience of dealing with risks enables you to adjust faster with the unexpected ones too. Also, if things go wrong within the list of anticipated cause-and-effect relationships, why would you wait to address these risks until the first indicators start to light up in red? That's why performance management and risk management go hand in hand.

Enterprise risk management is a process established by an entity's board of directors, management, and other personnel that is applied in strategy setting and across the enterprise. It is designed to identify potential events that may affect the entity and to manage risk so that it is within the entity's risk appetite, to provide reasonable assurance regarding the achievement of entity objectives.[1]

There are different types of risk: financial risk, operational risk, reputation risk, and strategic risk. Interestingly enough, this is very close to the perspectives of the balanced scorecard. Financial risk and financial performance are related; operational risk matches the process perspective; reputation risk is related to the customer perspective; and strategic risk can be linked to the growth and learning perspective.

Most performance management methodologies are "closed systems." They either ignore risk management as a related discipline or try to fit it into one area of performance management. Another way to look at risk management is to combine key performance indicators (KPIs) with the results of a risk management exercise, spanning all areas of performance. In this way every performance indicator has a counterpart, or a key risk indicator (KRI).

RISK MANAGEMENT

Risk management consists of multiple categories: operational risk, financial risk, reputation risk, market risk, and strategic risk.

The Basel Committee on Banking Supervision breaks down *operational risk* into a number of categories.[2] Although the Basel Committee focuses on the financial services sector, these categories are useful for most businesses. Fraud, such as circumventing regulations, theft, or inappropriate use of resources, can be committed both internally (by employees) and externally (by suppliers, customers, shareholders, and other external stakeholders). Workplace safety (or the lack thereof) is also distinguished as an operational risk. Damage to physical assets and system failures can potentially lead to business disruption. Losses arising from failure to meet obligations to clients are part of operational risk. There can also be losses from failed processes, both inside and outside the company, as in processes with partners and suppliers.

Financial risk consists of credit risk and market risk.[3] *Market risk* includes equity risk (what happens with stock prices), interest rate risk, currency risk, and commodity risk (the price of raw materials). *Credit risk* is the risk of loss due to a counterparty defaulting on a contract, or, more generally, the risk of loss due to some "credit event." Traditionally this is applied to bonds where debt holders were concerned that the counterparty to whom they've made a loan might default on a payment.

Reputation risk is more than the potential external result of operational risk or financial risk. It is also broader than customer reputation; it includes all stakeholders: suppliers, partners, regulators, shareholders, and society at large. Reputation risk is determined by three factors.[4] The first is the reputation/reality gap. Reputation is about perception and distinct from the actual character of the organization (as I also stress in the definition of alignment). The bigger the gap, the higher the risk. The second is changing beliefs and expectations. Once-acceptable practices may become frowned upon, leading to a bad reputation because of past action. The third is weak internal coordination, when one department makes public promises that other departments cannot fulfill.

Strategic risk is that the chosen strategy and decisions made do not lead to achieving the strategic objectives. This may have many reasons, such as uncoordinated management processes, political decision making, a lack of relevant and timely information, a lack of analysis or interpretation of strategic information, or bad strategy implementation (such as M&A integration or turning R&D into products). <u>Strategic risk management</u> is the link to performance management.

An organization's risk management is usually highly institutionalized and regulated. For instance, you cannot just combine a general risk management framework with a performance management framework, and create a single integrated framework. Risk management implementations are usually a very important part of an organization's compliance. Management can't just "fiddle" with the framework.

The point of integration between performance management and risk management is strategic risk. The less performance management the organization has, the higher the organization's strategic risk.

Case Study 1: IT Hardware Supplier

Consider the operational excellence strategy of a Web retailer of IT hardware, such as PCs, printers, and other accessories. Margins are very small in this business and therefore the company tries to create a continuous and predictable stream of orders from its customers, largely medium-sized companies. The way to do that in a price-sensitive business is to create customer preference by shipping overnight. The value proposition of the company is perfectly simple, recognizable, and measurable: "order today, deliver tomorrow." Because holding inventory is expensive, the company integrates its order channel (Web site and call center) directly to the systems of its suppliers. A combination of key performance indicators and key risk indicators in the context of a strategy map could look like Figure 8.1.

In order to realize world-class speed of delivery, the company measures the percentage of deliveries completed within 24 hours. It is currently installing a real-time monitoring system to improve that number. The risk in operating a process at this speed without holding stock is that the company doesn't control the complete process. Service level management is needed to control that risk. The customer pays after delivery; therefore, the average days-sales-outstanding (DSO) is an important performance indicator. The choice to allow customers to pay later also introduces credit risk, which needs to be managed.

Figure 8.1

Combining Performance and Risk Indicators

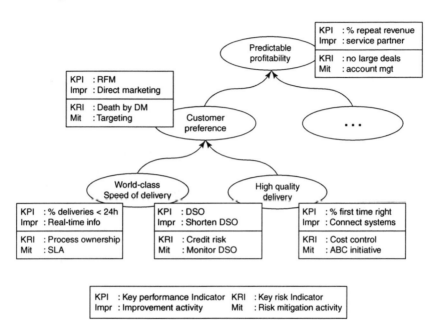

Monitoring the DSO is an activity that both improves the performance and mitigates risk. The company has found that if it makes mistakes, customers on average pay later, so the DSO is also a performance indicator for the quality of delivery. This is further measured by tracking the percentage of orders that are shipped completely and correctly. The risk is that high quality standards can lead to high cost structures, that is why the organization is introducing activity-based costing (ABC) to get insight into the cost of every step of the process.

The company aims for a high customer preference. It measures that by tracking RFM, or recency (how long ago was the last transaction), frequency (how often does the customer order), and monetary value (how big are the orders). It performs direct marketing to improve the RFM. However, too much direct marketing leads to either aversion or customers become jaded to the offers. A good process of targeting, based on the customers, needs, both mitigates that risk and increases the RFM.

Lastly, predicting revenues and profitability can be measured by tracking the percentage of repeat revenue as a result of customer preference. The focus on continuous revenue streams may lead the company to ignore large deals in the market that would increase the company's revenue. That's why it is also introducing account management for its larger customers.

Performance/Risk Map

The exercise of establishing both performance and risk indicators leads to insightful discussions. Do high rewards always have high risks? Do low-risk initiatives contribute enough to the objectives? Are there options that are low risk and high reward? Unfortunately, our current performance management practices and methodologies do not support that way of thinking. The structure of strategy maps, linking performance indicators with single lines displaying what-leads-to-what, tend not to recognize these dilemmas between risk and reward. They help us "optimize objectives," but easily lead to new problems in other areas. For instance, cost cutting leads to use of inferior materials. Inferior materials lead to a heavier burden on the environment and customer complaints of quality problems. Or, think of laying-off people, which negatively affects the knowledge base of the organization and the motivation of the people still left. It is good business to manage these risks when putting together performance management improvements.

The IT hardware supplier case showed how to fuse performance management and risk management, using an adaptation of a strategy map, originating in the performance management discipline. However, within risk management there is a useful visualization tool as well, called the *heat map*. See Figure 8.2.

A heat map has two dimensions. The vertical dimension shows if risks have a high probability of happening. The horizontal dimension shows the impact of that risk factor happening. Risks can then be plotted in the chart, based on the assessment of risk and impact. Risks that have a low probability and a low impact can safely be ignored. If they happen, there will be no material damage. Risks with a high probability but with low impact need to be included in the price of the products or services, to compensate for them. Risks with a low probability and a high impact should be monitored. They should be foreseen, for instance, through a scenario analysis, and a contingency plan should

Figure 8.2

Heat Map

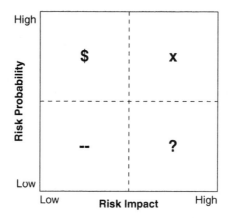

be in place to deal with the risk if needed. Lastly, risks with a high probability and high impact should be mitigated or, even better, eliminated. These risks require an active approach to steer the organization clear.

To fuse the heat map with performance management, you can plot strategies, objectives, or improvement initiatives instead of mapping risks. The risk dimension indicates the strategic risk: the chance that these strategies, objectives, or initiatives do not help the organization to reach its goals. Consider a fictitious family-owned midsized funeral business in a rural region, called Baker and Sons (B&S). Although business is relatively stable, margins have gone down due to large nationwide funeral businesses lowering prices. In order for B&S to stay profitable, it needs to explore different directions for growth and cost savings, to protect its bottom line. Figure 8.3 shows a number of possibilities plotted in a heat map.

B&S could start saving costs on the funeral services. It would certainly contribute to the goals, but the risk has a high impact—decreased quality of the service. It is hard to win from large competitors with an operational excellence model; it is probably better to differentiate based on high quality. Saving costs here would lead to a high strategic and reputation risk. B&S could improve its personalized service and cater for very specific cultures and religions. The margins on these tailored funerals are probably much higher, and the infrastructure

Figure 8.3

Margin Improvement Strategies for a Midsize Funeral Business

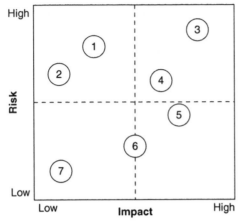

1. 25% cost savings services
2. 50% higher revenue new services
3. Acquire other undertakers
4. Collaborate with other undertakers
5. Being acquired
6. Increase spending on staff attraction
7. Cost saving on sponsor program

for performing personalized services is there, as the company is family-owned and highly flexible. However, there is a strategic and market risk. In a rural area there may not be that much demand for these services and the return on investment may not be very high.

Another option would be to acquire other small- to medium-sized undertakers. However, the strategic risk is very high as B&S are not experts in acquisition and integration. The impact of this betting-the-farm option is very significant: the company could go out of business. An option with a significantly lower risk, and less negative impact, would be to collaborate with various undertakers to create economies of scale while still operating as independent companies. The risk is still considerable because family-owned businesses tend to have developed their own specific ways of working and may not agree on common processes.

Another option for B&S could be seeking to be acquired. The company could, perhaps, retain its name and management, but the company would belong to one of the nationwide funeral businesses. The risk, in this case, is not high for B&S; it is the risk of the acquirer. It would also lead to growth and higher margins, which was the goal of the exercise. There is, however, a large market risk since personal service will most likely disappear under a new business model.

An option without much risk is to hire younger, more sales-oriented staff. The impact of such a campaign failing is neutral, it returns the company to the as-is situation. However, there is no reason why B&S couldn't do that in combination with most of the other options. The last option could look into other areas of its cost structure. For instance, if B&S sponsors the local theater, it could look to withdraw sponsorship. The risk of it is not high, but the contribution to the result is also not very high.

This exercise helps assess the risk of every performance improvement activity, instead of purely calculating the contribution to the goals. Instead of a single risky initiative, it might also be possible to construct a portfolio of multiple performance improvement initiatives, each without significant risk, which together can fully contribute to a positive impact.

However, to completely fuse performance management and strategic risk management, it is not enough to infuse elements of performance management into risk management or vice versa. An integrated tool for decision management is needed. Where performance management techniques are too positively oriented (not taking risks into account), risk management techniques are too negatively oriented (impact is about what happens if things go wrong). A performance/risk map solves both problems. The performance/risk map, like a heat map, has two dimensions. The vertical dimension is the risk dimension, which ranges from low to high. It shows how risky an initiative is. The horizontal dimension is the performance dimension, which also ranges from low to high. It shows the positive impact of an initiative and to what extent it contributes to the bottom line. See Figure 8.4.

Different organizations have different risk appetites. The more risk averse an organization is, the more the middle line could be drawn low on the risk dimension. Different organizations also have different levels of ambition. Highly ambitious organizations can draw the line high on the performance dimension. It creates four quadrants, each potentially with a different size. Initiatives with a high risk and low performance contribution are a no-go area, and they should be avoided. Where there is acceptable risk but not the expected return, the initiatives may be part of the solution, but by themselves they do not deliver enough of an improvement. Options that provide the full return but at a high risk, pose a dilemma. If things turn out well, you will reach your

F i g u r e   8 . 4

Performance/Risk Map

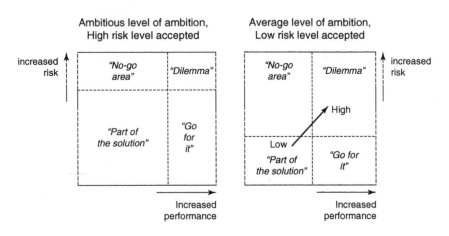

objectives, but failure will be a painful setback. It may become necessary to take such options because of the condition of the business. However, such action can often be avoided by diligent strategic risk management, not allowing conditions to go so far that these options are the only options left. Or there are other, less valid, reasons to consider the option, such as how it will be viewed by shareholders or even competitors. It represents the "bold move."

Obviously, it would be best to find options that have a low risk and a high performance contribution. The last option, low risk and high reward, tends to be rare. They are "hole in the market" strategies, and they are likely to lose their competitive differentiation because everyone will immediately copy the strategy. It is much likelier that a portfolio of initiatives will do the trick. However, just considering low-risk options may lead to too many small steps. That is why we need to add one more level of freedom in the model. Instead of plotting options as dots, we should plot them as a line (see Figure 8.4). The low side on the line shows the risk and performance if the initiative is implemented in a limited, tactical, or unambitious way. The high side of the line shows the position in the performance/risk map if the initiative is of a strategic nature and receives all the attention. Let's explore the case of an Internet bank to see how a performance/risk map drives the decision-making process.

Case Study 2: Direct Banking

How could we design an explicit process that balances opportunities and risk? Or, a process that leads to the right discussions while going through the various design steps? Consider a large global bank opening up direct-banking services in various countries. Its value proposition is clear: straight-forward standard products such as savings accounts and home insurance, with a low-cost structure, so that it can offer higher interest and lower premiums. The Internet and a call center per country will serve as the customer contact channel. Its bottom-line goal is to meet the return on the capital-employed goal of the parent company. This can be achieved by growing the assets under management, combined with a profitable reinvestment of the savings and premiums. Growth of assets under management, particularly for an Internet bank, is very dependent on the trust the target audience has in the bank. Trust depends first on the awareness level the general public has, as you can't trust somebody you don't know. This trust can be won by introducing transparency in the reinvestment processes, to show there is no customer risk. Another factor that builds trust is by having swift and reliable integrated operations, spanning the two customer contact channels. If we model these value drivers, it could look like Figure 8.5.

The rollout of direct banking is a great success, and the bank's ambitions grow. As part of these growing ambitions, corporate increases its targets for the return on capital employed (ROCE). The management team brainstorms and comes up with a few options. Trying to increase the operational excellence by centralizing call centers in multiple countries will certainly cut costs and increase margins. Another option is to reinvest the assets under management in a more aggressive way. The marketing director offers to start a large campaign to increase market awareness. Lastly, a junior manager brings in the idea to create a product for "Islamic banking,"[5] unlocking the large ethnic communities in various countries where the bank is active. The management team summarizes the four options as follows:

A. Cut cost by centralizing call centers: Easy.

B. Take more risk in reinvestments: Risky.

Figure 8.5

Value Drivers for Direct Banking

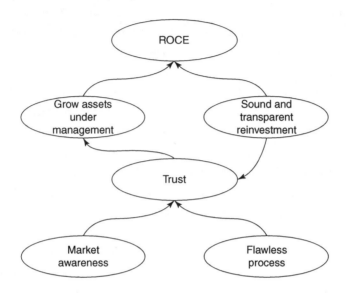

C. Raise market awareness: Too indirect to achieve the immediate objective.

D. Islamic banking: Great idea but with a long-term focus.

After a short discussion, the management team decides to go for option A. It is easy to calculate the cost savings needed to increase the return on capital employed and meet the new target.

The choice was made as a *single* solution *directly* solving the problem at hand—easy to oversee and relatively easy to control. But is this the right choice? Option B was dismissed because it was too risky. But all the other options have risks associated with them as well. Cutting costs by centralizing call centers negatively affects "trust" as it looks like the bank will physically retreat from certain countries, leaving only a Web site and a local phone number. Raising market awareness has the risk of being a victim of its own success. When meeting the stretch target, the scalability of the customer contact processes might not be enough. A decrease in reliability negatively affects trust again. Islamic banking may present a great long-term opportunity, but currently the company lacks the cultural capabilities to create an effective message; the risk of getting it wrong is too great. But why look for just one alternative to reach the new objective? Wouldn't a *portfolio* of improvement activities do the trick? The following three steps will lead to a better way of making the right decisions while addressing the associated risks.

1. *Determine the risk level and level of ambition.* The bank is not a particularly risk-averse or risk-seeking organization. It offers standard products to customer masses. However, the bank is very ambitious. As a result, it chooses a performance/risk matrix with the marking line in the middle between high and low risk, and the marking line between high and low performance toward the high end.

2. *Map the different options.* Each of the four options in our example has a different risk profile. The cost-cutting option will become riskier the more aggressively it is pursued. The Islamic banking option, on the other hand, starts out as rather risky, and follows through with building the capabilities. In that case, the risk compared to the potential gains dramatically decreases. The marketing awareness campaign is risk free as long as the processes and systems are scalable, in which case the risk would suddenly increase. Trying to increase the margin by creating a different reinvestment risk portfolio has a much more complex curve, as it will cost a certain segment of customers, while attracting a different type of customer. For the purposes of this example, we will assume a linear relationship (better performance leads to a higher risk). When we plot these options in the balanced performance/risk map, it would look like Figure 8.6.

   It helps to use lines with "low" and "high" instead of the usual dots because every option can be implemented in various degrees. Low here means only moderate changes are made, high means drastic redesigns are carried out. The line provides a visual explanation of how much impact the performance can have. The change in risk profile, according to the assessment that was made, would—by itself—barely meet the target even when executed with full force. The loss of customers and the addition of risk adjustments would take away much of the

Figure 8.6

Balanced Performance/Risk Map per Option

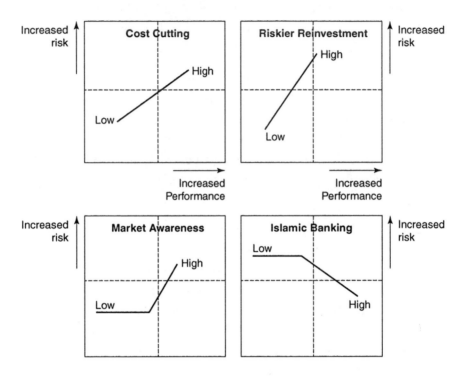

increased margin. At the same time, the angle of the line represents the increase or decrease of the risk associated with the level of ambition. The line can be horizontal, which means the performance improvement activity can be scaled up without additional risk. The line can go up, as it will do in many cases, to show how the risk will increase proportionately or disproportionately when the performance improvement initiative is implemented more aggressively. And there are cases where the risk actually goes down, at the same time as the initiative has more impact. This last case is preferable because the initiative reconciles the natural dilemma between risk and performance.

3. *Choose a performance improvement portfolio.* Changing the risk profile of the reinvestments was dismissed by the management for the right reasons. It would have a negative impact while the

returns would be marginal. But initially, guided by traditional performance management practices, the other options look different compared to the new approach. Making the decision to cut costs may seem very attractive because it is easy to calculate how much costs need to be cut, by centralizing call centers, until the new return on capital employed (ROCE) target is met. But at the point where cost cutting would lead to meeting the target, the risk becomes higher than would be acceptable. Going all the way may lead to serious problems. At the same time, improving the marketing awareness shows it leads to no additional risk, until the capacity of the current processes and systems is reached. Then the risk will increase quickly. The management rightfully decided to forgo Islamic banking as a means to contribute to the increased ROCE because management has no experience in that area. But the curve shows there is great strategic opportunity to tap into a large new market.

None of the options provides a perfect answer, as long as they are viewed separately. However, the picture changes once you consider multiple options, each contributing at an acceptable risk level. Instead of the point solution to performance improvement of the traditional way of thinking, a performance improvement portfolio emerges.

Cost cutting in call centers is still possible, not by closing call centers but by investing in an infrastructure that integrates call centers, so that local employees that speak multiple languages can also help customers in another country. By itself that may not save enough cost, so it helps to also increase market awareness, yet not so aggressively that the current processes and systems can't cope with the follow-up. The joint performance improvement more than makes the goal. The idea of Islamic banking remains. With the strongly improved contribution, a part of it can be invested in setting up an Islamic banking pilot in a single country and serving a single ethnic group. It allows the bank to follow the results and build up the necessary competency. The bank is investing in its next round of performance improvement. And the performance improvements are much more sustainable compared to the traditional approach because they improve the alignment of the organization. The external perception (the outside-in view) is explicitly considered as a boundary condition when designing inside-out strategies to improve performance.

Call to Action

To get started with aligning risk management and performance management, answer the following questions:

- What types of risk management do you distinguish? Do you separate out strategic risk as a category?
- What risk management methodologies do you use, and how can you integrate performance management into that?
- What performance management methodologies do you use, and how can you integrate risk management into that?
- What are your key performance indicators and your key risk indicators? Do they not only match your strategy but also match each other?

Take a few decision-making processes of the recent past and model them out using the performance/risk matrix. Look at the options of that particular process and see if using the matrix leads to different deliberations on what option to choose, or even better, an improved portfolio of smaller decisions and options. After having gone through the exercise of remodeling past decisions, and having built up your experience in the approach, use the performance/risk matrix for a new decision.

GUIDING PRINCIPLES FROM THE VALUES AND SOCIAL DIMENSIONS

—

Part II focused on the traditional dimensions of performance management and introduced the concept of horizontal alignment. Part III introduces two new dimensions from the performance leadership framework, the values and social dimensions. These dimensions encapsulate the traditional operational and analytical dimensions. In that sense, the performance leadership framework doesn't replace traditional performance management methodologies: it offers guidance on how to implement these methodologies in a better way. In the values and social dimensions, organizations align strategy according to what the organizations stand for and what the market is looking for. Understanding the sometimes conflicting nature of these internal and external requirements, and striking the right balance, is the key to being an aligned organization, where the self, self-perception, and external perception closely match.

Chapter | 9

VALUES AND CULTURE

How would you respond if your friend, who hit a pedestrian with his car, were to ask you to provide false testimony in court? Such a situation poses a dilemma, truth versus friendship. Some cultures tend to honor the law; others favor the friendship. But both types of culture feel their response proves a core value, integrity.
—Based on F. Trompenaars[1]

The Values Dimension

Where the operational and analytical dimensions aim to optimize business performance, the social and values dimensions of the performance leadership framework provide the guidance on how to optimize. Like people, organizations have values too. In fact, every organization has values, whether they are written down or not. People's values and organizational values relate to each other. Organizational values are an aggregation of the personal values of key people within the organization, and they attract people with the same values to the organization.

The values dimension provides strategic guidance from within, from what drives the organization to be in business, the *raison d'être* of the organization, to how it is recognized in the outside world. See Figure 9.1.

The shortest definition of organizational values is "what is good and what is bad in this organization."[2] They are normative and judgmental. Organizational culture is very much related to values; however, there is a difference. Organizational culture is the practical application of values in everyone's daily work; it's how people make decisions and

Figure 9.1

Values Dimension of the Performance Leadership Framework

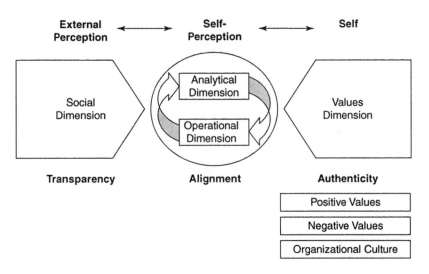

solve problems. Culture is more prescriptive, "the way we do things around here."[3] As evidenced in the opening illustration of a dilemma, people with different cultural backgrounds can share the same values, such as integrity. However, their culture can cause different — even opposite — behaviors. Behaviors are what people do. Behaviors are very tangible, they can be observed and influenced long before financial results. Behaviors that match an organization's values and cultures lead to alignment. Dysfunctional behaviors, behaviors that do not match the culture and values, lead to an alignment gap.

Although values and culture are not the same, for practical purpose in this book, I will not make a clear distinction. Organizational culture and values have a number of purposes in an organization.[4] These purposes include:

- *Boundary defining*. Different organizations have different cultures and values, and the differences create distinctions among organizations.
- *Identity builders*. Organization members derive a sense of identity working for a certain organization.
- *Commitment generators*. Strong culture and values generate commitment to something larger than a member's own personal goals.

- *Social system stabilizers*. Organizational culture and values are social glue, to keep the organization, or collaboration between organizations, together.
- *Sense-making and control instruments*. They guide and shape the attitudes and behaviors of organization members.

An understanding of an organization's values provides guidance to the right strategy. Let's look at an example. A large nationwide chain of car dealers needed to improve its cost structure. After years of spectacular growth through a number of acquisitions, it was time to reap the benefits of economies of scale. The business case for a project to centralize the back office for various administrative processes showed a very positive return on investment, which would greatly contribute to the strategic goal. The company went forward, but after a while noticed adverse effects. Customer satisfaction dropped and back office employees were not very effective in working certain back office processes. The problem was that the project did not support the values of the organization, which all revolved around catering to many very specific customer needs, ranging from special car options to specific financing needs. The back office people were distanced from the operations, and they were no longer able to be flexible. A new project was then started. The new project involved a somewhat more expensive virtual back office that local employees could log onto from their location; this proved much more successful. Although the cost savings for the second project on paper looked less attractive, the chance of achieving the goal was much higher.

This example shows how values guide making the right decisions. The top-down metric "return on investment" drove the wrong behavior. Understanding the corporate culture and values helps performance management in two ways. First, it helps predict dysfunctional behaviors when implementing new strategic initiatives or performance indicators. Up-front countermeasures can be taken. Second, it helps to put together initiatives or indicators to drive and reward the right behaviors from the outset.

Values and Culture Are Not "Soft"

Values and culture are often called *soft factors*, but in reality they are not. Values and culture have a very tangible impact on an organization's performance. New employees that join an organization and do not fit into its value system usually soon depart. They don't feel at home; they do not understand what is important and what is not. Even a known high-flyer in a previous company will not be effective in a company if there is no basic sense of shared values and culture between the organization and that person. Further, the example of the car dealer network showed that if a business initiative doesn't match the organization's values, it will not succeed unless it is forced through with extreme effort. Despite a positive business case, members of an organization simply do not accept the initiative. Also, values and culture are externally visible to customers. If an organization launches an initiative that doesn't fit the organization's perceived values, customers will not accept the initiative as authentic and attractive. For instance, a producer of SUVs will find it hard to launch a successful "drive clean and green" campaign. Yet a tobacco company may be very successful in being seen as authentic in setting up a system to prevent youths from buying cigarettes.

Understanding and using your organizational values can be a powerful source of management control. Traditionally, performance management is focused on bureaucratic styles of control, consisting of a number of standard processes, rules, and checkpoints to make sure all transactions are performed in the same way. This vertical alignment and a hierarchic approach works best in environments with low ambiguity (only one way to interpret things) and low uncertainty (stable environment). However, most environments are increasingly ambiguous and very uncertain. More control and more performance indicators would not lead to better results. In fact, they would lead to more dysfunctional behaviors. In ambiguous and uncertain environments, internalized control works better.[5]

Internalized control means that the members of an organization share the values and the objectives of the organization, and will seek to do the right thing and be open about it. Again, this principle is not soft. Internalized control is the basis of certification in certain professions, such as with chartered accountants or other types of auditors. Their certification is a first guarantee of integrity, although the integrity of the profession may not always be aligned with the goals of the organization. The values get internalized by years of training, initiation rites, and a strong status associated with the role. Obviously, values are not restricted to chartered accountants. Every organization has values. They may not be posted on the Web site, or even written down, but they live in the hearts of the people who work for the company . . . or not.

Identifying Values

An organization's values cannot be "set"; you can only discover them.[6] Values are not a change mechanism, where they are "rolled out"; they are already there. And although strategies, marketing messages, and practices change over time, values do not. When identifying organizational values, companies need to be real. Often, their list of values contains a few values that are aimed more at describing desired behaviors than the actual behaviors. For example, a company may want to focus its staff on teamwork, although in the past this has not been the case. You have to be careful with weaving in desired values. If values are not intuitively recognized by the staff, the response may be cynical and the result will be misalignment instead of a better understanding and performance.

Examples of organizational values are: accountability, quality-driven, ambitious, cost-conscious, compassionate, challenging conventional thinking, treating all equally, disciplined, trustworthy, highest levels of integrity, skillful, entrepreneurial, never giving up, flexible, or being innovative.

Values help understand the behaviors of people, they provide the necessary context. Figure 9.2 shows a typical balanced scorecard. Well-trained staff members run smooth processes, which lead to satisfied customers who keep coming back, resulting in healthy financial results. Successful companies have value drivers that make this happen. For instance, the organization may really care about working with customers; it is continuously busy with designing new and innovative products; or it is always looking to reach a higher level of operational excellence.

If your strategy is about cost leadership or operational excellence, most likely your values include thriftiness, efficiency, or discipline. Staff can have fun looking for ways to cut costs and create a more efficient operation. They pride themselves at having the most cost-effective production, which is recognized by the clients, leading to healthy

Figure 9.2

Strategic Context of Values on Performance Management

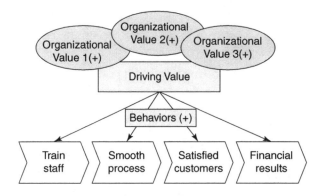

financial results. If your strategy is all about customer intimacy, it is probably based on values such as going the extra mile, flexibility, and empathy. If your strategy revolves around product innovation, likely it is driven by values such as quality, challenging conventional thinking, and never giving up. The staff looks for ways to create a superior product experience and perhaps pride themselves in a certain exclusivity. This leads to attracting clients that are willing to pay a premium price, leading to a profitable operation.

However, if we believe that values affect behaviors and behaviors drive what people do with performance indicators, the opposite should also be taken into account. Every organization, like every person, has a "dark side" too. Every organization has negative values as well; they are the other side of the coin of a positive value. It is important not to dismiss negative values; they have the same power the positive values have. After all, they're values. Here are some examples of negative values: opportunistic, greedy, stubborn, wasteful, doing things by half, bureaucratic, inflexible, overemotional, overengineered, and not invented here.

Positive values and negative values may correspond, as shown in Table 9.1.

Just as positive values can't be set, negative values cannot be avoided. They are something we have to accept as our dark side in the organization. However, we can be aware of them and accept them as part of the deal, as shown graphically in Figure 9.3.

Table 9.1

Corresponding Positive and Negative Values

Positive Value	Corresponding Negative Value
Skillful	Overspecialize
Compassionate	Overemotional
Cost conscious	Stingy
Quality driven	Wasteful
Ambitious	Greedy
Challenge conventional thinking	Not invented here
Highest levels of integrity	Inflexible, bureaucratic
Entrepreneurial	Do things by half
Never give up	Stubborn
Flexible	Opportunistic

Positive values drive performance for the organization. Negative values inhibit performance for the organization. Value inhibitors, from the standpoint of the organization, are the strategies we deploy to serve

Figure 9.3

Full Strategic Context of Values on Metrics

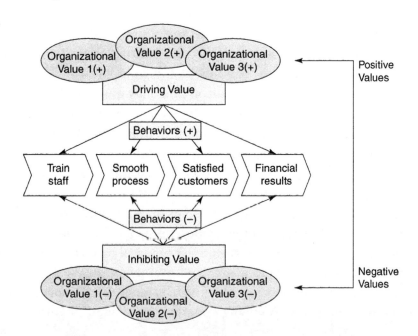

goals other than corporate objectives. Think of suboptimization, where we maximize our own targets, even at the expense of the overall strategic objectives. Or, think of gaming, where we start underachieving after making our targets, or overspending to secure a higher next year's budget.

Although this is a very logical thought, organizations typically do not have the same focus on the negative values as they have on the positive values. The most obvious reason is that it is politically incorrect to have a negative focus; understandably management might be concerned that the negative values become public knowledge. But measurement drives behavior and behaviors determine the effectiveness of any strategy. Determining negative values will provide greater insight in defining the correct and effective performance indicators. The behaviors (positive and negative) can be predicted once the performance indicators are implemented, and counteractions (such as incentives or punishment) can be defined up front. We don't have to be surprised.

Different Cultures, Different Behaviors

In my first job, as a 22-year-old, I had an interesting experience. I worked as a consultant in a subsidiary of an American firm. The local management, inspired by corporate practices, decided to implement a monthly incentive program. In a few performance categories, among which was "most billable hours," the best-scoring consultants would get a small bonus (enough for a nice evening out for two). The group of consultants rejected the program, as billability was considered highly dependent on the results of the sales force and only marginally dependent on the achievements of the consultants. Management insisted, and the group resisted. The group stated it would collectively put the bonus in a pool to then be equally distributed or awarded in a lottery. The incentive program was never put in place. It was my first lesson on how simple measurement and reward systems have a cultural context.

Values are defined as an organization's principal behavior on a high level; culture describes an organization's practical behavior that can be observed in similar situations over and over again. In the company I worked for, "fairness" and "equality" were values; "sharing success" was the cultural outcome. Applying generic management theories often creates undesirable outcomes, as they often do not take cultural differences into account. There are some areas of management that are truly objective and culturally independent, such as "operations research techniques" for process optimization, but performance management is not one of these areas. Organizational culture is often based on the values of a founder who is grounded in a certain national culture. Think of IKEA, which has a very Swedish culture, or General Electric, which is a very American company. The success of Toyota through its integrated value chain is also very much related to its Japanese culture.

An interesting study compared the American, French, and Dutch factories of a multinational conglomerate.[7] The three plants produced the same goods and used the same machines and processes, making cultural aspects a more easily distinguishing factor. The study described the American culture as very contract-driven. For every job there was a clear description of tasks, responsibilities, and review criteria — leaving it open to employees as to how to achieve the goals. It is no wonder "management by objectives" comes from the United States. The working relationships are hierarchic (you "work for someone"), based on a contract between free individuals. As a result, the controls are very formal. This top-down approach means there will be no problem connecting performance indicators to personal reward systems, openly publicizing ranked performance data, or using new objectives and metrics to drive change.

The French culture is about "honor." The staff does not focus primarily on who they work for, but rather their professional drive is based on being part of a social and professional group. This leads to a certain autonomy of decision making, where authority is based on the group that the professional belongs to. The French management style is hierarchic; however, the control systems are less formal. Changes are made on hints from management, and it is possible to massage and work the systems based on personal relationships. Openly sharing feedback information across the various professional domains in a French company will likely not work well, as it violates the honor of the groups. Having each group collect and share feedback among themselves will work much better.

The study described the Dutch culture as egalitarian. Decisions are fact-based, like anywhere else, but are not rolled out through the hierarchy. Instead, the decision-making process consists of extensive discussions on all levels of the organization, where employees feel free to disagree with their managers or top management. Decisions then are made based on a consensus, which is the objective of all participants in the discussion. When new data become available, anyone is free to reopen the discussion. This style is anything but hierarchic, and also not very formal. The controls, however, are formal; people do not appreciate shortcuts and cheating the system. Performance management is not a control instrument, but a platform for all employees to discuss.

There are several frameworks by which to describe and categorize cultures.[8] Often these frameworks use dimensions between two extremes to classify a culture on that specific characteristic. Most of the frameworks focus on describing national cultures, and deal with many social issues. However, some of the dimensions used also apply to corporate cultures, and they affect the way performance management should be implemented. These dimensions are:

- Group versus individual focus
- Meritocracy versus aristocracy
- Rules versus relational orientation
- Long-term versus short-term orientation
- Theory X versus theory Y
- Internal versus external orientation

For each of these dimensions I will describe the typical management processes, performance indicators, as well as feedback and reward mechanisms. And although the list of dysfunctional behaviors could be endless, I will provide some examples of what happens if you implement performance management in the wrong cultural way. The examples vary per dimension, but frustration, dissonance, lack of commitment, and underperformance can be expected in every single case.

Group versus Individual Focus

In individualistic cultures, managers seek information from various parties, take everything into consideration, and then make "the right" decision that is communicated to the rest of the group. People are held personally accountable for their results. Performance indicators are implemented top down, cascading into the organization. They reflect single corporate goals. Management information is not very public; feedback is given by management on an individual basis. Rewards are individualized as well.

Contrast this with group-focused cultures. The needs of the group to which that person belongs come first. Decision making in group-focused cultures is a process based on consensus. Managers facilitate the process and see "the right" decision as the one that has the highest buy-in. People take responsibility for each other, and the group is responsible for the overall results. Performance indicators come from the group and they are implemented bottom up. They are usually complex in nature and reflect the balanced needs of all stakeholders. Management information is created by the group and used by the group. Incentives are evenly distributed over the group.

If in a group-focused culture, an individual-focused performance management initiative is introduced, it will lead to ignoring the individual performance indicators, or all kinds of ways will be found to get around the system; for instance, by redistributing incentives. Conversely, if you implement a group-based system in an individual environment, it will lead to inertia. People do not see how their personal contributions are recognized and become demotivated. See Table 9.2.

Meritocracy versus Aristocracy

Meritocratic organizations recognize people based on their achievements. In a meritocracy based on specific competencies, people are drawn into projects that lead to strategic decisions. Performance indicators are zero-based. Every period there is another chance to prove what you are worth as a professional. A person's status is reevaluated every quarter on the basis of quantitative results. In a culture based on achievements, people are rewarded with a bigger domain to manage (such as a sales region), so that through higher targets and associated bonuses, they can become even more successful.

An aristocracy, where status is based on background, can also lead to high performance. In an aristocracy, where status is based on someone's background, performance is linked to influence. Hence, success is almost a self-fulfilling prophecy. Aristocratic environments are hierarchic. Status is measured in terms of the levels the manager oversees.

Table 9.2
_____

Group versus Individual Focus

	Group Focus (the needs of the group come first)	Individual Focus (the needs of the individual come first)
Management Process	Consultative	Directive
Key performance indicators	Bottom up, composite metrics to reflect balance of objectives	Top down, optimizing single goals, cascading into more details
Feedback	Organized by the group, for the group; no broad rankings	Privacy-sensitive, numbers not public
Rewards	Group-based, overall team performance	Personal rewards for each team member's performance
Dysfunctional behavior	Ignoring imposed metrics, gaming the system, misrepresentation	Inertia because "I am not appreciated here"

In the end, meritocracy and aristocracy lead to the same result: status based on the size of the operation the manager commands. However, the difference in how this success is achieved is vital. In a meritocracy, the best professional may earn more than the manager; in the aristocracy this is not common. Performance indicators in an aristocracy are based on continuous improvement; they are not zero based.

Implementing aristocratic performance management in a meritocratic environment will lead to disastrous results. To protect themselves, people will start building little empires to gain power, leading to suboptimal results. Others will become unmotivated, as they are not able to make the career progress they desire. Information and knowledge will not be widely shared because it is the only source of power the specialists have against the established order. Conversely, a meritocratic system will fail in an aristocratic environment. Managers will start to discredit the system, and to downplay the importance of the system if the actual performance is disappointing. If their direct reports can earn more than they do, they will find alternative ways to show their contributions of the past, instead of just their results for the most recent period. See Table 9.3.

Table 9.3

Meritocracy versus Aristocracy

	Meritocracy (what you've done)	Aristocracy (who you are)
Management process	Project-based, filled with the right competencies	Hierarchy-based, decisions made by the inner circle
Key performance Indicators	Zero-based, starting from scratch every quarter or year	Based on continuous improvement, accumulative
Feedback	Constant reevaluation, based on numbers	Coming from senior management, based on recognition
Rewards	Bonus, bigger domain	Salary increase, hierarchic promotion
Dysfunctional behavior	Suboptimization, hiding information	Downplaying the importance of performance management

Rules versus Relational Orientation

Rules-based cultures play it by the book. There are clear rules to make sure there are no exceptions and everyone is treated the same. This includes citizens, customers, and also employees. Contracts need to be kept, regardless of the circumstances. Every group has the same performance indicators, and the numbers speak for themselves. Feedback is based on a public ranking of results. The bonus schema is clear for everyone and has a predictable outcome.

In relationship-oriented environments, people focus on specific situations at hand. They speak of people in terms of relationships, such as "friend," "special customer," "loyal employee." Rules or not, the relationship needs to be protected. Contracts can easily be changed if circumstances change. Performance indicators are very personal, reflecting someone's unique position. The numbers don't speak for themselves; they are there to trigger a personal and qualitative discussion. Naturally, incentives are at the discretion of the management.

A rules oriented approach in a relationship oriented culture will lead to getting around the system; people will find alternative versions of the truth, showing their results are not comparable with anyone else's. A relationship-oriented approach in a rules-based culture is equally disastrous. It will lead to cynicism, with accusations of favoritism or even

Table 9.4

Rules versus Relational Orientation

	Rules Orientation (going by the book, obeying the rules)	Relational Orientation (building and sustaining relationships)
Management process	Focus on processes, controls, rules	Focus on who owes you; negotiation based on exchanging favors
Key performance indicators	Same clearly defined, consistent, and comparable metrics for everyone	Personal performance metrics that describe a person's unique position in the company
Feedback	Open feedback, public rankings; the numbers speak for themselves	Personal feedback; numbers trigger a qualitative discussion
Rewards	A clear bonus schema based on under- or overperformance	Incentives at the discretion of the managers
Dysfunctional behavior	Cynicism, no peer collaboration	Getting around the system, finding alternative versions of the truth

nepotism. There will definitely not be any collaboration, to avoid others getting credit for the work. See Table 9.4.

Long-Term versus Short-Term Orientation

Many current business cultures have a strong focus on the short term. Managers move on every few years, shareholders demand immediate return, strong competition demands shorter time to market, and product life cycles are become shorter too. Decision-making processes are very practical of nature, searching for swift and pragmatic solutions. Managers focus on immediate and tactical results. Performance indicators are very process-oriented, change often, and are measured as often as possible in real time. Feedback is immediate and focused on specific situations. In such environments people are rewarded with quarterly bonuses and awards such as employee of the month.

However, there are also cultures with a long-term orientation. In these environments, there tends to be more emphasis on tradition in decision-making processes and on finding the right solution. Decision-making processes tend to be slower, but also more balanced, taking long-term commitments into account. Some companies even have a vision where they would like to be in 20 to 50 years. Performance indicators are not based on immediate results, but on their contribution to longer-term goals. Feedback is important, but focuses on a person's potential as much as on results. Rewards are given in terms of more status within the organization.

A short-term approach in a long-term environment will lead to people ignoring performance indicators; there is simply a different sense of urgency. The opposite will happen when a long-term approach is used in a short-term environment. Middle managers will set up their own performance management systems and feel a lack of control. See Table 9.5.

Theory X versus Theory Y

McGregor's Theory X and Theory Y describes two extremes in people's work attitudes that are highly relevant for performance management.[9] Theory X states that people are looking for ways to minimize their effort

Table 9.5

Short-Term versus Long-Term Orientations

	Short-Term Orientation (pragmatic results)	Long-Term Orientation (contribution to the vision)
Management process	Tactical results, swift decision-making processes	Fundamental discussions, honoring long-term commitments and traditions
Key performance indicators	Process-oriented, fast-changing, real-time, specific goal-oriented	Periodic, focused on contribution to strategic goals
Feedback	Swift, specific	Periodic, holistic
Rewards	Awards, bonuses	Status, influence
Dysfunctional behavior	Setting up "illegal" systems due to lack of corporate processes and systems; procrastination (waiting for miracles to happen); unfocused behavior	Ignoring performance indicators

and avoid work. They need to be directed and controlled by management. Decisions are made and communicated. Performance indicators are a control mechanism, they are put in place to check if all the work has been done. Feedback is given in a negative way to those who do not work hard or good enough. Rewards consist of money. Additionally, Theory X environments also think in terms of punishments.

Theory Y states the opposite. People like to work; it gives them a sense of purpose and accomplishment. People are creative and look for better ways to do their job, maximizing the results of their resources and skills. They seek responsibility. Management's role is to coach employees, and the decision-making processes are participative. Performance indicators are used as a feedback mechanism to motivate people to improve. Rewards do not have to be monetary. They can also consist of public recognition or incentives aimed at building skills, such as training, leading to a higher job satisfaction.

A Theory X approach in a Theory Y environment will lead to many people quitting their jobs, such directive management is simply unacceptable. The people who stay will become inert, waiting for detailed instructions. In such organizations there is usually a very high level of passive-aggressive behavior, people like to see activities and processes go wrong. Conversely, a Theory Y management style in a Theory X culture leads to people taking advantage of the situation and avoiding work and responsibility. See Table 9.6.

Table 9.6

Theory X versus Theory Y

	Theory X (Control)	Theory Y (Feedback)
Management process	Directive, detailed	Participative, coaching, high-level
Key performance indicators	Measuring inputs, such as time and effort	Measuring outputs, such as achievement and results
Feedback	To management, for control purposes	To workers, for motivational purposes
Rewards	Bonuses, punishments (negative rewards)	Recognition, training
Dysfunctional behavior	Taking advantage	Passive-aggressive behavior

Internal versus External Orientation

Internally oriented cultures have a strong sense of independence; they shape their world themselves. Management processes are top down and sequential. There is a clear focus on a goal, but not much agility. Strategy sessions are translated into plans, plans are rolled out, and the results are measured. There is not much tolerance for uncertainty. The external world is carefully analyzed, but in terms of how to beat it. Performance indicators focus on a variance between actual and plan, and they have a strong deadline focus. People are responsible and accountable for their own actions and results. Feedback is based on the up-or-out principle, and rewards follow the same principle.

Externally oriented cultures believe their success is the result of the economy, the market in which they operate, or the weather. Management processes are very iterative. Many scenarios of potential futures are discussed. A desirable future is chosen, but in making decisions it is clear other potential future scenarios will not be closed off. Throughout a continuous process, the strategy is fine-tuned and updated. At the same time there is room for some experiments to test ideas a few people had in the meantime. A highly adaptive environment is tolerant of risk and uncertainty, yet not always fully focused. Performance indicators are relative, based on benchmarks, and aimed at agility. Feedback is based on what the external world thinks, and rewards are group-based, as everyone contributed to the success.

An externally oriented approach in an internally oriented world will lead to confusion. People expect clear goals, which they don't get. People will try to "fix" the environment, leading to gaming the numbers. An internally oriented approach in an externally oriented world also leads to problems. People feel unfairly treated. How can they be blamed for changes in the external environment? They will do everything to discredit the system. See Table 9.7.

Combining Dimensions

Looking at single dimensions one at a time, as we've done so far, provides very limited insight. It becomes really interesting if we start to combine dimensions. These cultural dimensions are not completely

Table 9.7
_____

Internal versus External Orientation

	Internally Oriented	Externally Oriented
Management process	Top down, sequential	Iterative and networked
Key performance indicators	Variance analysis, aimed at deadlines	Benchmarks, aimed at speed
Feedback	Up or out	From external stakeholders
Rewards	Personal	Group-based
Dysfunctional Behavior	Running numbers instead of running the business, trying to ignore external effects	Challenging the system with endless "what if" questions

independent. Multiple dimensions point, for instance, toward group-based or personal rewards, lead to the same dysfunctional behaviors. This reinforces the impact of not minding corporate culture or national cultural differences when implementing performance management. Chapter 3 discussed the example of the waste management company, where the CFO implemented all the best practices for performance management and saw performance of the best-scoring districts drop. This could have been avoided by understanding that the corporate culture was a combination of the following characteristics: group-based, aristocratic, relationship-oriented, Theory X. Openly publishing numbers would never work in such a culture.

Organizations should do a cultural performance management analysis before embarking on a performance management initiative. Or, they should do such an analysis where initiatives already under way are suffering from dysfunctional behaviors, to help get the initiative on track again. In a cultural performance analysis, we classify the organization on all cultural dimensions (see Figure 9.4).

It is important to realize that there is no right or wrong culture in the cultural performance management analysis. Every score is good; the key is that you are aware of the characteristics of your own corporate culture.

In the example, company 1, a manufacturer, is a classic public company with a strong U.S.-based business culture. The company has a

Figure 9.4

Cultural Performance Management Analysis

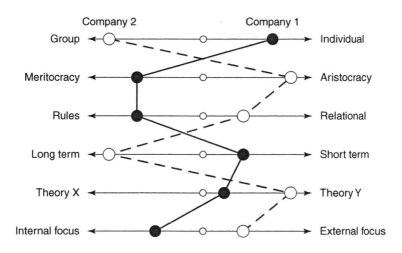

very individualized orientation, and through the meritocracy everyone has the chance to work himself or herself up. It is very rules-oriented; there is a process for everything. Given its public nature, it has a relatively short-term focus; new business strategies need to pay off within a fiscal year. The company tends toward Theory Y for the higher staff, but there are people whose job it is to just follow the process. The company is relatively internally focused, and plans its business using a traditional budget. This company benefits from the typical best practices of performance management: top-down strategy implementations, openly shared feedback with a ranking of the best-scoring people in sales. The bonus program, based on overperforming on the goals, can be found on the company's intranet, next to all other procedural descriptions.

Applying this style of performance management in company 2, a manufacturer about the same size as company 1, would not be successful. Company 2 has been a family-owned business for multiple generations. Senior management knows most of the employees; many of them have worked for the company their entire professional lives. The next generation of ownership is growing up and the company needs to secure their future too. The culture of the company is externally focused, and it can only survive in the market due to an extreme customer focus. This company has a very different decision-making process. Senior management will ask for input from a few trusted employees, and then the family will make a decision. There are performance indicators, but these are mostly aimed at how the company is performing in the eyes of the customers. Information is shared with the staff, but usually verbally in informal meetings. Rewards are not directly tied to performance in a specific period; the family rewards loyalty and provides bonuses when deemed necessary.

It needs to be made clear that cultural alignment doesn't always guarantee success. For instance, if company 2 is making a loss, perhaps some elements of the performance management practices of company 1 need to be adopted. Conversely, if company 1 is going through an extreme growth phase, key people need to be retained to manage that growth, and these staff members must feel part of the inner circle.

The cultural performance management analysis shows that the corporate culture drives how performance management should be implemented. But it also works the other way around, as measurement drives behavior. If there are cultural aspects that are undesirable, a measurement process might change that. If there is too much of a group focus, individual performance indicators may help. If there is too much of a long-term focus, short-term targets may help. If relationship focus turns into nepotism, more uniform reward processes may be needed. Performance management becomes change management, and dealing with undesirable behaviors is part of that.

In any case, ignoring the cultural aspects may easily lead to unpredictable behaviors. This will lead to misalignment between the self (behaviors) and the self-perception (management) of the organization. And if that continues long enough, that will lead to misalignment with the external perception (what we say we do versus what we really do).

Alignment

Understanding the values and the culture of the organization helps bridge the gap between the self and the self-perception of the organization. The values and culture of the organization represent the self of the organization; both drive behaviors, along with measurement. Performance management should take values and culture into account, so that the right behaviors are triggered. The impact of performance management, through instruments such as the budget and methodologies such as the balanced scorecard, should not be underestimated. What gets measured, gets done. If values and culture trigger different behaviors than performance management practices, then there is a serious misalignment problem. The actions of the organization will not reflect what the organization believes it stands for. At the same time, organizational values need to align with the external perception. Table 9.8 uses an auto industry example to show where organizational values match customer values.

Performance management has an impact on the customer value proposition. Misaligned behavior (perhaps even schizophrenic behavior) does not drive a positive external perception. Stakeholders become disappointed as the organization's daily behavior doesn't match the image the organization tries to convey. The organization will not be seen as authentic. Unless the organization truly has a unique product or service, or is a strong cost leader, what grounds are there left to ask for a premium or to expect any form of customer loyalty. The concept of alignment between self-perception and external perception is developed very well in the field of corporate communication as corporate identity and corporate image.[10] Corporate identity is the manifestation of the personality of the company.[11] Corporate image is the sum of all experiences that someone has with the institution.[12] This includes what people read in the newspaper, the reputation of a company as an employer, as a citizen of society, and obviously what the company has

Table 9.8

Organizational and Customer Values

Car Manufacturer	Organizational Values (Passionate about . . .)	Customer Values (Looking for . . .)
BMW (Germany)	Cutting-edge design, technology	High automobile performance
Volvo (Sweden)	Safety	Comfortable and relaxed driving experience
Toyota (Japan)	Operational excellence, quality	Reliability, minimal maintenance

to offer, the value proposition, what attracts stakeholders to the company. Aligned organizations have a close match between corporate image and corporate identity.[13]

One company whose success is based on a deep understanding of the alignment of its own values and the customer value proposition is IKEA. The company was founded in 1943 and had a 15.2 billion euro turnover in 2005. It had 221 stores at the end of 2005, which were visited over 453 million times worldwide.[14] Its value proposition is to "provide functional, well-designed furniture, at prices so low that as many people as possible will be able to afford them, creating a better everyday life for many people." The value proposition is carried out through the product concept. Design, in the beginning of the value chain, is completely in touch with logistics in the end (to make it efficient to ship goods) and customer experience. Customers assemble the furniture and accessories themselves, to keep down manufacturing costs. Customers pick up their items from the warehouse themselves (a mechanism originally born out of capacity problems). Customers take their items home themselves. Delivery is a separate service and is marketed as being reasonably priced. Even typical back office operations, such as inventory management, are part of the customer value proposition. Customers can use the IKEA Web site to view how many items of an article are in stock.

IKEA's customer value proposition is closely aligned with its organizational values, which are rooted in Swedish culture.[15] Founder Ingvar Kamprad is known for only flying coach, driving an old car, and taking the subway to work. There is even a story of how Kamprad took a soft drink from the minibar, and the next day went to the grocery store to buy a replacement. True or not, storytelling is a good way of conveying how important cost consciousness is. IKEA is very down to earth. Few IKEA managers at the corporate level dress in suits. Shop managers wear an IKEA sales uniform and manage by walking around. It's also significant that every employee can see local revenue numbers. One study[16] describes a conversation between Ingvar Kamprad and the first employee, in which they brainstormed about how to break the vicious circle between lower prices leading to worse quality. IKEA's value proposition is all about that. Cost control has a meaning beyond optimizing margins: it adds value to the customer through a lower price for a good-quality product. Although the performance indicators IKEA uses, for cost control for instance, are traditional, the difference is in how IKEA uses the insight. Revenue growth is seen as a measure of customer satisfaction, more than a measure of enhancing shareholder value. One of the largest cost items is staff, but IKEA is not aiming for employee cost minimization, like some retail discounters. There have been no massive layoffs to date and salaries are reasonable. IKEA instead looks for ways to control staff costs by making processes more self-service-oriented. It effectively reconciles the dilemma between cost and quality. Cost savings even lead to an improved customer experience. Self, self-perception, and external perception closely match.

Call to Action

The values of an organization can be discovered by asking questions. These questions should be directed not only to senior management, but also to the people on the work floor and customers that deal with the organization. Here are a few of the questions you can ask or answer for your organization:

- *For senior management*: If you are faced with a difficult business decision, a dilemma where two options each have positive and negative sides, how do you weigh the options? Most likely, the values guide managers to the right decision.
- *For middle management*: What behaviors help people advance their career in this company? Be careful what you wish for with this question, you might get answers you don't like.
- *For operational staff*: Which people in the organization do you admire for really getting things done, without banging heads? Most likely these people live the values of the organization.
- *For customers*: What does the organization stand for?

Compare the answers to these questions. The more the answers are the same, the more alignment between the self and the self-perception can be expected. Conversely, the more the answers are different, or the answers are cynical, the more misalignment there will be.

A good way of experiencing the impact of alignment, or lack thereof, on the performance of an organization is to look at failed as well as successful projects. Within your organization find, for instance, a certain marketing initiative, process redesign effort, or IT project that had great potential on paper, was implemented by the book, yet failed to deliver. Look at the original business case, such as cost savings, revenue enhancements, quality improvements, or time savings, and analyze why the target audience didn't accept the results and made the project fail. Chances are the project violated the values of the organization.

Next, with the first new project in mind, evaluate the business case with the positive and negative organizational values in mind. Can you predict behaviors that will endanger your project, and can you take measures to avoid that?

Chapter | 10

THE SOCIAL ROLE OF ORGANIZATIONS

For many centuries, business and society were highly intertwined. Take, for instance, the city of Utrecht in The Netherlands, where I live. For centuries, business was organized and regulated by the guilds. In the "guild letter" of 1304, a total of 21 of these guilds were instituted. Given the central location of the city and the high levels of trade, the guilds quickly gained power and influence. The guilds, professional organizations in which various craftsmen organized themselves, had important tasks. They took care of insurance and health care of the members, and they also acted as a social network. Additionally there were public tasks; every guild was responsible for defending a part of the city walls. This was in the best interest of everyone. A safe city leads to higher "consumer confidence," which leads to more trade, more wealth for the guilds, the citizens, and the church, and thus more money to invest in safety for the city. Creating value was a virtuous circle.

The Social Dimension

Business can only grow and prosper if the economy is allowing the organization to do so. A good economy leads to consumer confidence and a willingness to spend. Organizations benefit from a community's investment in security and infrastructure. That's why organizations pay taxes, as households do. And many organizations, like many households, feel that this is enough to cover infrastructure, security, social services, and other community services. But some people do more. They are active in society, as part of clubs, church, sports teams, their children's school, and other social structures. These people have a richer network than people that don't. They are respected and are held in high esteem by their environment, and somehow, opportunities—both private and business—come to them, as they are a known entity and a trusted party.

Like people, organizations do not stand alone. They are not independent, as big as they are. They have an interdependency with the communities in which they work, on many levels at the same time. It starts with common decency and being a good citizen. Many McDonald's restaurants require their staff—and pay for their time—to walk around the neighborhood and clean up litter, whether it has the McDonald's logo or not.

No organization operates in a void. Every strategic action of an organization has a social or environmental impact. Manufacturing goods or visiting customers produce carbon emissions. Although the impact of these emissions is debated by scientists, it is undisputed they do not contribute to a cleaner environment. If an organization needs to downsize, and close an office or a plant, or move operations to a different country, people lose their jobs, and need to find different jobs or rely on the social services. If a pharmaceutical company needs to set a price for a new type of medication, it implicitly decides who can afford the medication, and who cannot, affecting people's health.

Technology innovations have created numerous new companies that have had a profound social impact, making the world a smaller place. Search engines, such as Google, have changed the dynamic between customers and corporations, creating a new level of globalization and transparency. Community Web sites, such as MySpace or LinkedIn, have connected many people that have lost track of one another or people that have common interests.   no   Facebook ?

Clearly business and society affect each other, and the impact is only growing. Various studies have been done, comparing the GDP (gross domestic product) of all countries with the annual revenues of the largest corporations. Some even found that more than 50 of the largest economic entities are corporations, not countries. My analysis shows 29 of the top 100 are corporations, which is still significant. The largest corporation, Wal-Mart, holds position number 30 on that list, quickly followed by Exxon Mobil, General Motors, and Chevron.

Direct stakeholders, such as suppliers, partners, customers, shareholders, and regulators, as well as indirect stakeholders, such as the media and activist groups, offer their contributions. These contributions include their business or materials or their voice to promote you or regulations to ensure fair competition. At the same time, stakeholders have requirements, to satisfy their needs and objectives. Employees and customers are citizens as well.

However, most publicly traded organizations do not focus on stakeholder value, but on shareholder value. Shareholders do add value by supplying capital, but the other stakeholders provide value that is essential for the existence of the enterprise as well. Employees add value by driving activities and processes, customers take care of revenue and drive profit, suppliers take care of materials and services. The government provides the necessary infrastructure to do business. Focusing on creating value for shareholders only, neglects relationships with the other stakeholders that are also needed to survive. But there is a more fundamental problem. Shareholders, whether they are acting in the short or long term, are looking to maximize *their* returns, which is not necessarily the same as optimizing the performance of the organization. Shareholder value orientation is an effective instrument that provides guidance for the shareholders, but not for the organization. There is no saying if creating value is a sustainable virtuous circle or is about extracting value from the other stakeholders.

Measuring performance with a focus on a single stakeholder leads to dysfunctional behaviors, which in its turn leads to suboptimal performance. This is where the social dimension of the performance leadership framework comes in. It helps organizations determine how the actions and reactions of the organization's environment affect the business and how the business affects the organization's environment. See Figure 10.1.

Corporate Social Responsibility, a Debated Subject

It is impossible to think about the social dimension of the performance leadership framework without getting involved in discussions of corporate social responsibility (CSR). CSR is a highly debated subject and

Figure 10.1

The Social Dimension of the Performance Leadership Framework

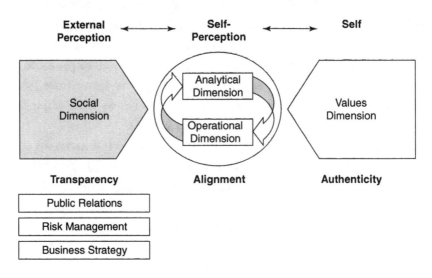

generally is not very well understood. It seems there are as many definitions of CSR as there are discussions on the topic. Some equate it with philanthropy, where organizations sponsor "good causes." Some talk about business ethics, others about "green investments," stressing minimizing carbon emissions and preserving natural resources. *The Economist,* the influential magazine, commented that for most companies CSR doesn't run very deep, and results are more about "good management" in general.[2]

Many organizations have coined definitions of CSR, such as these two:

- The International Standards Organization (ISO) defines CSR as "a balanced approach for organizations to address economic, social, and environmental issues in a way that aims to benefit people, community and society."[3]

- The European Union (EU) defines CSR as "a concept whereby firms integrate social and environmental concerns in business operations and in the interaction with their stakeholders on a voluntary basis."[4]

The ISO definition highlights the triumvirate of economic, social, and environmental issues, but focuses on benefiting not the organization itself, but people, community, and society. The EU explicitly mentions business operations, but fails to mention that CSR needs to be beneficial. My own definition of CSR is a combination of the two definitions:

Corporate social responsibility is a balanced approach for organizations to integrate social and environmental concerns in business operations in a way that aims to benefit the organization and its internal and external stakeholders.

The world's most influential thinkers disagree on how to position CSR. Nobel economist Milton Friedman is quite clear in his opinion[5] that the social responsibility of corporations is to maximize profits. Managers are legal agents of the shareholders; their sole duty is to maximize the financial return to shareholders. Hence if they spend corporate funds for social purposes, they are essentially stealing from the shareholders. The relationship between business and society is based on creating and returning funds to the owners of the business. It is up to shareholders to decide what to do with those returns—perhaps to allocate the returns for social purposes or perhaps not. Kaplan and Norton, the creators of the balanced scorecard, have a similar approach. They write, "The ultimate definition of success for public and nonprofit organizations is their performance in achieving their mission. Private-sector organizations, regardless of industry sector, can use a homogeneous financial perspective: increase shareholder value. Public sector and nonprofit organizations, however, span a broad and diverse set of missions and hence must define their social impact, their high-level objective, differently."[6] This implies that private-sector organizations do not have to define their social impact.

The well-known economist Peter Drucker comes from the same side as Friedman, but he offers a slightly more nuanced view.[7] Drucker starts out by saying that "a bankrupt business is not a desirable employer and is unlikely to be a good neighbor in a community; performance is the institution's first social responsibility." He then adds that "management must resist responsibility for a social problem . . . when the demand goes beyond the institution's competence." And further, an organization should ask itself, "do we possess authority in the area and should we have it?". In Drucker's view, an organization is not entitled to put itself in the place of government or to use its economic power to impose its values on the community. Managers are not elected officials. But Drucker introduces one exception, which is when contributing to easing a social problem creates an opportunity for performance and results. This is when the management has or should have the competence and authority.

Then there are the proponents of corporate social responsibility as a goal by itself. Organizations have a moral obligation to society. According to this school of thought, every organization needs to be social and green. Profit is important too, but it is only one of the three pillars of the triple bottom line: people, planet, profit. This nicely aligns with the ISO definition mentioning the social, environmental, and economic side of CSR. This view starts with the premise of the social responsibility corporations have as part of society. And as every stakeholder in society has responsibilities for the society, so do corporations. This school of thought defines CSR as a necessity, simply a cost of being able to do business. Environmentalists take this approach even further. Corporations need to invest in saving planet Earth, regardless of cost or loss of profit.

There are, therefore, two opposing schools of thought: some who feel CSR should not be part of a management agenda, and those who feel CSR is by default part of management's concern.

Porter sharply analyzes the shortcomings of both schools of thought because they focus on the tension between business and society rather than on their interdependence.[8] Running a business doesn't exclude being a good citizen. In fact these two objectives should be aligned. Unfortunately, the way organizations are structured and the control systems that are put in place make it hard to recognize this interdependency. Organizations are typically structured as bureaucracies in centralized or divisionalized forms. In the usual contrarian words of Henry Mintzberg, as early as 1983: "The economic goals plugged in at the top filter down through a rationally designed hierarchy of ends and means . . . [the] workers are impelled to put aside their personal goals and to do as they are told in return for remuneration. The system is overlaid with a hierarchy of authority supported by an extensive network of formal controls. . . . Now, what happens when the concept of social responsibility is introduced into all this? . . . Not much. The system is too tight."[9]

This typical style of vertically aligned organization uses the corporate hierarchy to implement strategy and to provide feedback. It is a top-down and bottom-up approach. However, if we apply the principles of horizontal alignment, the tension between business and society that Porter describes disappears. Horizontal alignment uses the value chain to create an efficient and an effective business, also called the *extended enterprise* or the *performance network.* On the strategic level it tries to reconcile different (even conflicting) objectives of the different stakeholders. Horizontal alignment looks like the market principle, where supply and demand regulate a price. However, within the performance network of stakeholders, relationships last longer than a single transaction. In order to run lasting relationships with different stakeholders, their trust is needed. Our actions need to be reliable, and our operations need to be transparent. We can only expect to receive stakeholder contributions, such as capital, labor, materials, infrastructure, business, and regulations, when we are prepared to meet stakeholder requirements, such as financial returns, a place to work, business, and being a responsible citizen. In this way, corporate social responsibility simply becomes just good management, as *The Economist* commented.

In order to understand how CSR affects performance management, it is important to distinguish different styles of CSR, ranked by their degree of integration with the business itself:

- Corporate philanthropy, sponsoring and contributing to good causes
- Risk management, making sure the organization's behaviors do not cause damage to the business
- CSR as an integral part of the business strategy itself

The Limited Impact of Corporate Philanthropy

Most companies have some kind of charity program. Many companies sponsor certain not-for-profit organizations, which fund research on serious illnesses, fight illiteracy, provide shirts for the local soccer team, or help in preserving an endangered species of animals. Alternatively, companies could allow their employees to work for charitable foundations or other "good cause" organizations on company time. Or companies could donate money after some kind of natural disaster. There is an endless list of possibilities for a company to be involved in corporate philanthropy. We already saw that influential thinkers such as Friedman and Drucker frown upon these practices. Although by far in most cases the costs for the organization are immaterial, the effort does not create shareholder value. This doesn't mean organizations shouldn't do it. If senior management decides that it is important to support certain good causes and the board approves, that is wonderful.

Strictly speaking, this approach to CSR does not really have an impact on an organization's performance management. It doesn't provide any guidance for a company on how to improve its performance. However, there is some intangible value, for instance, in improving an organization's employee satisfaction. Also, there is public relations (PR) value in corporate philanthropy; it can help create a more positive external perception of the organization. It makes strategic alignment somewhat easier, as external perception is one of the elements of alignment.

The Social Dimension for Managing Risks

The social dimension affects the organization because violating the rules and needs of the social environment leads to risks. Allowing negative values, such as greed, opportunism, and egoism, to drive the business is not good for business. If your business practices lead to environmental hazards, that upsets citizens. Shareholders and other suppliers of capital, such as banks, only want to be associated with a clean business. Challenging regulators and government officials can make corporate life very hard. There are pressure groups—with their own agenda—that have an impact on consumer perception, which then affects the business. A bad reputation, or a bad external perception, widens the alignment gap. And this is not restricted to the behavior of the organization itself. Organizations rely on suppliers for creating products and services, and rely on channel partners to sell products and services. Their behaviors can have a negative or positive impact on the brand as well. Behavioral risk spans the complete value chain. The social dimension of the performance leadership framework provides an outside-in view that forces organizations to look at the consequences of their actions on the outside world. The social dimension then acts as a boundary condition of doing business in a legal and socially accepted way.

Consider Nike, for instance, with over $12 billion in revenue in its fiscal year 2004, one of the largest and certainly one of the most well-known fashion and sports companies in the world. Nike has not always been a poster child for corporate social responsibility. For Nike, CSR has been a learning process for the last 10 years, growing from a defensive stage, to compliance, to a strategic adoption of CSR principles.[10] On its Web site Nike describes its social and environmental strategy in detail, using the guidelines of the Global Reporting Initiative (GRI; a global organization promoting a social, environmental, and economic reporting framework).[11] Nike's philosophy is that the social dimension is simply good for business. As Nike writes on its Web site:

> Nike's corporate responsibility (CR) mission is simple and straightforward. It is clear acknowledgement that CR work should not be separate from the business—but should instead be fully integrated into it. Our CR mission:
>
> - We must help the company achieve profitable and sustainable growth.
> - We must protect and enhance the brand and company.

Nike operates in an environment where almost all manufacturing is done by independent contract manufacturers that also produce for other global brands. A large part of the CSR strategy therefore lies in partner management. Transparency is a cornerstone to the strategy. Nike's latest achievement is that it has disclosed its manufacturing base, so that it is available for all stakeholders to see which other companies are involved in the Nike brand, and how they are adopting CSR principles. Nike has an extensive audit program in place to make sure its suppliers comply with the social and environmental standards that Nike has set, again based on the GRI framework. Given the nature of

Nike's business, there is a strong focus on waste management and monitoring the use of toxic components in the manufacturing process, such as polyvinyl chloride (PVC).

A large part of Nike's CSR strategy is about risk management, making sure the company cannot be compromised by its contract manufacturers and use of materials in product design. But auditing is not enough. Over the years Nike has learned that all parts of the internal Nike organization need to be aligned. Contract manufacturers need to be audited, but that process will only be successful if the procurement department conducts contract negotiations that focus on more than just price, quality, and delivery times. This will undoubtedly have an impact on price and on production methods, which affect product design and marketing. In the customer-facing part of the organization, CSR has an impact beyond risk management. One initiative is that customers can hand in their old shoes, and these will be recycled into material for running tracks or basketball fields. Also, the company sponsors a wide variety of sports-related community events, creating higher brand awareness and a positive corporate image for the brand. The complete value chain is affected by Nike's CSR initiatives.

The Social Dimension as an Integral Part of the Business Model

When we increase the level of ambition, the social dimension becomes an integral part of the business model. It stops being a boundary condition, and becomes part of the body of the business itself. In cases like this, CSR is not at odds with shareholder value, in fact, it drives shareholder value.

Typically, the more closely tied a social issue is to a company's business, the greater the opportunity to leverage the firm's resources—and benefit society.[12] For instance, at first glance, the first CSR program of TNT, one of the largest mail and express companies in the world, looks like a simple case of corporate philanthropy: it sponsors the World Food Program of the United Nations. However, this is not the case. TNT's support consists of more that just money; its main support consists of donated expertise and human resources. The effects of this are multiple. Of course there is good PR value, but the effect is felt throughout the organization. The company rose on the lists of "most wanted employer," among other things, because of this initiative. It attracts the type of ambitious staff TNT is looking for.

Employee satisfaction is positively affected, employees proudly talk about their employer, and about the partnership TNT has with the program as an integral part of the company. In some cases it can also be a soft investment. If one of the countries where TNT has been active through the world food program becomes an emerging economy, it will need to invest in infrastructure. TNT, being a trusted party, will likely get the opportunity to build a profitable business there. What makes the TNT example interesting is that it contradicts the view of Milton Friedman that charity is something for shareholders to do with their earnings, and not something the company should do for those investors. However, TNT contributes something no shareholder could ever do: deep expertise. At the same time it benefits from the partnership itself as well.

Another way of connecting CSR to the business is by creating meaningful products and services for previously unprofitable customer segments at the "the bottom of the pyramid," where there are immense new opportunities. For instance, Hindustan Level Ltd. (HLL), a subsidiary of Unilever, introduced an affordable detergent in small packages with a formula that allows poor people who wash in a river to get clean laundry. Another example is a bank offering microcredits in Bangladesh that had a 95 percent repayment rate, which is higher than most other banks have. Often, this requires radically different business models with different cost structures. Another example, Ruf&Tuf jeans, sells ready-to-make jean kits that are distributed through local tailors for around $6.[13] Another benefit of this type of CSR may very well be that rethinking product and business models will drive new innovation that is eventually profitable higher in the customer pyramid.

If CSR is about doing business, it needs to be managed like any other type of business. We can treat CSR as an objective. We can revisit the Direct Bank case study in Chapter 8, where two of the four options to increase the return on capital employed (ROCE) had social implications. Cutting costs by centralizing call centers for multiple countries would lead to layoffs and would likely negatively affect customer trust. Investing in an infrastructure to connect the various call centers would avoid layoffs and would lead to making at least part of the target. Islamic banking would have great potential for opening up a previously untapped market but would require significant investment and would only potentially contribute to the ROCE over the long term. A new matrix, plotting social/environmental performance against business performance, shows how these options can be compared. See Figure 10.2.

The lines in Figure 10.2 represent the effort Direct Bank could put in each of the options. If this is a low effort, it would only look at creating some efficiencies. If it puts in major effort (high), it requires a complete redesign. A horizontal line means the business performance increases, while the social/environmental performance stays the same. It means the improvement option is valid and that the initiative is environmentally and socially neutral. A decreasing line means the organization may reach its goals, but by extracting value from its environment. The organization's benefit is an environmental and/or social loss. This leads to risk and should be considered a nonsustainable solution. Increasing lines are to be preferred. It means that management is adding value by finding a way to reconcile the different requirements from the various stakeholders, such as society and shareholders. Both the organization and its stakeholders win.

Figure 10.2 clearly shows that centralizing call centers is not a good idea. If there is some moderate cost-cutting it is okay, but the moment it means closing a call center there is great social risk. The call center is the only physical presence the company has in the country. Laying off people

Figure 10.2

CSR as Part of the Business Model for Direct Bank

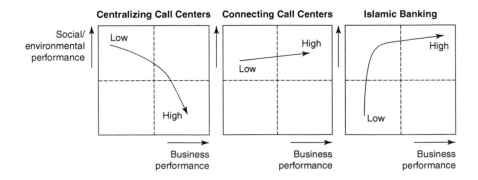

and closing the call center could be interpreted by unions, press, and customers as a tactical retreat from the market, affecting consumer trust negatively. Going for the bigger investment of call center virtualization by connecting the various call centers, there is actually a slight improvement in the social and environmental performance. The call center agents are encouraged to speak multiple languages, which improves their position on the market. The Islamic banking option still has considerable risk in terms of competencies. When the organization decides to invest in it, it will take a while before the organization starts benefiting from it. But when it has built the competencies, the business impact can be huge.

CSR and business performance are not opposites if you manage CSR as a business. That means CSR is an integral part of our performance management practices as well. If you use a balanced scorecard, it is part of that as well. There are various ways in which to integrate CSR into balanced scorecards.[14]

- Traditional balanced scorecards could contain a few indicators aimed at social and environmental factors
- A fifth dimension, the social and environmental perspective, could be added. Initiatives aimed at improving the bottom line should be balanced by, for instance, avoiding environmental pollution and child labor.
- A balanced scorecard approach, specifically and only aimed at a company's CSR program, perhaps as a special scorecard, could be cascaded from the organization's overall scorecard.
- An organization could choose to integrate elements of the social dimension in all other perspectives of the balanced scorecard.

When CSR is part of the business model itself, it makes sense to integrate the social dimension in the other perspectives of performance. CSR serves as a catalyst for improving performance in all areas of the business. See Table 10.1.

The Customer Perspective

Corporate philanthropy and sponsorship have a place in an organization's business model. It positively affects public relations, and it should have a role in aligning self-perception (wanting to do good) and

Table 10.1

Integrated Corporate Social Responsibility

Customer Perspective	Processes Perspective
• Adds to the customer value proposition	• Supports internalized control, compliance and transparency
• Is a source for trend watching	• Is a process optimization tool
• Should be treated carefully as PR	

Growth/Learning Perspective	Financial Perspective
• Adds to employee satisfaction	• Feeds CSR-weighted indexes
• Can be a soft investment	• Is a topic for long-term investors
• Enables organizational learning	

external perception of the organization (being recognized for it). But it's not only corporate philanthropy that builds external perception; it is the organization's complete strategy and practices.

Various influential magazines create rankings, such as *Fortune* magazine's annual "Accountability Ranking"[15] and Germany's *Manager Magazin*'s annual "Good Company Ranking."[16] These rankings incorporate a wide range of aspects, such as strategy (how a company includes social and environmental goals in its business decisions), governance (processes to hold executives and board members accountable), stakeholder involvement (how a company responds to its employees, communities, activist groups, and other stakeholders), and the impact of its CSR practices.

Shell has built significant experience with how to make CSR part of the overall business model over the years. During the 1990s it needed to close down its Brent Spar oil storage installation off the coast of Norway. It did a thorough analysis and decided the best healthful, economic, technological, environmental, and safest solution would be to sink it. Unfortunately, pressure groups did not agree with this, and the public opinion turned against Shell, leading even to a customer boycott. Shell learned quickly how pressure groups and citizens should be considered in its decision making. Perhaps the best example of Shell's understanding of CSR is the enormous success of Shell V-Power, a low-sulfur fuel for autos that was introduced in 2004. The product, priced at a small premium, is positioned as a performance fuel designed to help maximize engine performance while offering more protection for the engine. Shell could also have positioned the fuel as less environmentally impactful and more "green," something it tried with a different product, Shell Pura. Shell's success with V-Power teaches a very important lesson: Customers are not the same as citizens, even if they are combined within a single person. Environmental issues may be important for citizens (as was shown during the Brent Spar days), but as a customer, people can make different choices. Even for a more environmentally friendly product, a clear value proposition ("what's in it for me") needs to be articulated. CSR should be managed and marketed like any other business initiative: with the customer's need in mind and to make a profit.

In general, it's important for organizations to understand trends and customer behaviors. These are partly driven by society. As such, a socially responsible company would be more likely to recognize and respond earlier to trends. On the other hand, organizations should beware of picking up trends too early or placing too much focus on environmental issues, mistaking "buzz" for a large global trend. For example, the concept of "green electricity" has thus far not generated much success.

Public relations should not be the primary driver for CSR. There is also a PR danger with CSR. The more management boasts its good behavior, the more it will be exposed if there is even only a technical issue with, for instance, compliance to regulations.

The Process Perspective

Because of regulatory requirements, all organizations need a compliance strategy and an elaborate set of controls in their operational and management processes. Having a strong socially responsible culture contributes to internalized control. The members of an organization share the values and the objectives of the organization and will seek to do the right thing, and be open about it. Doing the right thing, in this case, means being socially responsible. It would be unwise to underestimate the efforts of organizations to be compliant, but organizations that are socially responsible will find that their compliance initiatives are easier to deal with, cost less because of lower internal political barriers, and provide higher-quality results.

The social dimension could also affect how organizations manage their processes not only for efficiency, but also for building a better value proposition. For instance, let's consider a manufacturer of self-assembly furniture. If prices are under pressure, a review of the raw materials used might be needed. Perhaps different materials should be used. If it is possible to use high-quality synthetic parts that are less environmentally invasive than using, for instance, wood, the benefits can be manifold. Not only is there an environmental advantage, but production and logistical costs decrease because of the lighter material. Using this new material might also affect product design, making it easier for customers to assemble the furniture. The decreased weight and easier assembly directly affect the customer value proposition, perhaps even warranting a price increase. The opposite, just being more efficient, would have been to simply save costs by using inferior and cheaper materials. A lower price, while keeping margins up might lead to more pollution as well as exposing customers to risk if the material breaks.

The furniture manufacturer provides a perfect example of people, planet, and profit being totally aligned. The performance improvement initiative added value, instead of extracting it.

The Learning/Growth Perspective

Good press and the opportunity to contribute to society leads to higher employee motivation, because employees feel proud to be working for the company. Better-motivated employees have higher productivity, lower staff turnover, and attract other staff like themselves. It allows companies to learn and to grow. Organizations need "genetic variation,"[17] people with different backgrounds, to inspire innovation. Growth and learning entails multidisciplinary teams within organizations, but the idea can easily be extended outside the enterprise. Many business cases for CSR are aimed at innovation:

The TNT example showed how giving expertise and human resources to the World Food Program of the United Nations was an investment that had a return on multiple levels. One part of it is that TNT employees that are part of the project team need to perform all kinds of activities in difficult environments, varying from specialist tasks to emergency response tasks. Innovative solutions the TNT employees come up with most likely can be applied within TNT too and affect the normal business. Volunteering helps build management skills. Being active in a different environment provides a fresh perspective on the work environment in general.

A consulting company allows and encourages some of its best and brightest consultants to teach at business schools and universities. The fees the school can pay do not compare to consulting rates, but the consulting company feels it is an excellent social activity. It teaches students about business, and they may remember their teacher when they are in the position to hire consultants. But there are other advantages as well. Consultants that need to teach students are forced to rethink the basics and essentials of their profession and work on their teaching skills. Teaching skills contribute to their professional development and allow the consultants to advance their career. The consulting company then can charge a higher rate for the consultant.

Encouraged by its CSR results, the same consulting company has recently decided to partner with a few banks, contributing to building a system to manage microcredits. This is interesting for multiple reasons. First, because it helps other organizations, the banks, to be successful with CSR, as part of the consulting firm's own CSR program. Furthermore, once the market opens for microcredits on a larger and more commercial scale, the firm will have a leading position.

In general, there are soft advantages of CSR to organizational learning too. Managers who are active in the community deal with different types of constituents; this provides them with a fresh perspective on their own organization and customers. Skills obtained during their community activities are likely to prove valuable within the company. Also, employees who in their spare time do community work, already show a collaborative attitude. This is bound to be applied in their daily jobs as well.

Financial Bottom Line

There is no demonstrated direct and positive link between financial performance and CSR practices. There are a few explanations for this.[18] For instance, most organizations have decided CSR is important, but don't know yet how to exploit it or how these smart strategies will affect market performance. Also, it is suggested there simply might not be a business case for some initiatives. There is also a different way of looking at the relationship between CSR and financial performance: there should be none. Using CSR as an important part of risk management allows organizations to avoid negative financial impact. It is desirable not to have a link. Also, the ultimate CSR is about having a sustainable business model itself. Singling out CSR as a separate contributor to financial performance defies the ultimate goal of CSR, to be inextricably connected to doing business.

There are indirect links between CSR and financial performance though. First, investors evaluate not only a company, but also its strategy and the capabilities of its management. A management team that has a strong vision of CSR that is embedded in the company most likely has a balanced decision-making process, indicating a highly conscious way of managing the business. Second, having a multiple-stakeholder approach and a balanced decision-making process may lead to less volatility in the value of the company. This reduces the odds of maximizing growth in the short term (perhaps by extracting value from the stakeholder environment), but it also reduces the chance of the company's value spiraling downward because it mitigates essential risks.

Third, many pension funds weigh the management ethics and social responsibilities of corporations before making their investments. As the former chief investment officer of ABP, one of the largest pension funds in the world, stated: "There is a growing body of evidence that companies which manage environmental, social, and governance risks most effectively tend to deliver better risk-adjusted financial performance than their industry peers. Moreover, all three of these sets of issues are likely to have an even greater impact on companies' competitiveness and financial performance in the future."[19]

Also, various CSR-driven financial indexes have emerged, such as the Dow Jones Sustainability Index, Ethibel, SERM, and FTSE4GOOD. In assessing the various organizations, these indexes look at a broad range of aspects.[20] They look first at the traditional economic measures of success. They evaluate the environmental policies of the company, how it reports on environmental impact, and if the firm monitors its suppliers as well. The indexes typically also track social-external and social-internal aspects, evaluating how the organization consults various stakeholders in decision-making processes, enforces equal opportunities for staff, fosters human capital development, minds health and safety regulations, has corporate philanthropy policies, and focuses on product safety.

Further, the indexes track corporate governance issues, such as board composition, policies on ethical behavior, and processes for risk and crisis management. As FTSE (Financial Times and the London Stock Exchange) states, "A broad range of stakeholders are challenging the corporate sector to take more responsibility for the ethical, environmental, and social impacts of their business operations. These stakeholders range from local communities to shareholders, customers, company employees, and even business partners. As companies respond to these challenges, many are finding that good corporate responsibility performance mitigates risks and brings opportunities that can have a positive impact on a range of key measures of business success: shareholder value, revenue, operational efficiency, customer attraction and retention, competitiveness, brand value and innovation."

Sustainability Reporting

Corporations today are being evaluated in almost every aspect of their performance. They are facing growing pressures to track and disclose nonfinancial metrics as well as financial metrics. A more environmentally and socially aware culture — a global community of stakeholders and average citizens — are demanding to know the impact a company has on the environment, the regions it operates in and serves, and its employees, among other things.

External reporting on social and environmental issues is not new. Particularly in the mining and manufacturing industry, health, safety, and environmental reporting has been required for many years. Today, integrated external reporting on economic, environmental, and social issues is called sustainability reporting (SR). With over 2,000 organizations using it, the leading framework for SR comes from the Global Reporting Initiative (GRI).[21] The GRI has representatives from business, accountancy, investment, environmental, human rights, research, and labor organizations from around the world. Started in 1997, the GRI serves as an official collaborating center of the United Nations Environment Programme. External reporting is either something we're forced to do, or it is something we choose to do, or embrace. If external reporting on social and environmental issues is only done to comply with legislation or to give the appearance that the organization cares, it will be minimal and done as cheaply as possible. Data quality and process controls don't really matter that much. However, if the organization embraces the concept, reporting can have a real impact on performance management. Measurement drives behavior. Having every business unit report on sustainability shows that senior management takes the subject seriously, and it will drive performance. Definitions, data quality, and process controls become very important. The GRI framework provides definitions, controls, and many best practices for implementing SR. The GRI lists numerous benefits of using the framework for reporting on corporate social responsibility:

- In today's "always-on" world where information is everywhere, a proactive approach to reporting is needed.
- The complex environment of all stakeholders that a company needs to mind requires a continuous "dialogue."
- Transparency builds trust.
- Sustainability reporting links all the parts of the business and challenges an insular approach.
- Reporting helps management in evaluating potential risks and in acting preventively.
- Sustainability reporting helps managers to create a more complete long-term overall picture of the business.
- Fuller and more regular disclosure of nonfinancial information can add stability to a company's financial condition by avoiding major swings in investors' behavior.

The sustainability reporting framework extensively describes a number of standardized performance indicators that help in understanding CSR benefits. There are core indicators that the GRI determined are relevant to most organizations and stakeholders, and additional indicators that represent a particular leading practice or are of interest for a specific stakeholder. Following these standards allows organizations to state that they are compliant with the framework, but perhaps even more important, to be able to benchmark the results against other companies, trying to become best in class. Table 10.2 provides an overview of the sustainability reporting framework.

Some organizations operate on the basis that minding the social dimension is part of the organization's "license to operate." In this way of thinking, every organization, as it is part of society, bears responsibility for that society as well. Corporate social responsibility

Table 10.2

Sustainability Reporting Framework

	Category	Aspect
Economic	Direct economic impacts	Customers Suppliers Employees Providers of capital Public sector
Environmental	Environmental	Materials Energy Water Biodiversity Emissions, effluents, and waste suppliers Products and services Compliance Transport Overall
Social	Labor practices and decent work	Employment Labor/management relations Health and safety Training and education Diversity and opportunity
	Human rights	Strategy and management Nondiscrimination Freedom of association and collective bargaining Child labor Forced and compulsory labor Disciplinary practices Security practices Indigenous rights
	Society	Community Bribery and corruption Political contributions Competition and pricing
	Product responsibility	Customer health and safety Products and services Advertising Respect for privacy

Source: Global Reporting Initiative (2002), "Sustainability Reporting Guidelines," www.globalreporting.org.

then is a necessity and considered even crucial for survival. Only companies who add value to all their stakeholders, instead of extracting value from their stakeholder environment, have a sustainable business model. But even if you don't buy into this school of thought, there is merit to GRI's sustainability reporting framework. As measurement drives behavior, adopting even a few metrics will create an awareness of the social dimension of performance management. Let's consider two organizations that have an outstanding reputation for corporate social responsibility, Metso Corporation and Rabobank.

Case Study 1: Metso Corporation

Metso is a global five-billion-euro engineering and technology corporation.[22] It has some 26,500 employees in 80 plants and 275 sales and maintenance units in more than 50 countries. Metso is a constituent of several sustainability indexes, including the Dow Jones Sustainability Index and the FTSE4Good Index. Metso has three business areas: Metso Paper, manufacturing equipment and machinery for paper and pulp production, power generation, as well as production lines for the panelboard industry; Metso Minerals, producing rock and minerals separation equipment, processing systems, crushers, screens, and conveyors; and Metso Automation, supplying flow control and automation systems for the process industry.

Metso's customer industries are significant users of natural resources, so Metso has major indirect impacts on the environment through the solutions it supplies. Metso sees optimizing its products and services for minimal environmental impact as a strong competitive differentiator, especially in developed markets. Here is how the company describes its environmental targets:

- We develop technology and solutions that support recycling and improve the environmental performance and operational eco-efficiency of our customers' production processes.
- We reduce the environmental impact of our own operations.
- We develop environmental cooperation with our key stakeholders.
- We promote the environmental awareness of our personnel and our partners.

Metso is already a major environmental technology provider. Over 50 percent of its sales can be classified as environmental business. It is interesting to see that Metso describes its value proposition as a close match between environmental and financial benefits; it positions its products as having high "eco- and energy-efficiency." Metso's solutions play a central role in reducing its customers' environmental impacts. Although the environmental impacts of its own operations are small, Metso needs to practice what it preaches and show its customers it is focused on environmental and social issues, next to economic health. For years now, Metso has had a comprehensive corporate social responsibility strategy, sustainable development management (SDM). SDM focuses on the "triple P" bottom line: people, planet and profit. Metso has a social, environmental, and economic responsibility.

Metso sees SDM as part of its risk management. Not in the traditional sense of financial, operational, or PR risk, but in terms of *strategic risk*. Lost opportunities are also risks. Environmental aspects affect Metso's operations over the long term through its customers. By systematically monitoring the development of environmental issues, Metso strives to find new business opportunities, which, if overlooked, would pose a strategic threat. Some strategic risks are related to competence development and employer image. All of Metso's businesses focus on innovation as a competitive differentiator. This requires the retention of high-quality staff.

This approach allows Metso to link CSR closely to its core business, selling equipment and machinery. For Metso corporate social responsibility is good business. Like every public company, the most important objective of Metso's strategy is sustainable and profitable annual growth. Metso's focus on CSR helps achieve that objective. Stricter emissions restrictions affect the operations of Metso's customers. The growing demand for energy and rising oil prices drive the need to improve production efficiency and to produce energy through alternative means. Increasingly tougher environmental legislation may present new business opportunities for Metso.

The growth of the company presents challenges for the development of Metso's staff. The controlled transfer of know-how to new markets is important. Human resources needs to make sure that the right people are in the right jobs, that Metso's know-how meets the changing needs

Table 10.3

Metso Environmental Reporting

Materials use	How much of materials used in production are recycleable metals?
	How much metal was used?
	How many hazardous materials and chemicals are used?
Energy use	How much electricity, district heat, fuel oil, coal, and natural gas were consumed?
Water consumption	How much water is consumed by the pilot paper machines in the technology centers?
	How much water was consumed for catering and sanitation? How much water was recycled?
Emissions into the air	How much carbon dioxide and volatile organic compounds (VOC) were emitted?
Waste	How much metal, wood, cardboard, paper, and municipal waste was generated?
	How much waste is recycled?
	How much hazardous waste is generated?
Storage and use of chemicals	What quantities of chemicals are stored and used?
Transportation	What is the impact of the transport of products?
	How do different methods of transportation rank based on environmental impact as well as volumetric efficiency targets for containers?

of its customers, and that best practices are shared within Metso. Metso's SDM helps Metso to be successful in the market, it improves Metso's own business, and it is seen as a prerequisite by Metso's customers. Metso publishes an annual sustainability report, for which it uses the GRI templates. In the sustainability report, Metso discusses environmental, social, and economic aspects. Table 10.3 lists environmental aspects the company reports on. The social aspects that are reported on are listed in Table 10.4.

Metso's economic reporting consists of the traditional performance indicators on revenue, profit, growth, and the different cost factors. However, Metso also discloses the monetary flow by stakeholder group. See Table 10.5.

At in Metso, different departments are responsible for the data reported in the sustainability report. The finance department is responsible for

Table 10.4

Metso Social Reporting

Personnel structure	Number of staff, broken down by function, gender, employment type, age, seniority, and educational background
Employee commitment	Overview of outflow of staff, broken down by number of people retired, disabled, laid off, voluntarily left, died, or finishing a temporary contract
Occupational health and safety	Costs and absenteeism broken down by illness and injuries, employee representation in health and safety committees
Leadership implementation	Percentage of staff having had performance reviews, which percentage of staff has a variable incentive plan
Competence development	Training days and costs

economic data, HR for social data, and the business areas for environmental data. However, the reporting is done through the financial consolidation system, managed by the finance department. This is because the reporting processes have great similarities. Data is collected from various departments, consolidated, and externally published.

Table 10.5

Metso Economic Reporting

Generation of value added	
Customers	Net sales
Suppliers	Procurements
Total added value	Net sales–procurements
Distribution of value added	
Employees	Wages and salaries
Public sector	Taxes and indirect employee costs
Creditors	Financing expenses
Shareholders	Dividends
Total distributed to stakeholders	
Retained in business	Total added value–total distributed to stakeholders

Although Metso has a comprehensive sustainability report, it still has ambitions for the future. Some parts of the environmental and social data could be collected and reported on more than an annual basis, preferably on a quarterly basis. These data could be utilized more for internal purposes as well, to make sure all managers keep seeing SDM as a priority. SDM could provide tools for better internal decision making, as well as contribute to the right management behavior. Another future requirement could be benchmarking Metso's performance indicators against those of its peer group that also make use of the GRI templates.

Metso is on the way to making CSR a competitive differentiator in its business model. The competitive differentiator doesn't just consist of being a responsible company itself, but—even more important— enabling Metso's customers to be more responsible. That's leverage. As a result, not only customers, but also investors rank Metso high on its CSR strategy.

Case Study 2: Rabobank

Rabobank is one of the largest food and agribusiness banks in the world. Rabobank's origins go back more than 100 years, to the Raiffeisen concept, in which farmers started a cooperative farmer's loan bank to avoid high interest rates by taking care of their own financial needs. Today, this concept is known as community banking. Although the cooperative structure of Rabobank has been modernized and is compliant with today's governance requirements, it still drives the organization's management model. Rabobank is not a public company. Corporate headquarters are owned by local banks, including Rabobank International and a range of other subsidiaries. The executive management of Rabobank reports to the Central Circle Meeting, which includes the directors of the local community banks. Headquarters is mostly a service organization, responsible for strategy, central processes, marketing, product development, and shared services, such as IT. Next to these services, it also functions as a control organization.

Rabobank has a long, stable history, with increasing profits. Perhaps the most visible sign of high performance is its AAA-credit rating by Standard & Poor's and Moody's. Rabobank is the only privately owned bank in the world to achieve such a high rating since 1981. The organization's management claims that its organizational structure, full of checks and balances, is responsible for this rating and performance.

In its GRI framework-based annual sustainability report, Rabobank describes how it is active in all facets of the social dimension.[23] Rabobank has all the environmental measures in place that fit a company in financial services. It tries to make use of recycled paper as much as possible, and it only allows company cars with low fuel consumption. But the impact of CSR goes much deeper into the business model. Like Nike, the CSR program is an instrument for risk mitigation. Rabobank will not involve itself with certain industries and countries, and it has an ethics commission to oversee these business restrictions. Risk management is also important on the microlevel. Rabobank's credit assessors are using CSR-related criteria as part of loan application reviews. To qualify for a loan, Rabobank's customers need to comply with certain labor conditions, regulations, and environmental standards.

But most important, CSR plays an important role in creating a competitive differentiation. Because Rabobank has strong ties to local communities, throughout its existence it has followed the principles of CSR. Corporate philanthropy, where local banks sponsor local cultural initiatives, sports clubs, and other events, magnify the bank's community roots, making the bank visible and accessible for all.

Rabobank has created a carbon emission reduction program for its credit card holders. Credit card payments are recognized and categorized, representing, for instance, clothing, food, or gas. Each category has a certain environmental rating, and the total of all credit card purchases is turned into "carbon credits." Rabobank invests these credits in sustainable energy and energy reduction projects.

Another initiative is Rabobank International Advisory Services (RIAS). RIAS is a consultancy division that supports banks in the field of rural banking and cooperative development. By infusing expertise into emerging markets, Rabobank will benefit by having access to these markets through the work it does with local banks.

Rabo Green Bank, one of Rabobank's initiatives, is the leading supplier of "green funding." The bank brokers between investors who want to invest in green initiatives and entrepreneurs who are looking to finance their green initiatives. Rabo Real Estate invests in affordable middle-income housing. In the food and agribusiness, Rabobank has special sale-and-leaseback constructions for glasshouse horticulture and hog farming, and it offers special long-term credit to farmers.

One of Rabobank's newer activities involves supplying microfinancing to entrepreneurs in disadvantaged urban areas. It provides microcredits of between 5,000 and 25,000 euros to largely ethnic minority entrepreneurs who are sidelined from traditional financing.

Corporate social responsibility is so connected to the business model that it is hard to distinguish CSR from the products the bank offers and how they are marketed. For instance, in its mortgage business, it offers customers a discount of a full percentage point on the interest charged for home renovations that reduce energy consumption. For Rabobank, CSR is about competitive differentiation and making a profit.

Call to Action

Even if you believe corporate social responsibility is all just PR and marketing, it still affects external perception. The social dimension is a key component in aligning the external perception and the self of the organization. In other words, the social dimension helps managing the difference between corporate image and corporate identity. An organization's environment has an impact on an organization's behavior. People, and consequently organizations, learn from feedback from the environment. Over time we find out which behaviors are desirable and rewarded, or undesirable and punished.

However, you need to organize the alignment of CSR. The finance department in particular plays an important part in this alignment. Although the finance department is traditionally not the source of intangible and nonfinancial matters, it plays a crucial role in organizing sustainability reporting. Data has to be collected each period, aggregated according to rules, and audited to support analysis and scenario planning. Overall, due to its experience with complex processes of audited external reporting, the finance department is a perfect place to bring financial reporting together with CSR.

The social dimension is not about CSR per se, it is about stakeholder alignment in general. Ask yourself which current strategies truly add value to your stakeholders. Contrast this to the strategies where you extract value from the stakeholder, only to benefit yourself. Adding value creates a virtuous circle, the value we create for our stakeholders, they can use in further adding value to our organization. Extracting value means the opposite. Extracting value is creating wealth for one stakeholder at the expense of one or more other stakeholders—stakeholders end up with less value and cannot add value to our organization. It speaks for itself that adding value is a more sustainable business model with less risk and greater recognition by all stakeholders as a solid business.

Start this strategic insight about alignment between the self (-perception) and the self of the organization, the corporate identity, and corporate image by organizing a dialogue with your stakeholders. Often, stakeholders have requirements that conflict with the requirements of other stakeholders. The only way to deal with these conflicting requirements is to be transparent. Open communication on what is driving the business and the strategies of the company. Seek alignment between what people do within the organization and what people tell the outside world, between how the organization is being perceived by the different stakeholders, and how the organization perceives itself. It is when conflicting requirements become visible and the different stakeholders can view the complete picture that an understanding of the different trade-offs takes place.

It makes sense to treat all stakeholders well. They each have their contributions without which your organization cannot thrive. And in order to get those contributions, their requirements need to be satisfied.

Chapter | 11

THE RETURN OF THE MISSION STATEMENT

Insurance company Interpolis has "crystal clear" as its motto. It means that doing business with Interpolis should be really simple. The company truly lives this motto in everything it does. I get an annual overview of all my insurances on one single sheet of paper. Reading the conditions is significantly easier than I am used to, as the company carefully looks at the language it uses. Last year I reported a stolen laptop. I called the insurance company to request forms and to inquire about how the procedure works. The friendly lady in the call center asked me for the brand of the laptop and wanted to know how old it was. She immediately told me the amount I would get for it and indicated that she would transfer the money within a day or two. She asked me to hold on to the police report, in case of a random check. I was amazed; it was really simple to work with the insurance company. I bet their fraud levels are even lower than at other insurance companies.

Rediscovering the Mission Statement

What drives us—our values, skills, strengths, and proven strategies—may not always be what our stakeholders are looking for. This might be temporal misalignment, as every change takes time. Or there may be more fundamental market changes, making our products and

Figure 11.1

The Mission Statement Reconciles the Social and Values Dimensions

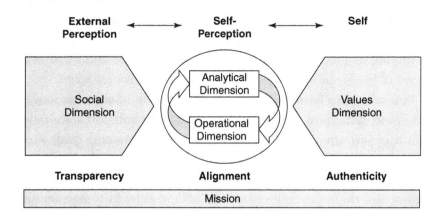

services out of fashion. Misalignment between the values dimension and the social dimension is very common. Both dimensions may provide different, even opposite, guidance to the operational and analytical dimensions. It is good that the performance leadership framework creates this tension because the tension exists in reality and needs to be addressed. But the differences need to be reconciled, a synthesis has to be found, and a way forward to satisfy both the organization and its stakeholders has to be created. This is the task of the organization's mission statement. See Figure 11.1.

Before industrialization most businesses were mission oriented.[1] Craftsmen were personally responsible for the quality of their work; and even when businesses grew, the owner would oversee business personally. This changed during the Industrial Revolution. The mission orientation was replaced by system goals, which are described in terms of survival, efficiency, control, and, most noticeably, growth. Systems goals are preferred by professional managers who are often not grounded in the business in which they work. Efficiency and control are concepts that can be used to run any kind of business. And growth is a goal that opens up promotion capabilities. However, systems goals, as optimized by traditional performance management methodologies, do not provide guidance.

The mission statement is an obvious tool to provide the needed guidance. A widely accepted definition of a *mission statement* is that it embodies "a broadly defined but enduring statement of purpose that distinguishes the organization from others of its type and identifies the scope of its operations in product (service) and market terms."[2]

According to a Bain survey, around 80 percent of organizations have a mission statement.[3] The problem with most mission statements is that they are often not implemented, because systems goals usually supersede them. Somehow the connection between the overall mission and everyone's daily activities is lost. The mission statement, vision, and the organization's values are published on the company's Web site, and they hang on posters at central places in the building; but the company's strategy—as people understand it—and performance indicators do not reflect them. In many organizations, this has led to cynicism or indifference about the mission statement, a typical behavior connected to misalignment. People do not recognize the mission of the organization and how it would affect their daily work; they do not know how their work contributes to achieving the mission. Consider the example of a European airline.[4] This airline publicly announced that environmental protection was a high-priority corporate goal. It stated that compliance to environmental regulations was not enough, that it wanted to use the best available technologies in the most economical way to continuously reduce the negative environmental impact that airline travel has. A look at the published scorecard of the airline showed financial goals, such as profitability and revenue growth; customer goals, such as loyalty, global presence, and image; and employee goals, such as a service-oriented culture, engagement, and a high level of skills. The strategic environmental goals were not given any consideration.

By themselves mission statements have limited impact. It is clear that there is no direct link between having a mission statement (let alone a good mission statement) and an organization's performance, but there is an association between mission statements and performance through organizational behavior.[5] Mission statements should not be seen as a direct input on business performance, but more as an output of good management and a solid business model. When articulated well, mission statements are useful to guide the strategic planning system.[6] The mission statement:

- helps not only to figure out what a right strategy is, but also which one has the tightest fit to what the organization stands for.
- defines the organization's scope of business operations/activities. It is often harder to decide what an organization should *not* do than it is to figure out what it should do. If the mission statement provides an overview of the scope of business, what it does for whom, it acts as a benchmark for new strategic initiatives.
- provides a common purpose/direction transcending individual and department needs. The mission statement is a short piece of text that should provide guidance to all employees on how their activities contribute to the overall goal.
- promotes a sense of shared expectations among all levels of employees, thereby building a strong corporate culture (i.e., shared values). Employees and managers need to make decisions every day. A well-designed and well-implemented mission statement helps people make the right decisions.
- guides leadership styles. The mission statement can be a benchmark for senior managers to make difficult choices when facing a dilemma. It provides the guidance to do the right thing.
- promotes the interest of stakeholders. The mission statement describes what the organization adds to the world, what stakeholders it recognizes, and how it believes it creates value for them.

Of course an effective mission statement is not about clever writing, but rather the implementation. However, if a mission statement doesn't follow a few basic guidelines, it won't work. First, mission statements should be to the point. In many cases this means the statement will be short, but this is not necessarily the case. Furthermore, mission statements need to have an external focus; mission statements describe a company's basic function in society. Next, mission statements must be both specific and broad at the same time. It is vital to be specific on *how* a company adds value, but in the broader terms of what the products and services achieve for the customers. Lastly, a mission statement needs to be inspiring and truthful; it needs to invite stakeholders to buy into the true value the company offers.

The Mission Statement Should Be to the Point

The more words that are needed to explain what the company stands for, the bigger the chance the company doesn't have a clear picture itself. It takes a certain level of maturity to boil the mission down to the essence, to understand the fundamental principles that drive the business.

Some examples of short mission statements are:

- "Provide the world's best communications solutions that enable businesses to excel" (Avaya, a U.S.-based telecommunication company).
- "We make food safe and available everywhere" (Tetrapak, provides packaging solutions for food).
- "To bring inspiration and innovation to every athlete* in the world. (*If you have a body, you are an athlete.)" (Nike).

But that doesn't necessarily mean long mission statements are bad. Consider Starbucks' mission statement, which is relatively long, but still to the point:

Establish Starbucks as the premier purveyor of the finest coffee in the world while maintaining our uncompromising principles while we grow.

The following six guiding principles will help us measure the appropriateness of our decisions:

- Provide a great work environment and treat each other with respect and dignity.
- Embrace diversity as an essential component in the way we do business.
- Apply the highest standards of excellence to the purchasing, roasting, and fresh delivery of our coffee.
- Develop enthusiastically satisfied customers all of the time.
- Contribute positively to our communities and our environment.
- Recognize that profitability is essential to our future success.

Starbucks is committed to a role of environmental leadership in all facets of our business.

We fulfill this mission by a commitment to:

- Understanding of environmental issues and sharing information with our partners.

- Developing innovative and flexible solutions to bring about change.
- Striving to buy, sell, and use environmentally friendly products.
- Recognizing that fiscal responsibility is essential to our environmental future.
- Instilling environmental responsibility as a corporate value.
- Measuring and monitoring our progress for each project.
- Encouraging all partners to share in our mission.

A Mission Statement Has an External Focus

Many mission statements focus on the company alone. One mission statement for a financial services company states: "We want to be the leader in wealth creation." Although "wealth creation" suggests the company is addressing the customer—who it would create wealth for—the focus is that the company wants to be the leader. The rhetorical question is, who wouldn't want to be a leader, or world-class, or highly regarded? As a consequence, the mission statement doesn't really mean a lot.

Consider how Nike improved its mission statement. On its Web site it writes that until 2001 its mission statement was to be the best sports company in the world. Nike further writes, "While it may have been a worthy ambition, it was focused only on the company; it was entirely about us." Earlier I already highlighted Nike's new mission statement: "To bring inspiration and innovation to every athlete* in the world. (*If you have a body, you are an athlete.)"

The Mission Statement Should Be Specific

Many mission statements do not explain what drives the company, what it excels at, or in general *how* it chooses to add value to its stakeholders. A typical example would be: "We strive to offer the best products and services, based on a superior understanding of the specific needs of our customers, while being operationally excellent to drive our costs down." This mission statement doesn't make sense. It tries to satisfy everyone's needs, but the lack of clarity achieves the opposite. Such a mission statement doesn't give any guidance as to the company's strategy system because it describes almost every possible strategy.

In reality, a focus on offering the best products means ensuring superior quality of raw materials as well as superior processes to assemble the product. It is unlikely that the company will be a cost leader at the same time. Having a strong operational excellence strategy means a high level of standardization. This in many cases conflicts with the understanding of the specific needs of customers, which would lead to processes aimed at a wide variety of specific customer demands, increasing the cost. There are ways to bridge these strategic opposites, but if a company succeeds in doing so, the mission statement should point out that unique position. "The soul of Dell" does a good job of explaining that strategic synthesis. Dell, the computer company, connects direct relationships with customers to its model of operational excellence, where customers have a superior customer experience putting together their own computers.

The Avaya mission statement, mentioned earlier in the chapter, has clarity. It says it provides the world's best communications solutions that enable businesses to excel. Avaya has a clear focus on quality. Let's look at another example: the vision statement of the logistics company Norfolk Southern. Its aim is to be the safest, most customer-focused, and successful transportation company in the world. It not only focuses on the customer, but particularly on safety. It gives clear guidance on where to invest, not on squeezing cost of service, but on maximizing safety and customer focus.

A Mission Statement Should Be Defined in Broad Terms

The mission statement needs to be specific on *how* it adds value to its stakeholders, but it can't be too specific, as strategies come and go over time, and products and services change as well. It is best if the mission statement is formulated in terms of what the stakeholders achieve with the products and services of the company, instead of what the company offers. For instance, Nokia doesn't speak about telecommunications; it talks about "connecting people." Its newly released navigation systems, for instance, fit perfectly within that mission statement. Google, the company behind the search engine, states that its mission is to organize the world's information and make it universally accessible and useful. That mission goes way beyond the main product of Google (the search engine) and allows Google to find many alternative ways of contributing to the mission. A company offering diet products can describe its mission by stating that it contributes to the health of its customers through nutrition.

The Mission Statement Should Be Inspiring and Truthful

The effectiveness of a mission statement is largely based on how people refer to it. Many mission statements are not implemented within the organization, so they are "hollow" or a product of "wishful thinking," conveying a message of how the organization should be instead of its reality. As a result, the employees ignore the mission statement or, worse, treat it with cynicism. The cynicism appears as the employees have a different picture of the organization than the mission statement portrays. For a mission statement to contribute to organizational alignment, truthfulness should be the starting point and inspiration should be the journey.

When managers and leaders are thinking about the best strategy for the organization moving forward, the mission statement should be the lighthouse. Over time more managers will develop ideas in which direction to go; it could be that many different directions seem attractive. An inspiring mission statement makes it easier to decide what *not* to do as well. The mission statement is meant to provide a common purpose, direction, and shared expectations across all stakeholders.

Without the support of the shareholders, there is no capital. Without the support of the employees and the suppliers, no exceptional work will be done. Without the strong acceptance by customers, there is no business. Some mission statements focus completely on the shareholders. In fact, one fashion brand's mission statement only says: "Management's primary objective is to create value for the company's shareholders." It may be truthful and (potential) shareholders may be inspired, but shareholders expect that as a given and therefore it does not need a mission statement to spell it out. Employees most certainly will not be inspired by it. And it will also not appeal to customers. This brand misses an opportunity to use the mission statement as an instrument to build customer awareness and preference. The only purpose of the mission statement is to focus top management, and it doesn't even provide the guidance on how to achieve the goal.

Again, consider Nike's mission statement. It is short, externally focused, and broad enough to capture many different ways to serve the customer. It is specific enough to focus on innovation for athletes, and it even uses the word inspiration—and inspiring it is. According to Nike, everyone with a body is an athlete. And the hidden message is clear, the more Nike products you use, the more of an athlete you will become. Let's also look at Southwest Airlines' mission statement, which is equally as strong as Nike's. The mission of Southwest Airlines is to be dedicated to the highest quality of customer service delivered with a sense of warmth, friendliness, individual pride, and company spirit. This mission statement clearly focuses on service above anything else. The choice of words is remarkable, as many of the words have an emotional appeal. As management literature and management theory can be full of jargon, being able to bring a complex set of thoughts to human proportions, is quite an achievement.

A Stakeholder Analysis of Mission Statements

Organizations are facing multidimensional competition. Not only are we competing for the best customers, but also for the best talent and the best partner network. We compete for the best stakeholders and actively need to work on our relationship with them. I've made an analysis of over a hundred mission statements to see how they reflect which stakeholders are considered important, and how the company adds value to them.[7] My analysis of mission statements across different industries revealed that most mission statements do a good job of identifying an organization's key stakeholders.

Figure 11.2 shows the result of this analysis. Part A shows how often each group is mentioned in the mission statements. The pie chart in part B shows the cases where only one stakeholder was mentioned in the mission statements and which stakeholder that was. Part C shows in how many cases each group was mentioned first in the mission statements and in how many cases it was mentioned last.

For the purposes of the analysis, it is assumed that if a group is mentioned first, it is more central to the success of the business. If a group is mentioned last, this can mean multiple things. The stakeholder could be less important than those mentioned first. Another option is

Figure 11.2

Stakeholders Analysis of Mission Statements: (A) how often mentioned (B) only stakeholder mentioned (C) mentioned first or last (D) distribution of groups

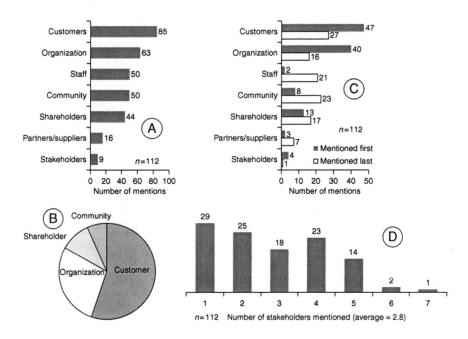

that the benefit for the stakeholder mentioned last is the result of servicing the aforementioned stakeholders well, like a cause-and-effect relationship. Finally, the stakeholder mentioned last could present a boundary condition. This means the company has to operate within the limitations this stakeholder poses on the organization, such as the law. Part D shows a distribution of how many stakeholders are mentioned, ranging from 1 to 7. The average mission statement contains about three stakeholders.

To show how the stakeholder analysis works, let's look at the mission statement of Virgin Atlantic, a British airline. It reads: "To grow a profitable airline that people love to fly and where people love to work." The mission statement has three stakeholders. The first stakeholder that is mentioned is the organization itself. The customer is mentioned next, and lastly, the employees are referenced. In this mission statement, the organization is seen as the most important stakeholder. The customer is the most important external stakeholder, and the employees come third. The mission statement follows a compelling order of importance.

Lehman Brothers, a U.S.-based financial services firm founded in 1850, states: "Our mission is to build unrivaled partnerships with and value for our clients, through the knowledge, creativity, and dedication of our people, leading to superior results for our shareholders." The mission statement mentions again three stakeholders. First, the customer is mentioned. Although the mission statement doesn't really directly focus on the needs of the employees, it describes their knowledge, creativity, and dedication, which should be appealing to current and future employees; therefore, staff is the second stakeholder to be addressed. Shareholders are mentioned third, in a cause-and-effect relationship.

The overall analysis revealed a total of seven stakeholders: customers, the organization itself, staff, the community, shareholders, partners and suppliers, and, lastly, some mission statements use the umbrella term *stakeholder*.

Customers

It should not be a surprise that most mission statements, 76 percent to be precise, mention the customer as a crucial stakeholder. In 42 percent of all mission statements, the customer is even mentioned first. Further, in more than half of the cases (55 percent) when only one stakeholder is mentioned in the mission statement, it is the customer. In 24 percent of cases, though, the customer is mentioned last. In the majority of cases where this happens, only two stakeholders are mentioned. Typically, in those mission statements the organization is mentioned first. For instance, Avery Dennison's mission statement reads, "To be the world leader in products, services, and solutions that enable and transform the way consumers and businesses gather, manage, distribute and communicate information." In this case, the customer is considered the most important *external* stakeholder.

This analysis shows clearly that the customer is considered the most important stakeholder. Peter Drucker is widely quoted to have said that "The purpose of a business is to create a customer, and the stakeholder analysis shows that the mission statements at least acknowledge that." In complex value chains, the people or organizations a business sells to directly are not always consumers. In many cases there are intermediaries, such as hospitals, pharmacies, or doctors (in the case of pharmaceutical companies), supermarkets (in the case of fast-moving consumer goods companies), and importers or car dealers (in the case of car manufacturers), and so on. However, most mission statements define the customer as the end consumer.

Organization

A company can be compared to a living organism, where the main objective is to stay alive, to sustain. That is why organisms reproduce, evolve, and display certain characteristics of resilience in the environment in which they live. Following this philosophy, it is no wonder that 56 percent of organizations mention themselves as a key stakeholder in the mission statement, and 36 percent of organizations mention themselves first in the mission statement. In the typical mission statement, the company is typically referred to in terms like this, "We are here to build and to sustain a great organization, in order to. . . ." In mission statements that mention only one stakeholder, 28 percent mention the organization. These are often statements that say, "We aim to be the global leader in . . ." or something similar. Such statements are not very effective.

Staff

Employees are a key asset of any organization. About 45 percent of mission statements mention staff. Traditional accounting has limited means to reflect the value of staff; employees show up as a cost factor in the profit and loss statement (often a sizable or even the largest cost factor) instead of on the balance sheet. But like capital, raw materials, and facilities, employees are a key production factor. Staff is often mentioned last in the mission statement. Some mission statements mention job security, but most mission statements refer to employees by offering "a great place to work."

Community

The community in which organizations work is mentioned in 45 percent of mission statements as well. In two mission statements it was even the only stakeholder mentioned, although I strongly suspect that if I would actively search for mission statements in the nonprofit sector, that number would be higher. And it looks like community is becoming more important as a stakeholder. An increasing number of organizations produce annual sustainability reports, often based on the Global Reporting Initiative guidelines. Many mission statements address the community as a boundary condition, typically last in the mission statement, such as ". . . while being a responsible citizen." There are a few examples of mission statements that mention the community first, typically in the case of health providers or insurance companies. For instance, insurance conglomerate Achmea aims to be a socially responsible, leading, and innovative provider of financial services, financial security, and health care (All Finance, All Care). Our goal is to offer our customers the right product/service combinations and in so doing to shoulder their burden. A human approach to our customers will play a central role in achieving this goal."

Shareholders

Shareholders are ranked fifth in the list of most mentioned stakeholders; only 39 percent of mission statements even mention the shareholder. At first glance, this would suggest that shareholders, according to the mission statements of organizations, are not the primary stakeholder. However, if we look at in how many cases the shareholder is mentioned first, the shareholder ranks third, after the customer and the organization itself. We found a small number of mission statements that mentioned the shareholder as the only stakeholder.

In a good number of cases, the shareholder is mentioned last in the mission statement. For instance, consider pharmaceutical company Merck's mission statement: "The mission of Merck is 'to provide society with superior products and services by developing innovations and solutions that improve the quality of life and satisfy customer needs, and to provide employees with meaningful work and advancement opportunities and investors with a superior rate of return.'" The shareholder is mentioned last in the mission statement, but this is not to imply a lesser degree of importance. Being mentioned last can also mean the mission statement describes a cause-and-effect relationship. Oil company Sunoco, in its description of its stakeholders, states that it aims at "managing all parts of our business in a manner that builds value into the investment of all shareholders, confirming their confidence in participating in the ownership of this company." The earlier mentioned Lehman Brothers mission statement is another good example of a cause-and-effect relationship of stakeholders, mentioning the shareholder last.

It is clear that shareholders play an important role, together with the customer and the organization itself. However, it is also clear that shareholders are not the only stakeholder that should be considered.

Partners/Suppliers

Partners and suppliers are ranked sixth in the number of times they are mentioned as a stakeholder. They are mentioned in only 14 percent of cases. Dell understands it is part of a value chain when it writes: "We believe in being direct in all we do. We are committed to behaving ethically; responding to customer needs in a timely and reasonable manner; fostering open communications and building effective relationships with customers, partners, suppliers and each other; and operating without inefficient hierarchy and bureaucracy." It seems as if other technology companies also share this belief. Lexmark states that employees, customers, and partners are reminded daily of Lexmark's operating philosophy. However, fast-moving consumer goods companies also rely on partners. Unilever's mission is to add vitality to life. On its Web site it writes about "our road to sustainable, profitable growth, creating long-term value for our shareholders, our people, and our business partners." Personal care company Colgate states: "The company cares about people: Colgate people, customers, shareholders, and business partners." As no organization can stand alone, for alignment of the value chain, the role of partners and suppliers is becoming increasingly important, and it will be interesting to see if this will be reflected in future mission statements.

Implementing Mission Statements

The stakeholder analysis revealed that many mission statements are excellently formulated. The problem is that they are often not implemented. Organizations that have done a good job of turning a mission statement into an effective guiding force for decision making concentrate on the process of alignment.[8] The mission statement needs to be connected to the performance indicators of an organization. Measurement makes the mission statement work. It puts into place solid measurement practices to help the organization discover which of its objectives and strategies have succeeded in bringing the organization closer to achieving its mission. Conversely, the mission statement makes measurement work. It helps the organization to focus on what it is trying to achieve. This focus should be directly reflected in the metrics, the processes, and the communication about an organization's value drivers.

Different organizations have various value drivers. Some organizations are all about brand value, defining their own organization as the main stakeholder. Brand value can be defined as the premium consumers are willing to pay over that of a comparable product. Other organizations see customer value as their main driver. In other words, what they contribute to the life of consumers or the business of corporate customers. The customer is the main stakeholder. Another driver can be shareholder value. In these cases it is the main purpose of the business to maximize the return on investment within any legal means possible. Obviously, in this instance the shareholder is the main stakeholder.

The mission statement should be translated into tangible metrics that describe the value driver of the company. If the mission statement is well understood, and the company is serious about it, many of the key performance indicators will present themselves.

Brand Value

Nike's mission statement again provides an excellent example. Nike tells consumers that it brings the inspiration for everyone to be an athlete. It makes consumers want to be associated with Nike. As a consequence, it is more important for consumers to be part of the Nike world than it is for Nike to be part of its customers' world. Nike takes the lead in customer relationships, as it provides inspiration and innovation. Nike's mission statement indicates that it is the brand that drives the value creation.

Nike's performance indicators should reflect this. From a customer perspective, "customer satisfaction" makes less sense than consumer "mind share." Mind share would be measured by asking guided and unguided questions as to which brands consumers associate with various sports, such as basketball, soccer, golf, and jogging. The more Nike is mentioned in the unguided questions, the more consumers are willing to purchase Nike products over other brands. The higher Nike's mindshare, the more people are willing to pay a premium for the products, compared to other brands or unbranded products.

Mind share would be a leading indicator; it could predict sales and margin preservation. If Nike's mind share increases in the market, sales should go up. And as customers are willing to pay a premium, less markdown is needed. A complementary indicator would be a cross-sell ratio: in other words, in how many cases do consumers use multiple products? This could be tracked within a certain sports product line but also across various product lines. Because many consumer products are not registered, as insurance or software would be, it is often hard to measure this exactly. However, a market basket analysis can be used, which analyzes cash register data for which products are bought together. Alternatively, statistically significant market research can be done that allows making assumptions about the complete market. Cross-sell is a lagging indicator; it shows to what extent a certain objective has been reached. In the case of mind share and cross-sell, the objective would be to see if "inspiration" is a successful value proposition.

Innovation could be measured on an aggregated level, such as the product line, and on a divisional or corporate level. A lagging measure that is often used is the percentage of revenue coming from new products. If this is high, Nike has a high ability to execute with its innovations, whether they are functional with products such as golf clubs and soccer shoes, or more fashion-based, as with apparel. Of course the percentage should not be too high, because that would indicate the product life cycle is going too fast and there is not enough time to get a good return on investment on new product development.

It is also possible to measure how successful the positioning of the combination of innovation and inspiration is in the market. It would be interesting to know if consumers buy Nike products when they start practicing a certain sport (bringing the inspiration), or if Nike products are seen as more advanced and are bought when the consumer reaches a higher level of competence. This then would be seen as innovation and an upgrade from other brands.

Without knowing Nike from the inside, examining and interpreting its mission statement provides us with some powerful information about its value drivers and how to manage the organization.

Key performance indicators of brand value for Nike would be:

- Percentage revenue of new products
- "Mind share"
- Cross-sell
- First product bought

Shareholder Value

Most performance methodologies focus on maximizing shareholder value. If the mission statement states the same, there is alignment between the organization's mission and how to track the results. The following mission statements focus on shareholder value only. A fashion brand states, "Management's most important objective is to maximize value for the company's shareholders." A hardware and building supplies chain says: "The Board of Directors is committed to maximizing long-term shareholder value while supporting management in the business and operations of the Company, complying with the highest integrity standards and laws of the jurisdictions within which the Company operates."

These mission statements are very straightforward. They address the stakeholder, in this case, the shareholder directly. They are also formulated in broad enough terms. However, these mission statements are not particularly inspiring, nor do they give guidance on what the right or best strategies are. For long-term sustainable performance, having a strong identity is important; it guides difficult decisions in tough times. What happens in pure shareholder-driven organizations, if in this case the fashion brand predicts the trend wrongly? It is hard to fall back on the recognition of brand identity and brand loyalty, as one of the instruments that can be used to strengthen the brand if it's not in the mission statement.

Economic value added (EVA) can be of help in creating the right focus. EVA is a financial formula: the net earnings minus an appropriate charge for the opportunity cost of all capital invested in an enterprise (capital charge). It requires management to focus on margin and invested capital. One can focus on margin by rigorous cost control in combination with minimizing price erosion. For strategic initiatives, there should be a concentrated discussion about whether they are to be funded by capital expenditure or out-of-pocket expenses, to maximize the return. It is also important to perform a compliance benchmark once in a while, to determine if the company indeed is complying with the highest standards.

Although the mission statement can be translated effectively into the right performance indicators, we do not gain any insight on the specifics of the industry or the business model of the company from the mission statement.

Key performance indicators of shareholder value include:

- Margin
- Profitability
- Return on capital employed (ROCE)
- Compliance benchmark

Customer Value

There is a gray area between brand value and customer value. The subtle difference would be in how the customer value proposition is translated. Brand value propositions describe the customer advantages in terms of what the products will do for them. Nike will bring innovation and inspiration. Anheuser-Busch brands will bring enjoyment. Customer value is just slightly different — it describes the *result*, such as a pleasant customer experience, or more tangible results, such as having to spend less effort, cost, or time on a certain service. Let's look at the mission statement of British Telecom: "Primarily, we are passionate about customers. Every time we have contact with a customer, our aim is to deliver an excellent experience." It is the excellent experience that counts. This is really important for British Telecom. In BT's traditional business, landlines, statistics suggest that there is, on average, a customer contact opportunity every seven years. It had better be good; there are not many chances to correct that first impression.

Customer satisfaction is an important driver, but there may be a difference between what people say and what people do. Share of wallet might be an alternative performance indicator. This metric looks a bit like market share, but on a micro level. Instead of tracking the total market, it looks at what a person spends on telecommunications, and which portion of that amount goes to British Telecom. It would be impossible to track that on the personal level, so there will have to be aggregates for customer segments. Another performance indicator tracking the consequences of an excellent experience is the adoption rate of new products. If BT routinely delivers an excellent experience, customers could expect this in new business as well. This metric also serves a different purpose: focusing on expanding the business, because landlines are not a growing business.

All of these three metrics are lagging indicators; they describe a result. A leading indicator would have to be used as well. For BT this would be the service levels, particularly for more established products, where customers have a relatively transactional relationship with the company. In such relationships the customer experience is strongly determined by meeting service levels, such as the time to solve out-of-service problems, installing new landlines, accuracy of invoices, and so forth. These service levels should preferably even be externally communicated, so that customers have a certain level of expectation. If these service levels are routinely met, preferably with a significant profit margin, this should drive high customer satisfaction and meet the requirements of the mission statement.

Key performance indicators for BT could include:

- Customer satisfaction
- Share of wallet
- Adoption rate new products
- Service levels

Value Synthesis

Procter & Gamble's (P&G) mission statement requires special attention. It matches all the characteristics we described, and manages to synthesize all value propositions in a meaningful way. Procter & Gamble states: "We will provide branded products and services of superior quality and value that improve the lives of the world's consumers. As a result, consumers will reward us with leadership sales, profit, and value creation, allowing our people, our shareholders, and the communities in which we live and work to prosper."

The mission statement has an external focus, as it addresses the crucial stakeholders. First, the customer is mentioned, and, second it refers to the company ("us"). Then the other stakeholders are mentioned: employees, shareholders, and the community. It provides some clear guidance on how to formulate the right strategies. It is clear that the business is about branded products. The P&G label stands for superior quality and services. This indicates P&G is, for instance, not seeking cost leadership. Yet, the mission statement doesn't describe which consumer markets P&G addresses; it is broad enough to allow for brand stretching. However, this should take place within the confines of the strategic focus: consumer products of a high quality. Lastly, the inspiration comes through using the verb "to prosper." This means more than money alone, it implies doing well in both tangible and intangible forms.

Within two sentences P&G describes the cause-and-effect relationship of its value proposition. The core is brand value. Through brand value customer value is realized, an improved life for consumers. If this is done well, then other types of value, such as shareholder value, will follow. The field of strategy formulation typically asks for choices. An intuitive reaction would be to ask P&G to focus on one value driver, instead of multiple. However, P&G is very clear that for P&G the various value drivers are synthesized. Shareholder value is the result of customer value, which, in turn, is created by brand value. The value propositions are not competing, but follow each other sequentially.

Based on P&G's mission statement, designing the first set of strategic performance indicators is not hard. Brand value can be measured by establishing that premium consumers are willing to pay for the P&G brand. After that, there should be metrics in place that track the quality of the products and services. For instance, product characteristics can be benchmarked with the product characteristics of the competition, such as the absorption power of paper toweling or protection against bacteria for baby diapers. Then, the mission statement suggests improving consumer's lives. For instance, this could be done by measuring how much time and effort consumers save in cleaning the house and changing a baby's diapers. Lastly, the mission statement even suggests a few core lagging performance indicators, such as market leadership, sales, and profit. P&G shows how an effective mission statement helps create alignment.

Call to Action

Most organizations have a mission statement, so I will assume your organization has one too. Answer the following questions:

- Is your mission statement to the point? Specific and broad at the same time?
- Does it have an external focus, explaining your basic function in society? What do you achieve for others, and who are your stakeholders anyway?
- Is your mission statement truthful?

A truthful mission statement reconciles the sometimes conflicting nature of the social and values dimensions. The external focus should be heartfelt and recognized by the outside world. If the market or society at large don't recognize the value you describe, the mission statement is hollow and cannot be implemented. At the same time, if the mission statement doesn't reflect your values, implementation will not succeed.

With a good mission statement in mind, you can start thinking about how to implement the complete performance leadership framework in Part IV of the book.

IMPLEMENTING THE PERFORMANCE LEADERSHIP FRAMEWORK

Performance leadership aims to achieve results through all stakeholders (within and outside the organization) by bridging the different and sometimes conflicting objectives of the various stakeholders and building a common purpose. The performance leadership framework shows the dilemma between the outside-in approach of the social dimension (what the external world wants from us) and the inside-out approach of the values dimension (what our company stands for and is good at). These dimensions may pose conflicting requirements. A good mission statement reconciles that dilemma by taking a stakeholder approach. Part IV focuses on how to implement the performance leadership framework in a practical way by creating a performance network.

Performance networks take performance management to the next level. Horizontal alignment is important across the complete value chain, not just within the organization. And performance management should not be used only to drive personal behaviors within the organization, but to drive how the entire organization behaves across the complete performance network. It's the mission of a performance leader to optimize the results of all stakeholders, not just the leader's own performance.

Chapter | 12

PERFORMANCE NETWORKS

Shareholder value, profit, and market share are not goals; they are rewards.

It's a Networked World

There is a fundamental shift in the organizational model of firms. Organizations have evolved from corporate hierarchies to networks. They have morphed from large corporate silos to more informal, agile alliances of people and firms. The examples are manifold.

Fifteen years ago a typical German car manufacturer built most of its cars itself in Germany. Every model would have its own design, a separate engineering team, and its own production plants. Today the manufacturer builds multiple models on one platform. Plants and platforms are even shared between multiple brands. Only a small part of the car is built in-house; most often complete assemblies are delivered from suppliers from all over the world. On average, manufacturers offer more than three times the number of models they did 15 years ago.

As another example, the vast majority of branded sports products never see the brand's office from the inside. The brand is responsible for the design and the marketing and for managing the complete value chain between production and sales in independent stores. But most, if not all, products are manufactured by contract manufacturers and distributed directly to contracted warehouses and retailers. The same is the case with many consumer electronics brands.

Many telecom companies are so-called mobile virtual network operators (MVNOs). They do not have their own mobile infrastructure; they buy excess capacity at large quantities at a discount from other telecom companies that do own the infrastructure. Because these MVNOs have minimal overhead, they can sell this capacity to their clients at lower prices than the original telecom company can and still make a profit. The advantage for traditional telecom operators is that they can sell their overcapacity. The same can be seen in other infrastructure-related businesses that are usually highly regulated. To enhance competition, infrastructure and distribution are split. The national railways are split into an infrastructure and multiple operator companies. The electricity companies are split into an infrastructure organization and a sales company, and multiple vendors of electricity can deliver through the same infrastructure.

Increasingly, innovation comes from the collaboration of different companies. For example, Senseo is a coffee pod system, codesigned by Philips and Douwe Egberts. Philips contributed the hardware, a special coffee-making machine, while Douwe Egberts developed the supplies, coffee pods filled with coffee according to a special brewing method. As another example there is the Nike+ system; a collaboration between Apple and Nike. Nike designed shoes that hold a sensor that, through a bluetooth connection, sends jogging statistics to an Apple iPod, so users can track their average speed, distance covered, time spent jogging, and an approximation of the calories burned. Such initiatives can be shaped traditionally through a joint venture, but that is not needed. Production and marketing teams of multiple companies can simply work together and develop new products and services. An agreement simply specifies how to allocate the costs, the revenues, and the profit.

Financial services have also become networked. For instance, there are many alternatives to straightforward mortgages. Usually they come with a package of insurance, supplied by the insurance unit of a financial services conglomerate or a business partner, such as homeowner insurance and life insurance. The insurance company invests money and reinsures the risks it takes. Furthermore, the mortgage itself contains investment components. The payments on the mortgage are reinvested, enabling the homeowner to pay off the house faster—and at a higher risk obviously—while making use of all tax benefits. Some of the mutual funds in which the mortgage is invested may not even belong to the bank where the mortgage is closed. And in some cases, the complete offering doesn't even carry the name of the financial services institution, but has the label of a large intermediary. In the case of one mortgage, five or more parties are involved.

On top of all these types of collaboration, outsourcing has become commonplace.[1] Organizations routinely outsource facilities services such as cleaning, cafeteria services, and security. Increasingly information technology tasks, such as helpdesk services, complete data centers, and even system development have been outsourced as well. The same trend can be observed in areas such as finance, human resources, logistics, and other business domains. In many cases, cost savings are an important driver.

These forms of collaboration need to be managed. There is an extensive body of theory we can draw on called *transaction cost economics* (see the sidebar below). The term *extended enterprise* is fairly widely used and understood. Others speak of business webs[2] or value networks.[3] In Japan, the term *keiretsu* is somewhat related, describing a group of firms having strong financial relationships with one another. Strangely enough, however, the concept of an extended enterprise has not had a substantial impact in the field of performance management. The traditional ways of performance management, using the hierarchy and focusing on vertical alignment, clearly do not work in these networked environments. What is needed there is a performance network.

TRANSACTION COST ECONOMICS

In economics, transaction cost economics (TCE) is a very well-established discipline.[4] However, it seems to be totally unused in performance management. Despite a more networked approach to business, accounting research to date has largely ignored the increasing importance of supply chains, planning, budgeting, and control processes flowing from one organization into another, as well as their implications for financial decision making and control.[5]

TCE helps organizations understand which activities should be undertaken within the walls of the organization itself and which should be left to the market. Where it is easier, or better, or more efficient to interact with others than to coordinate activities yourself, relationships should be forged. If transaction costs between parties or on the open market become too high (due to complexity and/or uncertainty), TCE recommends that those activities take place within the organization.

TCE emphasizes the risks of doing business. It describes the concept of "bounded rationality," which means that suppliers and customers (contractors) cannot predict every event and cater for that within a contract. This introduces risk. TCE also describes "opportunistic behavior" among business partners, and the impact of those behaviors on cost and pricing. Sometimes, a customer dictates new terms after the supplier made a specific investment in doing business. If the customer leaves, the supplier would have to write off the specific asset investment. TCE refers to customer-specific investments, such as product adaptations, administration, machinery, or account management, as *asset specificity*.

To deal with the risk, precautions need to be taken, leading to transaction costs, such as search costs, identifying potential partners that the organization feels confident about; contracting costs, negotiating and writing an agreement; monitoring costs, setting up a governance system to ensure obligations are met; and enforcement costs, bargaining if the contractual obligations are not met.[6] The applicability of TCE goes beyond cost, however, to include other areas of value. Potential advantages of participation in interorganizational relationships include[7]:

- Access to a particular resource, such as capital, skills, intimate knowledge of a (foreign) market, production facilities
- Economies of scale, finding partners to expand production volume, and share risk, and volume
- Codevelopment of a product or service, learning from each other
- Speed to market, involving, for instance, contract manufacturing
- Flexibility compared to one's own organization
- Collective lobbying power to influence government agencies
- Neutralizing competitors and building combined market power

In transactional relationships, price is the most important component, and switching costs are generally assumed to be low. For new transactions, new partners could be contracted. However, an argument can be made for considering longer-term, less cost-oriented relationships, based on trust, ease of doing business, competence, speed of delivery, and so forth. More continuous relationships have a positive effect on transaction costs. A continuous relationship is often in the best interest of all parties.

Performance Networks

All the examples show that multiple business partners are stakeholders in business. They have all kinds of different relationships. Some may be formal, such as joint-venture organizations, most of them will be more informal, based on agreements that may change over time, or are simply created on a per-project basis. Agreements for cobranding, code-velopment, comarketing, or simply sourcing agreements may intensify over time as relationships become tighter, or the opposite may happen. As innovation continues and market demands change, new stakeholders may enter the network and existing stakeholders may disengage and seek collaboration with another network. And firms may be part of multiple networks at the same time.

Unfortunately, most performance management methodologies do not reflect that new reality. They are aimed at optimizing the results per company in the network of stakeholders. Methodologies such as DuPont analysis, economic value added, and balanced scorecard look at optimizing the needs for the shareholders, which are typically connected to a single entity in the network. Also, beyond budgeting and critical success factors are rarely implemented in a networked way. In other words, the focus is on the question "How do I optimize my own performance?"

In order for performance management to be effective in fueling growth or supporting any other strategic imperative, it needs to support the business trends instead of hinder them. With business operating as a network, needing more horizontal alignment, how to optimize your own performance is the wrong question, as it leads to suboptimal results. Optimizing the results of a single stakeholder doesn't necessarily mean optimizing the results of all stakeholders involved in the value creation process. Also, it doesn't take into account how other stakeholders contribute to the organization's performance. Performance management should start by focusing on the impact of the other stakeholders on the organization: "What do my stakeholders contribute to my success?" This question leads to a much higher leverage. This question can only be asked if the opposite question is asked as well: "And what do I contribute to the success of my stakeholders?" These questions are the key to the performance network.

A *performance network* recognizes all stakeholders in a value chain, and it aligns their objectives in order to optimize the performance of the overall network, not the performance of each stakeholder by itself.

The performance network is taking "measurement drives behavior" to a whole new level—from collaboration between people within an

Figure 12.1

Example of a Performance Network

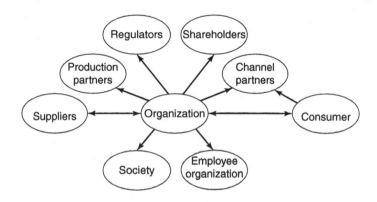

organization to connecting complete organizations; from personal behavior to organizational behavior; from vertical alignment using the hierarchy within the organization to horizontal alignment managing information, business processes, and business disciplines across the value chain. See Figure 12.1.

The analytical dimension of the performance leadership framework focuses on figuring out how to get where you want to be. Applied to a performance network, this means finding the right stakeholders and creating an *understanding of the right type of relationship*. All parties need to have the same understanding of the business relationship. If one party is looking to invest in a relationship and actively seeks partnership, while another party treats the relationship as transactional, both parties will become frustrated, and no productive results will come out of the relationship.

The operational dimension optimizes the current day-to-day processes, which always start with a certain *transparency* between stakeholders. Information is an asset, to be deployed and optimized like other assets such as capital and materials. Information is shared as much as possible to optimize relationships, transfer knowledge, and traffic other assets as efficiently as possible between all stakeholders in the performance network. By sharing information, the stakeholders can identify opportunities and inhibitors (bottlenecks) in the performance network, and they can move from suboptimization to optimization. Together, the operational and the analytical dimensions of the performance leadership framework constitute traditional performance management.

The social dimension demands the relationship between stakeholders to be *reciprocal*. The performance of the enterprise depends on the performance of its partners in the value chain. Not only should we measure to which extent we are making our targets, but also to which extent we enable our stakeholders to make their targets. This tells us how effective we are in our collaboration.

The values dimension suggests that there is more to a relationship than contracts and deals. Based on the understanding of the relationship, transparency, and reciprocity, the other stakeholders are either comfortable working with the organization or not. Stakeholders have a choice of whom they would like to work with; their *trust* needs to be earned. Trust exists when stakeholders understand each other's motives, values and—in general—their way of thinking. In summary, the four pillars of the performance network are: understanding the nature of the relationship, transparency, reciprocity, and trust.

Nature of the Relationship

At the core of the performance network is the belief that not all relationships are the same, although all of them are important. Some relationships are very transactional, such as managing the cafeteria in facilities management, or desktop management in IT, or some forms of logistics. These can often simply be outsourced. Other relationships are more strategic, as these support the core competencies of the firm directly or involve innovation through cocreation. These types of relationships require more advanced management. Within the performance network, we distinguish three types of relationships: transactional relationships, added-value relationships, and joint-value relationships. See Figure 12.2.

Transactional relationships have a clear customer/supplier basis. Usually the switching costs, the costs incurred when you move from one supplier to another, are low. The customer simply will evaluate the speed, quality, price, and convenience of doing business with the supplier and, if there are any problems, find another supplier. The supplier will try to optimize profit and growth from the customer, and it is not overly interested in a continuous customer relationship, other than

Figure 12.2

Three Types of Relationships within the Performance Network

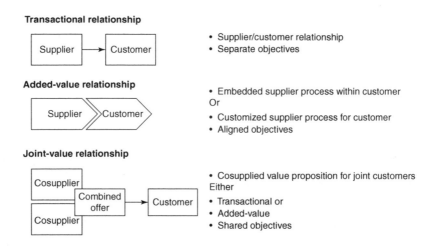

Transactional relationship

Supplier → Customer

- Supplier/customer relationship
- Separate objectives

Added-value relationship

Supplier › Customer

- Embedded supplier process within customer
Or
- Customized supplier process for customer
- Aligned objectives

Joint-value relationship

Cosupplier, Cosupplier → Combined offer → Customer

- Cosupplied value proposition for joint customers
Either
- Transactional or
- Added-value
- Shared objectives

to secure repeat business. Each party in a relationship focuses on its own performance, managing its own processes.

Although transactional relationships are scalable (because they can be repeated for every single customer) and can be very profitable, they are becoming decreasingly competitive. Within transactional relationships, competing on price is not likely to be a good option. Most likely you have invested in becoming operationally excellent already, or there will always be someone else who can do it even cheaper. Or perhaps price competition doesn't fit your brand. Also, competing on product quality is becoming less differentiating: There are hardly any really "bad" products left in the market. Many organizations therefore look to provide additional value.

In *added-value relationships*, profit and growth are still important for the supplier. But there is a clear need and wish to create a long-term relationship. In some cases, products or services are tailored to meet the needs of a specific customer. Think of printing a customer's logo on a standard product, or building a product from scratch according to a customer's specifications. Another form of adaptation can be found in logistics and administration, connecting systems to monitor stock levels or to perform joint planning. A certain level of trust is required by the customer to allow another party into the operation. Once this is a fact, switching costs will be higher. Both parties are committed to the relationship and seek alignment, benefiting from mutual success.

Table **12.1**

Performance Network Relationship Examples

Type of Relationship	Examples
Transactional relationship	• Outsourcing company cafeteria, cleaning services • Leasing contracts for company cars • Minimal healthcare insurance or car insurance • Internet ordering service for branded consumer electronics
Added-value relationship	• RFID-tagged supply chain integration • Management reporting as a service from leasing companies for fleet managers of their business-to-business customers • Usage reporting of mobile phone companies • A travel agent allowing corporate customers direct access to their flight booking systems
Joint-value relationship	• Companies from different industries codeveloping a new product, such as Nike and Apple (Nike+), Douwe Egberts and Philips (Senseo), Adidas and Goodyear (sports shoes with special soles) • Complementary companies from the same industry offering a joint service, such as airline alliance loyalty programs (OneWorld, Skyteam, StarAlliance) • Competing companies collaborating on a common objective, such as competing insurance companies starting a trusted third party, collectively having a majority market share, to entice car repair shops to adopt standardized processes, systems, and pricing, driving average claim size down.

In *joint-value relationships* there is no clear supplier/customer relationship anymore. This means that both partners aim at managing the profit and growth of their combined activities. There are shared objectives toward a joint target audience, to which they are cosuppliers. On the basis of equality, switching is not an option. Table 12.1 provides a few examples of each type of relationship.

In each of these relationships, there are different strategic themes (see Figure 12.3). Within a transactional relationship, we focus on the organization itself and its standard products and services, which we seek to sell in a profitable way to as many customers as possible, making use of standard processes. This doesn't mean there isn't a lot of innovation.

Figure 12.3

Performance Network Themes*

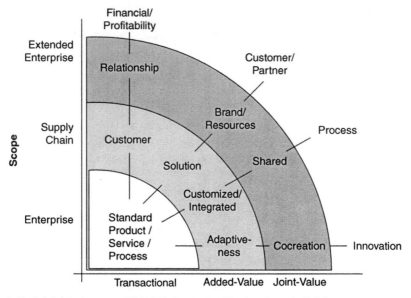

*Inspired by: Prahalad, CK.; Ramaswamy, V. (2003), "The New Frontier of Experience Innovation." *MIT Sloan Management Review*, Vol. 44, No. 4.

In fact, many highly innovative organizations focus on these types of relationships, creating technological breakthroughs for others to use. A prime example of this is the Dolby Surround system, which is licensed by most consumer electronics firms.

Added-value relationships focus on the supply chain, moving from product selling to solution selling, often involving multiple firms to complement the solution. The solution should become part of the customer's everyday life or business processes, creating a high level of customer loyalty and sustainable customer profitability. Not every customer is the same. In many cases the solutions need to be adapted to specific conditions. A partner network helps to create these adaptations. Think of the Apple iPod product "ecosystem," involving many third parties offering accessories. Although every party may have its own objectives, they are aligned, leading to mutual success.

Joint-value relationships focus on the extended enterprise. Multiple parties collaborate to create a new product or service that they could not have created on their own. They share the same objectives: joint success in the market. Think of Senseo, a one-touch-of-a-button espresso system where the machine is built by Philips, and the coffee pads with special coffee are supplied by Douwe Egberts. Each of the two firms offers unique skills to this joint-value proposition. The profitability comes from the special relationship, which started without a finished product or service. Specialists of both firms combined forces and cocreated a new product, where each firm also contributed their brand name to make the product a success, and created collaborative processes to maintain the offering over time and perhaps also created new collaborative products and services.

Power or *dominance* is an important factor connected to the level of the relationship. There are different factors that allow a stakeholder to become dominant. These can include the size of the organization (like a huge oil company), the brand value and recognition it has (to attract customers), a certain legal protection (state-regulated organizations or unions), a crucial position in the network (for instance, owning customer information), or technological advantage (offering a unique product). A dominant organization in the performance network can effectively drive transactional relationships; others have little choice but to follow the dominant partner. Suppliers that have a dependent relationship with a more powerful partner may wish to seek a more added-value relationship, to increase customer loyalty—being embedded in its customer's processes, raising the switching cost. In many cases, cocreated products and services come from a power-neutral relationship. Each partner has its own unique skills and resources, and it contributes its brand name.

Regardless of how powerful one organization is, all parties need to agree on the level of relationship they have, in order to collaborate well. If there is no agreement on the level of a relationship, it is most likely not sustainable over the long term and may succumb to opportunistic behavior. For instance, one of the partners opens up to the other, trying to build a relationship, which then is immediately returned by the other in terms of a new opportunity for price renegotiation. This will teach the first partner not to be that transparent anymore, whether it has the power or not. If there is no agreement on the level of relationship, reciprocal performance indicators put in place by one of the partners will not be recognized or appreciated for the value they provide. When there is

Table 12.2

Key Characteristics of a Performance Network

	Transactional Relationship	Added-Value Relationship	Joint-Value Relationship
Strategic focus	Standard products and services	Adaptive customer focused solutions	Cocreation, joint value proposition
Scope	Enterprise	Supply chain	Extended enterprise
Stakeholder objectives	Different	Aligned	Shared
Switching cost	Low	High	No switch possible
Power balance	All power balances	Improving power balance between unequal stakeholders, where the dependent stakeholder builds brand preference and tries to increase switching cost.	Neutral, interdependent, building joint brand preference

no clear understanding about the level of a relationship, there is most likely also little trust, especially when the behavior of one party doesn't fulfill the other party's expectations. The parties need to agree whether they have a transactional, added-value, or joint-value relationship.

With organizations being structured as networks, and business models aimed at collaboration within the network, managing the relationships between the stakeholders becomes a strategic part of performance management. Understanding the relationship, sharing information, reciprocal metrics, and a trusting relationship are the key components of managing that relationship.

In summary, Table 12.2 describes the key relationship characteristics of a performance network.

Transparency

In a performance network, there is no single CEO who hands out the marching orders that are then cascaded into the organization. Unless there is one dominant party in the network of business partners, there is no clear command and control model. Creating and sustaining business performance is achieved through communication and collaboration.

There cannot be collaboration without information exchange. Information is an asset, to be deployed and optimized like other assets, such as capital and materials. Information should be shared as much as possible to optimize relationships, knowledge transfer, and traffic of other assets as efficiently as possible between all stakeholders in the performance network. By sharing information, the stakeholders can identify opportunities and inhibitors (bottlenecks) in the performance network and can then move from suboptimization to optimization.

There are many examples of business enterprises that changed their industry by aggressively adopting transparency and raising the bar for their competition. Transparency affects most of our stakeholder relationships, such as society (sustainability reporting, extensively discussed in Chapter 10), our suppliers, shareholders, and customers. Here are a few examples:

- *Shareholders.* There is no direct causal link between the timeliness of external reporting and the valuation of the overall company. However, it is commonly accepted that the two factors are somehow related. Enterprises that report quickly come across as decisive, shareholders are better informed about them than about enterprises that report more slowly. Furthermore, early and accurate reporting is a sign of having good controls in place, one of the main targets of corporate governance regulations and guidelines. Organizations that invest in shareholder transparency show they are good managers of the capital supplied by the shareholders.
- *Suppliers.* Many organizations go through a supplier rationalization exercise and, as a part of it, create supplier scorecards. In the beginning these are designed to make the relationship with the suppliers more objective, as part of an effort to decrease the number of suppliers the organization deals with. The suppliers that score best will see their purchasing share increase. Others will see it decrease, or they will be let go. At first most suppliers are skeptical, as they think the scorecards will be used to squeeze even greater discounts out of them. However, these attitudes tend to change. Supplier scorecards improve relationships. Performance indicators help in pointing

out that there are more competitive factors than just price and discount. Both the supplier and the procurement department have a more equal position, since the scorecards provide a discussion platform. It also gives the suppliers more insight up front as to what their client is looking for. Sharing performance indicators creates a win-win situation, when positioned as a collaboration-and-communication instrument.

- *Customers.* The killer business case comes from being able to share information with customers, as this is related to customer retention, lifetime value, and competitive position. A European asset management firm has introduced individual personalized annual reports for their highest-valued customer segments. In these reports the performance for that specific customer is benchmarked.

There are many examples of "information as the product." Competitive differentiation for car lease companies does not come from the cars, but from the management information the company shares with their customer's fleet managers. HR departments that outsource benefits programs to insurance companies demand solid management information. One telecoms provider offers a Web page where consumers can view simple personal reports. The list of the most-dialed numbers helps make better use of the discount program. There are hardly any vertical relationships in which "information as the product" is not relevant.

Within transactional relationships, transparency consists of operational and financial information exchange, derived from the flow of transactions. The operational information would typically consist of status information on transactions: for instance, tracking and tracing information within logistical environments or approval status within backoffice departments in administrative environments. The financial information would typically be contained in invoices and other payment records.

When managing added-value relationships, in addition to the operational information, there is also management information, aimed at enabling the stakeholder to manage the relationship better. The examples all focus on creating added value on top of the core product or service.

Within joint-value relationships, transparency consists of a full set of management information, which is similar to what any company would require from internal operations. There is also operational information exchange as well, but too much emphasis would lead to transactional behaviors. In addition to the management information, transparency consists of a certain free flow of organizational capacity. Think of an exchange of capital, contribution of skills and staff, materials, and use of facilities. These can be formalized within a joint venture, but this is not necessary. Managing joint-value relationships requires a voluntary and open exchange. See Table 12.3.

The effects of sharing information are dramatic. Transparency drives behaviors in a positive direction. Recall the example in Chapter 3 of the claims department of the insurance company. Hanging a poster with a few graphs every week at the message board near the coffee machine showing the average processing time of a claim had tremendous impact. I am not suggesting disclosing the organization's complete strategy. But a good strategy is based on the skills, resources, market position, and other unique characteristics of an enterprise. This is not easily copied by the competition. And even if it is copied, a copied strategy doesn't fit the competition

Table 12.3

Information Exchange

Type of Relationship	Examples
Transactional	• Information on orders, inventory, sales, promotions, invoices and other transactional topics
Added-value	*In addition to transactional information:*
	• Benchmark information for customers or suppliers, comparing themselves with others
	• Management information on cost savings, or generated opportunities
	• Integrated processes and systems for processing and controlling transactions between the organizations
Joint-value	*In additional to information and integrated systems and processes:*
	• Full set of management information on the joint activity
	• Flow of capital between partners
	• Allocated staff resources to the joint initiative
	• Sharing facilities and materials

and will not lead to the intended results. But the overall strategic direction should be known to, and understood by, all within the company and all other stakeholders. Otherwise it cannot be made actionable.

Reciprocity

Next to sharing information in order to collaborate better on a day-to-day basis, the relationship needs to be managed. Key performance indicators are needed, but they should not be focused on how to optimize the organization's own performance only. Sharing the same top-down metrics the organization had before, but with a wider audience of stakeholders, doesn't make sense. Performance indicators should be reciprocal, showing what the stakeholder adds to the organization's performance and how the organization contributes to its stakeholders' performance.

A huge contribution to managing stakeholder relationships comes from a methodology called the *performance prism*.[8] One of the key messages of the performance prism is that stakeholders have requirements and offer contributions. This methodology describes in great detail, among other things, what stakeholders could (and perhaps should) expect from each other. With this in mind, it triggers the right strategic, planned discussion. The requirements of different stakeholders, or the requirements between a single stakeholder and the organization, may not align, or may produce some tension, or may even be conflicting. Without realizing this, we may act on assumptions or, worse, we may be ignorant of these needs. By understanding these objectives, we can find a solution to reconcile these differences, which probably will lead to much smarter solutions than optimizing a single set of objectives. Figure 12.4 and Table 12.4 provide an overview of an organization's stakeholders and their needs, according to the performance prism methodology.

Figure 12.4 clearly shows how customer/supplier relationships are the basis of all value creation in the performance network. The suppliers of an organization view that organization as a client, while the organization itself has its own clients. Organizations are looking for profit, growth, favorable opinions, and trust downstream in the value chain. They are also looking for fast, cheap, and easy products and services upstream in the value chain. Other stakeholders, such as employees, the community,

Figure 12.4

Graphical Representation of Performance Prism

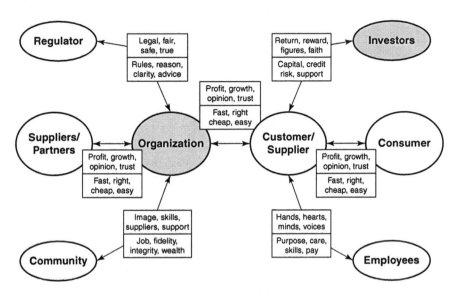

regulators and investors supply the means to propel value creation, thereby making it possible. Regulators ensure fair competition; the community provides a platform to work in, such as infrastructure; investors supply the necessary capital to operate; and employees provide the needed labor. With this view in mind, it is quite clear that none of the stakeholders can be ignored, as each represents a vital component in making the value chain flow smoothly. Traditional performance management usually aims at optimizing results for the shareholders. But if you follow this visualization, it also is immediately clear that investors are not the central stakeholder in a networked business model. Managing customer-supplier relationships is central. Optimization for investors alone will disrupt the reciprocity of good stakeholder relationships.

Reciprocity is even important within transactional relationships. Companies need to track what is important for their stakeholders, to make sure they are still on the right track. Failure to do so will lead to a reduced level of stakeholder satisfaction and, where switching costs are relatively low, to outright stakeholder defection. However, measuring what is important to the stakeholder is done with a focus on optimizing one's own performance toward the stakeholder.

Table 12.4

Needs of the Organization and Its Stakeholders, According to the Performance Prism

Stakeholders	Needs of Organization	Needs of Stakeholders
Investors	*Capital*, to operate and invest	*Return*, capital appreciation
	Credit, facilities from banks	*Reward,* dividend
	Risk, to be taken by investors	*Figures*, justification
	Support, loyalty and advice	*Faith*, confidence in management team
Customers	*Profit*, to sustain the business	*Fast*, rapid delivery
	Growth, increase of sales	*Right*, high-quality products and services
	Opinion, feedback on performance	*Cheap*, reasonably priced
	Trust, for repeat business	*Easy*, no barriers to buying
Employees	*Hands*, headcount, productivity	*Purpose*, support, direction
	Hearts, loyalty, commitment	*Care*, respect, fair treatment
	Minds, qualifications, teams	*Skills*, training, knowledge
	Voices, suggestions, diversity	*Pay*, compensation package
Suppliers	*Fast*, rapid delivery	*Profit*, to sustain the business
	Right, high-quality products and services	*Growth*, increase of sales
	Cheap, reasonably priced	*Opinion*, feedback on performance
	Easy, no barriers to buying	*Trust*, for repeat business
Regulators	*Rules*, for fair competition	*Legal,* compliance to laws
	Reason, sound purpose and reasonable to implement	*Fair*, no monopolistic or anticompetitive behavior
	Clarity, unambiguity	*Safe*, no endangering society
	Advice, on implementing rules	*True*, be open and honest
Community	*Image*, be viewed in a positive way	*Jobs*, regional employment
	Skills, availability of workers	*Fidelity*, sustain and grow employment
	Suppliers, local vendors for particular needs	*Integrity*, open, honest, responsible
	Support, supportive of aims	*Wealth*, making the community healthy and prosperous

Reciprocity within added-value relationships has a bigger impact on an organization's performance management. The organization needs to track what it achieves from its stakeholder's performance. This of course is the bottom line for one's own performance as well. There should be performance indicators that point out how much in costs was saved for the stakeholder, how much return was generated, and how much opportunity was created, as well as any other measure of success.

Within joint-value relationships, organizations measure what they would measure for themselves as well. With shared objectives, all parties involved look for the same measure of success. The difference is that the organization does not measure what it has achieved for the other, but what it has achieved for the joint relationship. Table 12.5

Table 12.5

Performance Indicators

	Transactional Relationship	Added-Value Relationship	Joint-Value Relationship
Supplier Requirements			
Profit	Shareholder value and profitability	Partner margin	Revenue and profit joint initiative, compared to internal profit
Growth	Market share	Share of wallet	"Blue Ocean" growth*
Opinion	Customer satisfaction survey	Personal, more qualitative, feedback partner	Continuous operational and management feedback
Trust	Cross-sell ratio	Percent process integration	Growth in investment in joint initiative
Customer Requirements			
Fast	Average time own process	Average time overall process	Time to market
Right	Percent transactions "first time right"	Meeting partner requirements through customization	High asset specificity
Cheap	Price benchmark	Cost savings for partner	Low transaction costs
Easy	Channel availability	Channel preference	Crossover resources (capital, staff, material, use of facilities, information exchange)

*A "blue ocean strategy" is a strategy aimed at creating a completely new market, as opposed to a "red ocean strategy," which aims at competing in an existing market. See Kim, W.C., Mauborgne, R. (2005), *Blue Ocean Strategy: How to Create Uncontested Market Space and Make Competition Irrelevant*, Harvard Business Press, Cambridge, MA.

shows how performance indicators in supplier/customer relationships differ per type of relationship.

Case Study 1: EnGen

EnGen (a fictitious name[9]) is a manufacturer of generic car parts, such as parts of engines, windshield wipers, car chair covers, and so on. EnGen sells through retail chains, but mostly through independent garages. EnGen has a difficult position, end-consumers are not really aware of the brand, and garage holders mostly care about profit margin. Price competition would build preference from the garages, but there will always be a supplier who is willing to discount more.

The traditional approach, witnessed in many different industries, is based on the classical focus: "How do I optimize my own performance?" EnGen would start to build a brand preference with its target audience, whereby consumers would ask the garage for EnGen parts, instead of just for generic parts. This would be a multiyear effort at a considerable cost, and the return on investment would be uncertain. Asking how EnGen could optimize the performance of its complete performance network, and how the stakeholders would help improve EnGen's performance, leads to an entirely different, more effective, and much more economic approach. EnGen realized that in order to be successful in building loyalty with the garages, while maintaining high margins, it needed to find a way to make the garages more successful in the market. See Figure 12.5.

Figure 12.5

EnGen's Performance Network

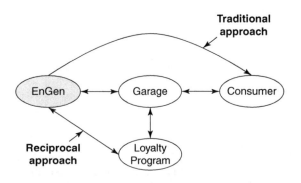

The key to success for EnGen is to realize that most independent garages are small businesses, run by excellent mechanics, but lacking professional marketing. This is something EnGen can offer through its economies of scale. EnGen created a marketing program for the independent garages. When a garage guarantees a certain amount of business, it can apply for membership with a trusted third party, something the company charges the garage for. The third party runs a marketing factory to produce mailings and a customer database to analyze and benchmark information. All customer-facing activities are done under the label of the garage, which basically outsources its marketing. The result is a "double whammy" loyalty program. Loyalty between consumer and independent garage is increased by reminders from the third party to have the oil checked, tires changed, and so on. The consumer is more likely to come back to the same independent garage for maintenance, probably before any problems arise. And, perhaps such a visit is a good trigger to see if the customer is interested in buying a new car as well. At the same time, EnGen creates a much more meaningful relationship with the garage that is based on process integration (through the trusted third party) instead of pure price negotiations.

Success is primarily measured in terms of return on investment for the garage. This produces a triple win: The garage increases its business performance, EnGen secures its revenue stream and can improve its market share through better service, and the trusted third party is paid per subscription, so it needs to keep the garages happy.

The next step in the program is to move beyond just marketing. Through a Web site, powered by EnGen, customers could directly book appointments in the calendar of the independent garage. By using purchased data and data from the garage itself, the Web site allows customers to see an estimate of the costs, based on what the customer selects from a wide range of maintenance activities. For it to be worthwhile, this system contains much more than just EnGen products.

EnGen's focus on what it can contribute to the success of its channel partners, the garages, instead of just optimizing its own performance, has created a competitive advantage.

Trust

Within every organization there should be trust. Employees should trust the management and vice versa. Without a basic level of trust, there would be no productivity at all. The same kind of trust, and probably even more, is needed between organizations. All relationships, even the most transactional ones, require trust. However, there are multiple levels of trust between stakeholders.[10]

Contractual trust is the most basic form of trust. It occurs when all parties involved believe that contractual obligations will be met. In most societies this is a prerequisite for doing business, and it's a key element of transactional relationships. *Competence trust* is displayed when parties believe that their partners will not only meet the minimum contractual obligations, but also have the right skills, technologies, and other resources to do the job well. Competence trust is needed within added-value relationships, when organizations rely on processes and systems that are managed by other organizations. Lastly, there is *goodwill trust*, where parties know others will represent them fairly and will make the same decisions as they would when representing them. This can only take place when the parties involved share the same norms and values. Goodwill trust involves joint-value relationships, where organizations share intellectual property and resources such as capital, staff, information, and facilities, and materials flow freely between the organizations—an intrinsically vulnerable situation.

Trust, more than control, fuels the performance of the relationship. In more strategic relationships, *too much accountability* hurts. An atmosphere of strong accountability does not fit well with the creation of trust, whereas an atmosphere of open commitment does.[11] Without an open commitment between parties, the relationship can be terminated at any moment because at all points the accounts can be settled. This leads to lower switching costs and, in general, to more transactional behavior. It doesn't mean there should be no control and no measurement. The aim of performance indicators and management processes should be to build that trust, lowering the transaction costs within the relations.

Trust and transparency have a complex relationship. For instance, an increase in trust may sometimes lead to an increase in transparency, when more information is shared voluntarily. In other cases, however, an increase in trust might lead to less transparency, as formal controls to compensate for an earlier lack of trust become less needed. Transparency and performance don't lead to trust immediately. In order to trust one another, stakeholders should be aware of each other's strategy, and more importantly, their values, what drives their business model. The link between performance and trust is influenced by many other factors.[12]

- Different stakeholders have different expectations. If the strategy is aimed at cost leadership and the organization is doing a good job, the cost-related performance indicators will show it. However, this doesn't necessarily mean that the organization is trusted. If it is quality or speed that is expected, the company will get bad grades regardless of the success of its own chosen strategy. Trust is earned only if there is a fit between the organization's strategy and the external stakeholder's expectations, not by good performance per se.
- Customers may have a certain brand perception, regardless of how the organization is performing. A well-known anecdote (the story is not true, but it makes a great point) is about Mercedes and Brand X each doing a similar recall of a specific line of cars that contains a certain defect. All owners are advised to report to the car dealer and have the car serviced, free of charge. Mercedes sends its customers a recall letter and gets applauded for being diligent and quality oriented. Brand X sends a similar letter but gets a negative response because quality problems were exactly what was expected of that brand.
- Large enterprises often have a broad portfolio of products and services. The perception of performance is made up by the overall performance of that organization, and not the performance that is delivered by the business unit a customer may be dealing with. If a quality-oriented upscale manufacturer of watches is bringing a new line of products on the market priced more attractively for middle-class consumers, it will be trusted, even if the market has no experience yet with the new product line. Conversely, an underperformance business unit will affect the trust that external stakeholders have in a well-performing business unit.

- Business performance is not the only thing that stakeholders evaluate. Shell took a hit on its image during the Brent-Spar affair. The company felt it was the most economical and environmentally friendly solution to sink the Brent-Spar oil platform, but the general public and environmental organizations did not agree. Although the products and services of Shell were not compromised, the company suffered from decreased trust. Or, on more of a microlevel: The shopping experience in a store that has great products for low prices is still a negative one if the staff is not friendly.
- Performance and the trust scale do not always have a symmetric relationship. Good performance for some services tends not be noticed, while bad performance leads to immediate distrust. Think of an outsourcing company that processes payroll. Their service is either normal or bad.

Within daily life, trust grows when people share the same values. It gives people the feeling that they understand the motives and behaviors of their colleagues, friends, or partners. It works the same way within business, where people work with people. An understanding of an organization's values provides guidance if we feel comfortable in being open with our partner. If we provide a transparent view, we should have the feeling that our partner will have the same understanding that we have. If we integrate our processes, we need to have the feeling that our partner will make the same decisions on our behalf as we would.

This trust is built by understanding each other's organizational values. Understanding the values does not necessarily mean both parties need to share the same values. There needs to be a basic overlap: otherwise the parties would probably not be attracted to each other. But the values could also be complementary. If your strategy revolves around product innovation, likely it is driven by values such as quality, challenging conventional thinking, and never giving up. However, there is no need to apply this way of thinking to all parts of the company. In this particular case, it makes sense to source logistics to a partner that is driven by efficiency and discipline and with those values has perfected an operationally excellent distribution business, something you could never achieve since it is not part of your particular passion.

At the same time, for other relationships, the values need to match. In order to codevelop, cobrand, and comarket a product or a service, the product or service needs to be recognizable to the market. If people do not share the same passion for the customer or for innovation, the result will be a noncompetitive product or service that is not recognized in the market. A values exercise, to uncover the positive and negative values that stakeholders have, helps predict many of the collaboration problems we can imagine. It also helps stakeholders to read each other's intentions and read through the performance data alone.

Case Study 2: IT Department

Externally and internally, different stakeholders have different values and objectives. One of the business areas that in many organizations is most exposed to having to manage many different stakeholders is the information technology department.

This IT department, depicted centrally in the performance network consists of two parts. As in most IT organizations, there is an IT development part, which takes care of implementing new applications, and there is an IT operations part, responsible for maintaining all existing applications. It is important to also understand the values and the cultural context of performance management, to understand the behaviors and assumptions people have, in order to have a trusting relationship. The IT performance network shows this, first between the two parts of the IT department, then between IT and a few external stakeholders. See Figure 12.6.

In this IT department, IT development is driven by an "all-the-way culture." Perfectionism is seen as a good thing. The department is very innovative; it is always looking for the next generation of technologies. As a downside, there is also a negative value: the department has trouble accepting standard applications. It suffers from the "not-invented-here syndrome." The IT operations department has a very distinct set of values too. It is very thorough. Every change will be checked, double-checked, and checked again. The department aims at keeping a stable status quo; it has a "don't touch attitude." It is more open for change, though, when there is a cost-saving opportunity.

Figure 12.6
_____

Performance Network of an IT Department

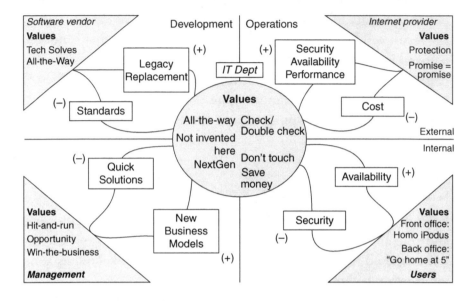

A crucial part of the success in the relationship between development and operations is an understanding of each other's motives. It then becomes predictable that there will always be tension between the two departments about which technologies to use. The development department will always look for the new technologies that operations see as a potential disruption. The relationship can improve if development, for instance, applies its innovative all-the-way skills to a new way of testing. It is easy to predict that introducing a rigorous test process that already runs at the design phase of new implementation and monitors all development from there will be accepted easily by both. It is an innovative methodology, and it is aimed to save costs and to improve the quality of developments.

Of course, the IT department does not operate on its own. It interacts with its stakeholders on a continuous basis. The IT department is funded by the management of the company, which is very opportunity-driven. It tries many different ways to win more business, and is open to all kinds of ideas. Sometimes this leads to a "hit-and-run attitude" and a somewhat short-term focus. The management and IT department get along quite well when discussing new business models; the

IT department always knows about a new technology that would help. However, there are continuous discussions on how to do things "well" and how to measure "success." IT likes to take a thorough approach and build robust systems and processes. Management wants to be the first mover and win the business at hand.

Part of the systems landscape is based on packaged enterprise resource planning (ERP) software. The software vendor enjoys working with the IT department and provides special treatment as the IT department is always willing to act as a beta-test site. The company also engages with the software vendors as codeveloper for new, business-specific modules. The measures of success seem to be straightforward: it is about shortening implementation cycles while having a good match between the new implementation and the functional requirements of the business. Despite the clear business case, often discussions flare up during the design phase. The software vendor is pushing for the use of standards, to make sure it can resell the codeveloped software to a broader audience. The IT department usually proposes innovative technologies to go the extra mile.

Where the relationship with the software vendor is based on joint value, the relationship with the Internet provider is much more transactional. There is a service-level agreement that provides clear commitments on availability, scalability, and performance to run the Web-based applications in the field. There is not much discussion between the Internet provider and the company, except with regard to the cost. Both parties agree that security is of the highest importance. But whereas the Internet provider sees that as an area where it can charge a premium on top of the standard service, the IT department feels such security should be a basic service included in the price. Although the Internet provider claims it provides transparency by introducing various pricing levels based on completeness of service, the cost-saving mentality of the IT department leads to the feeling that the IT department should switch to another provider that provides a complete package for a single price.

The relationship between the IT department and users is somewhat complex. The IT department services both the front office as well as the back office. The back office users are looking for reliable, fast solutions so that IT is not a bottleneck and everyone can go home at 5 p.m. Although the front office users want the same reliability, they also want much more IT know-how. Users want support of all kinds, from hand-held devices on which to receive information to the ablility to buy their favorite brand notebooks that could simply be connected to the corporate network. Both the users and IT agree on how to measure the reliability of the service, but this does not drive customer satisfaction very much. The front office requires more flexibility.

Despite clarity on performance indicators and policies, the example of the IT department shows that the *intentions* are equally as important as the *results*. Different stakeholders have different intentions. And this starts within the IT department, between development and operations. Even with the right performance indicators in place, it will be a struggle because both parts of IT have fundamentally different beliefs and different cultures. Understanding the IT department's performance network creates a picture that can be used as a basis for the right discussions. Natural behaviors will be better understood, leading to stakeholder alignment, and a more optimized value chain.

Case Study 3: Athletixx Sportshoes

Performance networks are not static. Partners come and go, based on new innovations and collaborations. Market dynamics change, affecting the power of the various stakeholders. Because of fluctuations in the economy, buyers' markets may change into sellers' markets or new business models, and intermediaries need to reinvent themselves. Athletixx Sportshoes (another fictitious name) shows the impact of changing market dynamics on the performance network.

Athletixx Sports is a global brand of footwear and sportswear. It started as a brand specifically for soccer players, but it is now active in many different sports. The company sponsors a rock band, and many of the fans want to wear the same sneakers and shirts. The company was very traditionally organized and operated a traditional performance network (see Figure 12.7). (In reality the performance network also includes other stakeholders such as regulators and activist groups, but this is a simplified example. The numbers in the figure show where the process starts at step 1 and how it consequently flows). Athletixx works with contract manufacturers; they are supplied with the designs and have to produce the products in high quantities to cater to the various

Figure 12.7

Athletixx Footwear's Performance Network

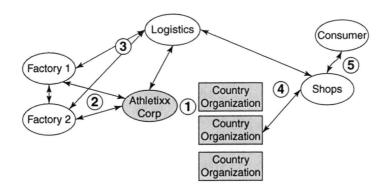

markets. When needed, the contract manufacturers also jump in for each other. Athletixx has a global contract with a large logistics firm to ship all produced goods worldwide. Athletixx sells through different retail chains in the countries where it is active and doesn't really interact with customers directly. In each of those countries, Athletixx has a "country organization," an office that manages the contracts with the local retail chains and also helps design a country-specific collection. In different countries different colors and styles are fashionable.

A new business initiative significantly changed Athletixx's view of the world. Athletixx introduced a service where customers, through a Web site or a kiosk in the shop, could design their own shoes or shirts. Different colors, different materials, different design elements can be combined. Customers can even upload their own text or logo, which will be placed on the side of the shoes. Customers can also design their own apparel. Customers can choose from the many different types of shirts, deciding between various prints and colors.

Athletixx has introduced a mass customization business model, next to the traditional mass production business model it has had for many years. The popularity of the service is enormous and a growing percentage of revenue and growth comes from the new service. The performance network of the firm has changed dramatically, as shown in Figure 12.8 (the numbers show the flow of the process in the performance network).

The dynamic between the various stakeholders has totally changed. The role of the country organizations has been greatly diminished;

Figure 12.8

New Performance Network for Athletixx Footwear

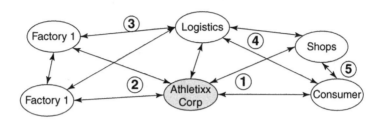

customers design their own personal product, and there is no need to assemble a season's collection. New elements and colors can be added, but this is done centrally; there is no need to filter out all possible combinations into a small set of products to be produced in large quantities. This dramatically changes the way Athletixx works with its contract manufacturers.

Instead of a relatively off-line relationship, where there is a contract to manufacture a previously planned number of shoes, there needs to be tight systems integration between Athletixx's design systems and the manufacturing systems. The manufacturing processes needs to be redesigned, and logistics processes need to be revamped; the average size of parcels being shipped becomes a lot smaller and the shipping process needs to be more precisely planned for efficiency. Every order needs to be completed and delivered within seven working days. A new operational excellence model emerges, not based on squeezing costs by economies of scale, but based on tight integration between the stakeholders. In the old situation, the most important metrics would be growth and revenue, to produce the economies of scale.

The model has changed from a single order of large quantities to a large number of orders for a quantity of one or a few; therefore, it is contribution margin or profitability that becomes the primary driver, to make sure every order (of which the product characteristics are unpredictable) is profitable. Planning cannot take place anymore based on capacity, it has to be totally demand driven. Seasonal plans are replaced with a continuous monitoring process. The role of the customer changes dramatically too. The first buyers' collectives have been identified already, bargaining for a better price or an even higher degree of customization, if an entire sports club or student organization is to be outfitted in shoes with a specific logo.

The key success factor for Athletixx moves from the quality of the product—people testing if the shoes fit well, to brand trust. Is Athletixx a brand one would trust to buy shoes from without having seen them in person first? Is the brand so powerful that people buy a personalized pair of shoes just because their peers have them too?

That leaves the question of transparency. It is clear that the new performance network can only work if there is a high degree of transparency between Athletixx and its business partners in manufacturing, logistics, and the shops, to make sure there is a seamless customer experience. It remains to be seen how high the transparency toward the customer is. Athletixx is a brand with a certain brand value, which means it can, and should, ask for a premium. On the other hand, different customers have different expectations and spending power. As a consequence Athletixx will introduce a few price categories between which customers can choose. The choices in product design by the customer will be restricted to what remains profitable within that price category.

Given the high level of uniqueness of the design, the business model is bound to attract competition that offers "white-label footwear" to be customized. White labels do not have the brand value Athletixx has, and they will have to compete on price. Most likely, the competition will choose a high-transparency business model. As with pizza toppings, customers are charged a basic price, and during the design process the additional cost of every step will be shown, so that the customer can exactly balance price and level of customization.

The best way for Athletixx to respond to competition is to create a community of intermediaries, each representing their own brand or lifestyle. Athletixx products can be tailored and cobranded to appeal to many different customer segments.

Alignment

All stakeholders—business partners, shareholders, governmental agencies, unions, customers, and employees in the performance network— are interdependent and need each other to be successful. The interesting turn that the debate on social issues takes here is that the social dimension is not about environmental issues and people's rights anymore as a boundary condition or even as a competitive differentiator, but about the fundamental core business model: collaborating with stakeholders to get something done, to innovate, to add value for the customer, to be profitable in the first place. The values dimension guides us in picking the right partners and other stakeholders.

The idea of the performance network as a means to optimize the performance of the organization enables organizational alignment. Alignment is the extent to which the self, the self-perception, and the external perception of the organization match. When you think about your business model in terms of a network of stakeholders, the circle of control and influence that you have immediately becomes bigger. A large part of what used to be "external perception," as organizations traditionally focused on their own performance optimization, now becomes "self-perception" as well.

The contributions of the stakeholders are part of the organization and its strategies too. When the relationships between various stakeholders become deeper and grow from a transactional to an added-value relationship or even a joint relationship, where appropriate of course, the self and the self-perception of the network align as well. We are discussing not only the objectives themselves, but also what motivates us in achieving them, what we expect of ourselves and of our stakeholders, what stakeholders can achieve for us, and what we can achieve for our stakeholders. This in the end leads to trust. Transparency is the major driver in achieving that alignment.

Alignment doesn't happen by itself. Organizations that realize they are part of a performance network and see the interdependency between the various stakeholders typically have relationship managers in place. Relationship managers, not procurement officers or account managers, are responsible for the overall relationship with a certain group of stakeholders. Large organizations often depend heavily on a few IT suppliers, if IT services are outsourced. Or they depend heavily on a financial shared services center. Or they cannot manufacture products without tight integration with a few business partners that deliver preassembled parts.

It is the task of the relationship manager to make the relationship and the collaboration successful. The relationship manager needs to make sure the stakeholders are successful, realizing that this is the key to making the manager's own organization successful. The relationship manager reconciles the conflicting requirements between account managers and procurement officers, who each have a clear business domain goal. The sales manager needs to fight for margin; the procurement officer for a low as possible price and favorable delivery terms. The relationship manager realizes that the business partner needs to have a fair profit and that it is in the best interest of both for the business partner to grow. The success of the relationship contributes to the profit of the organization.

Measurement drives behavior. If you have or desire an added-value or joint-value relationship, but you put a transactional service level agreement in place, you will experience dysfunctional behaviors. People fall back on transactional behavior. Conversely, if you desire a more strategic relationship with a stakeholder, it may help to turn to progressive performance indicators, to start driving the more strategic behaviors.

Call to Action

Given specific stakeholder dynamics, performance networks will look different in various industries, and even for different companies within a certain industry. Industries have different maturity levels, and organizations have different strategies. In the following chapters, I will describe typical performance networks for insurance, retail, and telecom. However, every organization has a performance network.

Identify your stakeholder relationships and for each relationship determine the current level as well as the desired level of relationship. Although transactional relationships are scalable (because they can be repeated for every single customer) and can be very profitable, they are becoming increasingly less competitive. See where added-value or joint-value relationships build more competitive differentiation and advantage.

Start designing your performance management initiative around your stakeholder contributions—what do they have to offer in addition to your own performance improvements? Remember that this question may only be asked if you are prepared to ask the opposite question as well—what do you contribute to your stakeholder's performance?

If you manage added-value or joint-value relationships using transactional performance indicators, you will have to deal with dysfunctional behaviors by both parties. Implement performance indicators that reflect the current as well as desired nature of the relationships to drive behaviors toward an improved and more profitable relationship.

Chapter | 13

THE INSURANCE PERFORMANCE NETWORK

There are worse things in life than death. Have you ever spent an evening with an insurance salesman?
—Woody Allen

Trends in Insurance: Multistakeholder Collaboration

Insurance is often regarded as a dull industry, but from a business model perspective nothing could be further from the truth. The health of the collective insurance industry has a material impact on society, and as such, the industry is highly regulated. Also, in delivering the insurance product itself, multiple parties are involved. Risks are reinsured with other insurance companies. In many countries, there is a trend not to reward claims with cash, but "in kind." For instance, insurance companies replace or repair the damaged, broken, or stolen insured goods instead of paying out money. Insurance becomes a mass customization product. With some insurance companies, customers can go online, tailor the exact coverage they wish from a large number of categories, and buy the insurance on the spot. At the same time, insurers still control their business in a very hierarchic way, instead of optimizing their performance network.

Figure 13.1 shows a typical performance network of an insurance company.

Figure 13.1

A Typical Insurance Performance Network

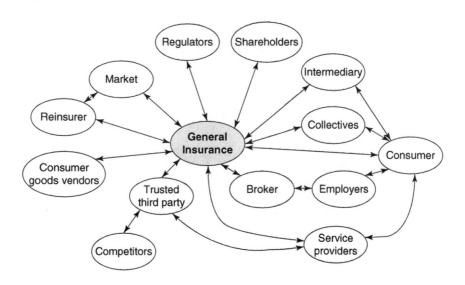

I will primarily focus on the insurance performance network "downstream," given the high dynamic that insurance business models show in the channels to reach the customers. This doesn't mean the performance network doesn't stretch upstream: How an insurance company reinsures its risks, works with other financial institutions, and relates to its shareholders and regulators. For practical reasons, in this chapter, I will focus on general insurance, such as fire insurance, travel insurance, and health insurance.

Managing Channel Stakeholders

In order to manage this performance network for each of the stakeholders in the performance network, we need to have an understanding of the following:

- The nature of the relationship between the stakeholders
- Which level of transparency is needed to be able to collaborate
- Which reciprocal metrics are needed to manage the relationship
- The trust between the stakeholders in order to form a single value proposition

Selling insurance, until recently, was a relatively straightforward process. Based on actuarial calculations, insurance companies designed a few products per insurance category and either sold those products to consumers via intermediaries or through a direct channel (direct writing). Most of the relationships were very transactional, as many intermediaries are independent and work with multiple insurance companies. The trust levels within the performance network were usually based on contractual trust: the conviction that both parties would deliver what was promised, based on a minimal exchange of information. Communication would be about product information, transaction status, and commission. In many cases, to protect their domain, the intermediaries did not even share all customer data. Today this process looks very different.

Intermediaries

Insurance companies have invested heavily in building tighter relationships with intermediaries, particularly by sharing information. Intermediaries can make use of information systems developed by insurance companies to guide customers through more complex products. Insurance companies allow intermediaries to do professional direct marketing under the intermediaries' label, using the "marketing machine" of the insurance company. Also, insurance companies allow intermediaries to access administrative systems directly, eliminating paper-based processes and speeding up the underwriting, claim, and renewal processes. These are all examples of how insurance companies have moved away from transactional relationships and toward added-value relationships. This also requires a different kind of trust: competence trust, where the intermediary should have faith in the insurance company's ability to run a professional direct-marketing campaign or allow the insurance company in any other way within its business processes.

Brokers

New channels and different value propositions have emerged. For instance, usually through brokers, insurances are sold to human resource departments as part of the employer's compensation packages offered to employees. The HR department outsources the insurance part of the employee benefits program to the broker and insurance company. "Employee benefits" programs are a completely new value proposition for insurance companies, offered through a new channel. Without brokers with professional account managers, many insurance companies would have trouble building up such a sales process. Together with the brokers, a joint-value relationship is built. There is no such thing as a strict supplier/customer relationship; both parties go to market together. This requires goodwill trust that is based on shared values and go-to-market strategies.

Service Providers

Another type of joint-value relationship comes from working with "service providers." In many cases, claims are not paid out in cash. Instead of cash payments, insurance companies have built networks of service providers that "fix the problem." Think of car repair shops or craftsmen that can repair damage to the house. It is in the best interest of the service providers to move away from a potential transactional relationship and create an added-value relationship, where the switching costs for the insurance company would be higher. In order to build up a provider preference, service providers need to look for ways to adapt to and integrate with the systems and processes of the insurance companies they work for, particularly something the larger chains are able to achieve.

Some initiatives are bigger than one insurance company can achieve. The major cost of general insurance is in claims. As it is a price-sensitive business, the best bet on how to bring costs down is in trying to decrease claim size. Whereas a single insurance company would have trouble imposing a single process and systems standard, as well as single pricing for car repair shops, for example, a group of insurance companies with a collective dominant market share can. In one case, the third party is financed partly by the contributing insurance companies that also each appoint a member of the board. Car repair shops, a total of 600, each pay a membership fee. They receive all the business from the insurance companies, but need to adopt the standard processes, systems, and prices. Insurance companies can benchmark their average claim (per car brand, driver age class, geography, cause of damage, and a variety of other angles) against the best-of-class and average-in-class of all contributing insurance companies. The trusted third party represents the joint-value relationship between the insurance companies based on goodwill trust. In order to enable that, the board, consisting of managers of each participating insurance company, is an important governance structure. Collaboration, even with competitors, is an important means of innovation in the insurance market.

Consumers

Some insurance companies allow their customers to build their own specific coverage, based on various product components, into a single unique policy with a single unique price, much like a "mass customization" process that can be found in the automotive industry. Direct writing, a process that has existed for many years, where customers deal with the insurance company directly without going through an intermediary, is now an entirely different process. The insurer needs to move from product sales to a framework in which various product components can be combined, overseeing risk factors and legal issues. You could even think of virtual insurance companies, combining product components from multiple insurers, creating unique packages.

Building the Performance Network

Insurance performance management and its networked business model should be better aligned. The current misalignment between performance management and the business model leads to suboptimization, which is particularly impactful in a low-margin business such as general insurance. Therefore, actively seeking opportunities to evaluate how an insurance company's stakeholders could contribute more to the performance has much greater leverage than focusing on the insurer's performance optimization. Also, the performance network supports the business model. Implementing the performance network will drive the insurer's management toward a more outward-looking and collaborative mindset, leading to more innovation and a competitive advantage. In this case, the performance network drives the further development of the business model.

Table 13.1 shows an overview of reciprocal performance indicators between an insurance company and its intermediaries, brokers, and

Table 13.1

Reciprocal Metrics for the Insurance Industry

	Transactional Relationship	Added-Value Relationship	Joint-Value Relationship
	Insurer Requirements from Channel		
Profit	• Shareholder value • Profitability • Commissions paid	• Incremental cost of customization • Channel margin	• Revenue and profit joint initiative as percentage of overall revenue and profit • Profit benchmark against internal profit
Growth	• Market share • Customer retention • Percent conversion	• Share of channel wallet • Percent of product portfolio customized	• Percent transactions going through new process • New market growth
Opinion	• Customer satisfaction	• Qualitative feedback from channel "council" • Continuous operational feedback	• Continuous operational feedback • Continuous management feedback
Trust	• Market share • Cross-sell ratio • Customer retention	• Channel process coverage	• Growth in investment in joint initiative • Brand trust
	Insurer Contributions to Channel		
Fast	• Average time underwriting • Average time claim processing • Average time policy renewal	• Average time lead-to-policy • Average time accident-to-claim-closed	• Time to market • Time decision-making process
Right	• Percent transactions "first time right" • Data quality	• Meeting partner requirements through customization	• Revenue growth • Brand preference
Cheap	• Benchmark policy premiums	• Cost savings in channel • Added opportunity in channel	• Joint customer benefits • Joint process TCO
Easy	• Call center, Web, account manager availability	• Channel preference	• Crossover resources (capital, staff, material, use of facilities, information exchange)

service providers—its "channels." The performance indicators for the three different types of relationships are listed. In added-value or joint-value relationships, managing the transactional elements of the relationship is still important. The stakeholder contributions and requirements are based on the performance prism methodology discussed in Chapter 12.

Managing Transactional Relationships

Insurers cannot rely on their traditional performance indicators. Even within transactional relationships, reciprocal metrics are important. An insurance company's set of measures to see what it adds to its channel partner's requirements is mostly process oriented. It needs to have a short average time for critical processes such as underwriting new policies, renewals, and claims, as these are primary drivers for customer satisfaction within the insurance industry. A claim that is accepted after six months will still lead to low customer satisfaction; it places the channel partner in a defensive position too. At the same time, a rejected claim that is processed really quickly has a limited effect on customer satisfaction.

Not only do these processes need to be efficient, they also need to be of high quality. The insurer should have metrics in place to track data quality and the percentage of transactions that are completed without any rework. From a marketing point of view, it is wise to compare policy premiums with the competition and track this. In a price-sensitive business such as insurance, and within transactional relationships that have low switching costs, it is easy to switch to a different insurance company. Lastly, to make sure it is easy to do business with the insurance company, the different ways to communicate with its channel, such as the call center, the Web, and its account managers should be easily available.

In addition, there should be some transparency between the insurance company and its channel partners. In transactional relationships information exchange is fairly operational. It consists of limited customer information, because the intermediary owns the customer data; the status information on claims, policies, and renewals; and straightforward management information on intermediary commissions. Although steering on commissions is enough for the revenue side of the business, higher levels of relationships are needed to manage the cost of claims. Within transactional relationships, there is no incentive for intermediaries to drive down claim size.

Managing Added-Value Relationships

For added-value relationships different performance indicators are needed. Insurers can add value by opening up and adapting their processes for the channel partners. Think of decision support systems that help channel partners sell the right insurance or allow channel partners to use the insurer's direct-marketing capabilities under their own names and labels.

Insurers obviously need to measure the costs of these special systems and processes, and weigh these against the competitive benefits and margins. Particularly when processes need to be customized for specific channel partners, it becomes important to measure the incremental costs of customization. The results of embedded or adapted processes should be measured in terms of "share of channel wallet." In other words, how much of the portfolio of the channel partner is trusted to the insurer, because of the convenience of the embedded or adapted processes. Also, on a more qualitative level, customer satisfaction surveys do not suffice; a council of its channel partners is needed to give more strategic feedback.

Channel partners have requirements as well. It is important for the insurer to track those in order to keep the right focus on the relationship. The measures to track how the channel partner requirements are met are again very process oriented, but aimed at the complete process, not just the insurer's part. For instance, what is the average time in the lead-to-policy process or the accident-to-claim-closed process? These processes start with the customer, go through the channel partner, move to the insurer, return to the channel partner, and end with the customer again, involving possibly multiple customer contact moments, using multiple customer contact channels, such as the Web, call center, and channel partner itself.

Particularly in the case of adapting an insurer's processes for the specific purposes of a channel partner, the end result should be measured in terms of cost savings for the channel partner, or in the monetary value of additional opportunities generated. The measure of success for the channel partner, showing the ease of use in doing business with the insurer, is the same as the measure of success of the insurer itself: the channel preference leading to a higher share of channel wallet.

As in every relationship, there needs to be transparency between the insurance company and its channel partners. In addition to transactional information, there should be an information supply that helps the channel partner to evaluate the business relationship with the insurer, or even better, that helps the channel partner in its own business. For instance, think of benchmark information that allows the channel partner to benchmark itself against its peers. The insurer has all the information from all the parties it works with in a certain channel — such as the intermediaries — and can provide additional value by comparing each specific intermediary with its peers within a certain region and of a certain type (such as small, medium, or large). Also, both parties may exchange operational information on marketing campaigns that the insurer ran for the channel partner. Think of follow-up lists, response rates, or conversion rates. Lastly, of course, the insurer needs to supply management information about the costs it saved for the channel partner and the opportunities it generated.

Managing Joint-Value Relationships

In joint-value relationships, the insurer and one or more channel partners work together to create a joint-value proposition and bring it to the market. Whereas in transactional and added-value relationships each party has its own objectives, within a joint-value relationship they have the same objectives. This means each participating party should have a full set of management information, similar to what it would demand within each organization.

The bottom-line metric for joint-value relationships is obviously profitability; however, each of the parties should compare the joint profitability with his or her own. The joint-value relationship may be profitable, but may not bring the same percentage of return. Or it may bring more, and the partnership could be extended. It is also important to measure the percentage of revenue and profit that the joint initiative brings to the overall result. The initiative should be material, but if it has too much impact, perhaps a different relationship is needed, such as a merger or acquisition.

Insurers should measure growth by measuring what percentage of overall transactions goes through the new process, and should also measure the growth of any new market or new business model created with the joint innovation. Think of the collaboration between different insurers to create a network for car repair shops, to create a new value proposition. As with any relationship, feedback between the parties is needed. Within such a close collaboration, this is done best by having a process for continuous operational and strategic feedback. The trusted third party that runs the insurer's network has its own brand; it is necessary to measure the brand value and the brand trust of the initiative.

Although the parties share the same objectives toward their mutual customers, insured people, they also have requirements toward each other. Collaboration needs to be fast, right, efficient, and easy. Particularly in joint-value relationships, collaborative processes should be designed very explicitly. For instance, insurers should evaluate their contribution to a fast time-to-market, and they should track the time needed to make strategic decisions through their joint management channels. If they do this right, market share and brand preference are the bottom-line indicators. Lastly, insurers should track how much each contributes to the joint initiative in terms of management attention and skills. Ideally, it should be as easy to deploy resources within the joint initiative as within the insurance company itself.

Chapter | 14

SUPERMARKET PERFORMANCE NETWORK

Recently I wanted to buy a very well-known soft drink in the supermarket where I usually shop. Instead of bottles, there was a letter hanging on the shelf. The letter explained that since the soft drink producer had drastically increased the price of the product, the supermarket decided to stop offering the product for the time being. The note further advised buying a different brand.

Stakeholder Dynamics in Supermarkets

Supermarkets and general stores offer perishable and nonperishable goods, and they focus on offering a wide variety of brands—in other words, "one-stop-shopping." Turnover speed needs to be very high; margins tend to be low and are driven by optimizing the supply chain. Supply chains in retail can be either plan-driven or event-driven. In plan-driven environments, all parties plan distribution based on the availability of products, anticipated demand, and an optimized distribution plan. The opposite approach is called event-driven. Based on buying patterns, new products are ordered and distributed in a just-in-time fashion.

Supermarkets need to have an iron discipline in logistics and an operational excellence strategy for their supply chain in order to compete effectively on quality and cost. Many business functions are involved, some may be outsourced and others belong to the supermarket's organization. Individual supermarkets may be owned by

Figure 14.1

An Example of a Supermarket Performance Network

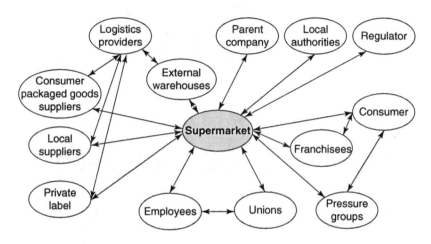

franchise holders and many transportation tasks might be outsourced to logistics providers. There are many, many different suppliers.

However, management information is still very inward focused, and procurement and logistics departments still operate very separately from each other, leaving opportunities for value-chain integration or further innovation unused.

Stakeholders for a supermarket include the many suppliers, logistics service providers, external warehouses, local authorities (e.g., for location planning), customers, pressure groups (e.g., lobbying for social responsibility, healthy products, or other causes), employees, unions, parent company, and regulators. Figure 14.1 shows a typical performance network for a supermarket. I will focus on the relationships between a supermarket and the different types of suppliers it has.

Managing Supplier Relationships

In order to manage a retail performance network, we need to have an understanding of the following for each stakeholder:

- The nature of the relationship between the stakeholders
- Which level of transparency is needed to be able to collaborate
- Which reciprocal metrics are needed to manage the relationship
- The trust between the stakeholders in order to form a single value proposition

Consumer Packaged Goods (CPG) Suppliers

Full-service supermarkets cannot afford not to carry the A brands in their assortment. At the same time, distribution, pricing, promotions, and eye-height shelf space compared to their competitors is crucial for the CPG suppliers. Sometimes this power balance is disturbed. For instance, if supermarkets start a price war and try to recover part of the loss of margin from the CPG suppliers or if private labels come close in quality to CPG trademarks. CPG suppliers and super-markets often have a very transactional relationship, focusing on price and quantities for special promotions. The relationship is primarily based on contractual trust, or, in order words, basic ethical behavior.

At the same time, the relationship between CPG suppliers and the supermarket has one important characteristic of an added-value relationship: value-chain integration. The large brands are delivered on a continuous basis to the distribution centers of the supermarket based on online sales and stock information. For some brands, the suppliers even manage their shelf space in the individual supermarkets themselves, a concept called *rack jobbing*. However, within this transactional relationship value-chain integration is simply needed to deal with the large volume of products being delivered on a daily basis, not a better relationship per se.

If both stakeholders are happy with the relationship, there is no need to change. However, from the supermarket perspective, there are ways to intensify the relationship. For instance, there are examples of relationships where a retailer and a few strategic suppliers discuss their mutual margins, creating a deeper level of transparency. The retailer understands that by leaving more margin for the supplier in the price negotiation process, the supplier is able to invest in a process and information exchange to improve the logistical process, leading to cost savings far beyond the savings achieved by squeezing more margin out of the supplier. In this case the supplier has an added-value relationship with the supermarket.

Supermarkets should also consider sharing point-of-sale (cash register data) analysis. Consumer packaged goods (CPG) suppliers can save some money on the data they obtain from the market research agencies. But more important, supermarkets can share sociodemographic information with CPG suppliers, where their products are sold for local marketing purposes, and also buying patterns throughout the week, for media advertising reasons.

Local Suppliers

Often supermarkets make use of local suppliers for nonbranded perishable products such as vegetables, bread, and dairy products, or for specific local brands connected with local traditional foods. As their products do not really have a brand value, the supermarket can easily switch to another supplier that offers a comparable quality for a lower price. It is in the local supplier's best interest to create an added-value relationship by investing in logistical and administrative value-chain integration.

It can be a competitive advantage for local suppliers to be very transparent in the production process of the goods they deliver, in terms of the ingredients or materials used, or the food preparation techniques. This helps to build competence trust, and allows supermarkets to be confident that they are selling healthy foods and environmentally friendly products.

Also, it is important for local suppliers to invest in integration with the supermarket, for order receipt, invoicing, and tracking and tracing. Putting an electronic tag on every product aligns the supply chain so that it has almost perfect real-time information, very much like the just-in-time delivery mechanism in the automotive industry. An aligned supply chain is a large driver of supermarket profitability.

Private Label Suppliers

Having their own brand, or private label, is of paramount importance to many supermarkets. The margin on private label products is bigger, and they also have strategic importance in changing the power dynamic to the CGP suppliers. If the supermarket's name is an A brand, it can develop its private label to have a certain brand value as well.

Supermarkets can have all types of relationships with the private label suppliers. Sometimes these suppliers deliver a standard product, with standard packaging, that has space for the label of the supermarket. This represents a classic transactional relationship. Sometimes packaging can be codeveloped, so that it matches the brand experience of the supermarket. This would be an added-value relationship from the private-label supplier point of view. One way to evolve the private label into a joint-value relationship is to develop completely new products, exclusively available under the private label, such as a line of low-calorie fresh ready-made meals. In joint-value relationships, ideally there is no customer/supplier relationship, but all stakeholders involved create a new product or service that none of them could have created alone.

Building the Performance Network

Retail, despite the impact of the Internet and all forms of e-business, is a very traditional industry. It is very product- and bulk-transaction oriented. Supermarkets are used to being the spider in the web, and have no problem displaying their power during price negotiations. However, the variety of relationships is increasing, and a supermarket's performance management needs to display that. Table 14.1 shows an overview of reciprocal performance indicators between a supermarket and its suppliers. In added-value or joint-value relationships, managing the transactional elements of the relationship is still important. The

Table 14.1

Reciprocal Metrics in the Supermarket Performance Network

	Transactional Relationship	Added-Value Relationship	Joint-Value Relationship
	Supermarket Requirements from Supplier		
Fast	• Replenishment frequency • Order-to-replenishment wait time	• Time to respond to required changes	• Time-to-market new products • Time for intercompany decision-making processes
Right	• OTIF (on time, in full) • Quality of shipment, % deliveries accepted • % orders accepted first time	• Percentage of first-time-right transactions through integrated process • Fit of product in overall brand experience • Quality of information on ingredients	• Market share • Brand preference

(continued)

Table 14.1 (Continued)

	Transactional Relationship	Added-Value Relationship	Joint-Value Relationship
	Supermarket Requirements from Supplier		
Cheap	• Margin • Price flexibility for promotions	• Cost savings through value chain integration	• Price difference with CPG brands
Easy	• Customer service responsiveness	• Level of logistical and administrative integration	• Crossover resources
	Supermarket Contributions to Supplier		
Profit		• Fair profit	• Revenue and margin joint initiative as % of overall revenue and profit in product category • Margin benchmark against CPG margins
Growth		• Percentage of revenue of supplier within product category	• Percentage of growth of revenue within product category
Opinion		• Supermarket satisfaction • Support calls on integrated processes	• Continuous operational feedback • Continuous management feedback
Trust		• Growth of using added value services • Growth of revenue within product category	• Growth in investment in joint initiative • Brand reputation/ value

stakeholder contributions and requirements are based on the performance prism methodology discussed in Chapter 12.

Managing Transactional Relationships

The metrics for managing transactional relationships with suppliers are very traditional. The speed of service (fast) is measured in terms of replenishment frequency—in other words, how many times per week or per day new products can be delivered. It is also important that the time between ordering new products and delivery is very short. The higher the frequency and the shorter the order time, the more demand-driven the value chain can be, making use of minimal stock levels. The standard metric for the quality of shipments (right) is OTIF (short for "on time, in full"). This is very much connected to being fast, in order to run an efficient demand-driven value chain. But there is more to the quality of an order than being complete and on time. Particularly with perishable products; factors such as the temperature of products are vital as well. Products should also not be damaged. If there is a continuous stream of orders, the supplier should not make many mistakes in receiving and handling the orders. Supermarkets need to have high turnover, as they have small margins. Next in importance only to the speed of the relationships and the quality of transactions, price negotiations should focus on margin. However, this should not be done only for day-to-day replenishments, but also for special promotions. For instance, the supplier should be willing to fund promotions. Lastly, it should be easy to do business. If there is a continuous stream of orders, there should be a customer service desk, or an account manager, or what is sometimes called a *flow manager* available, especially, during off-hours.

In other types of relationships the set of metrics is reciprocal in that both supplier performance and its requirements are taken into account. However, in transactional relationships there is not much incentive to take this into account. Supermarkets typically are not concerned about the profitability of their suppliers or their growth. They are, however, willing to provide their opinion, especially if there are problems. Other than on a contractual level, trust doesn't seem to be a strategic theme. That is why the column in Table 14.1 for supermarket contributions to suppliers for transactional relationships is left empty.

Managing Added-Value Relationships

In added-value relationships, relations are strengthened typically by additional services. Suppliers can offer special packaging for private label products, integrate with logistical and administrative processes, or provide extensive information on product origin, ingredients, or how the item is prepared. The quality of the added-value relationship can be measured in terms of how well those adaptations are done. How many transactions go through an integrated logistical or administrative process successfully in the first pass? How well do the possibilities for special packaging fit in with the brand experience of the supermarket? How extensive (and correct) is the information about the products? And in general, how fast is the supplier at responding to required changes to packaging, processes, and information supply?

In transactional relationships from a financial point of view, margin is key. In added-value relationships there should also be a focus on realized cost savings through value-chain integration. The more a supplier is capable of doing that, the more valuable the supplier becomes, and the easier it is to do business with that supplier. This should be a trade-off in contract negotiations. Metrics in added-value relationships should be reciprocal; the supermarket should also consider the requirements of the supplier. As in added-value relationships, the switching costs tend to be higher, and a good relationship is also in the best interest of the supermarket. If a supplier makes a fair profit, it can invest more in product innovation, value-chain integration, customer service, and other areas that improve the quality of the supplier, leading to cost savings potentially much higher than a slightly better margin through tougher contract negotiations.

It is the objective of the supplier to grow its revenue, and the supermarket should monitor this growth. It is helpful to support the growth of the supplier because both parties benefit if this is based on mutual growth of the product category. However, if growth is based on the substitution of other suppliers within that product category, this could be a problem. If this is happening marketwide, the supermarket is simply following market trends in its portfolio. If substitution is a targeted action, the supermarket should be careful as it impacts the supermarket's formula. The supplier is also interested in the supermarket's opinion, and it is in the best interest of both for the supermarket to build such an opinion in a more strategic way. It is not enough to air opinions only if there are operational problems. The themes in the relationship with the supplier (fast, right, cheap, easy) impact the transaction cost of working with that supplier, impacting overall margin. Proactively sharing opinion on satisfaction, and guiding the supplier on how to do a better job, improves the relationship.

It is not only important for a supermarket to build contractual and competence trust in the supplier, the supermarket should also focus on being a trustworthy customer. Being a trusted customer lowers the transaction costs of doing business, as the supplier feels comfortable with less stringent monitoring systems, payment agreements, and other control processes. These lower transaction costs translate into a higher margin.

Managing Joint-Value Relationships

In joint-value relationships, there is no strict customer/supplier dynamic anymore. Both partners contribute unique characteristics to codevelop products to a mutual set of customers. Particularly with private labels, there is an opportunity to cocreate a unique supermarket label with products that are not sold elsewhere, effectively lifting a supermarket label to an A-brand level. Both partners, of course, measure profit of the joint initiative. From the supermarket's point of view, the profit margin should be compared to the margin on other products, and other suppliers, to optimize the margin of the overall portfolio. The more successful the partners are with building the private label, the higher the margin created by asking A-brand prices.

A true measure of success is revenue growth within the product category. The private label should substitute for unbranded or lesser-known brands, and grow its market share within the particular product group. If the private label introduces a completely new product, that has no alternative, it is a product group by itself, with 100 percent market share. Less market share and other brands entering the market are good things. They are a validation of the strategy, and all brands collectively grow the overall market.

Next to profit and growth, the partners seek each other's opinion and trust. Opinion is not based on customer satisfaction surveys, or any other once-in-a-while initiative. Opinions are shared continuously on an operational level, with people working together on a daily basis, as well as on a managerial level, as a continuous theme through combined management meetings. Trust grows from contractual trust to goodwill or relationship trust, in which the partners feel that each would make the right decisions while representing the joint initiative.

Of course both partners have relationship requirements as well, and the interaction needs to be fast, right, and easy, and the price needs to be right. Fast interaction leads to a low time to market, and a short time for interorganizational decision-making processes, ideally as efficient as within an organization's own hierarchic structures. Getting it "right" is measured by joint success in the market, with a good market share, and by building brand preference.

The economics need to be right too. The margin should be higher than CPG-supplied brands, but, more important, in a joint-value relationship, the price for the end consumer needs to be right, typically lower than a CPG brand. Although in added-value relationships ease of doing business is measured in terms of value-chain integration, in joint-value relationships the bar is raised again. Within a partnership there should be an easy crossover of resources. The more capital, staff, material, use of facilities, and information exchange that cross organizational borders, the more depth and meaning the relationship has.

Chapter | 15

TELECOM PERFORMANCE NETWORK

Mr. Watson, come here, I want to see you.
First phone call of Alexander Graham Bell, inventor of the
telephone (1876)

Market Dynamics in Telecom

The telecomunications market has gone through a profound transformation. In almost nothing does it resemble the market of 15 or 20 years ago. In many countries, the telecom business did consist of large state-owned (regional) monopolies managing landlines. The business model largely consisted of two sources of income: subscriptions and selling minutes of phone time. In most countries telecoms are now privatized, public companies, listed on the stock exchanges. The shift was needed to encourage competition and to create more efficient organizations, offering better prices for their services. Many telecom companies also acquired other telecoms in other countries, in order to expand their business.

Telecoms have experienced a huge growth because of mobile telephony and digital subscriber lines (DSLs). In many countries there are now more mobile phones than inhabitants. The traditional landline business has negative growth, an increasing percentage of customers and households do not have a landline at all anymore. At the same time, new uses for the traditional landline "backbone" infrastructure has emerged, through fixed/mobile convergence, broadband, and "local loops." Competition is fierce, from direct competitors but also from unexpected angles, such as financial services firms, i.e., banks, who want to have control over business-critical infrastructure for mobile banking. Another source of competition comes from providers without an infrastructure, who just buy minutes in bulk from established telecoms and sell them at a low price to end consumers; or from cable TV providers and even electricity providers, who also have an infrastructure reaching many households, and through modern technology, offer telecommunication services using their infrastructures.

The way for telecoms to survive and to maintain margins is to offer an ever-expanding range of subscription types, ranging from prepaid offers, to a multitude of "value packs," including text messaging, data access (Internet), special rates for international calling, and discounts on special phone numbers, all based on different consumer behaviors and life styles. Although it would be in the best interest of consumers for all these subscription types to be comparable, telecoms deliberately differ enough from the competition to make sure consumers cannot choose a provider purely on price. In other words, the margins of telecoms partly exist due to the lack of transparency for their customers.

Next to expanding the capabilities of the telecom infrastructures, telecoms also aggressively enter other businesses, to compete with the firms that enter the telecom market. Almost every telecom has invested in being an Internet provider as well. And in the corporate world, telecoms increasingly compete with systems integrators by offering integrated information and communication technology (ICT) services.

One of the most interesting areas of expansion is in product and service integration, offering cable TV access as fixed-price packages to customers—"triple play": Internet, (Internet) telephone, and TV.

At the same time, within the various products and services, there is an extreme differentiation with many different types of subscriptions and marketing campaigns. In this hypercompetitive environment, execution must be flawless. In order to manage this complexity and speed of business, telecom organizations need to focus on their internal alignment, even before aligning with their external stakeholders in their performance network. Figure 15.1 shows how the internal performance network of a telecom company that offers triple play is organized into

Figure 15.1

An Example of a Telecom Performance Network

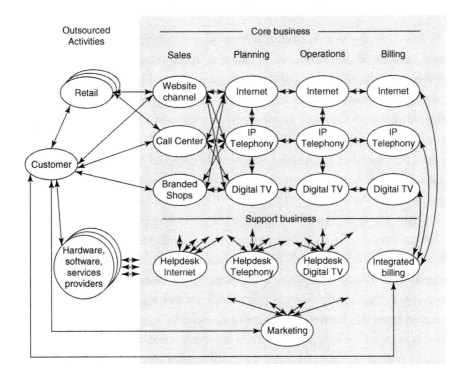

separate product divisions. Although the figure looks complex, it is a highly simplified version of reality.

Managing Internal Relationships

Traditionally, internal relationships in telecoms—and in many other divisionally oriented organizations—are rather transactional. The style of alignment is often vertical, senior management treating the divisions as a portfolio. However, with the telecom market becoming more integrated and product offerings being combined, horizontal alignment becomes more important. In order to manage the internal performance network, we need to have an understanding of the following:

- The nature of the relationship between the stakeholders
- Which level of transparency is needed to be able to collaborate

- Which reciprocal metrics are needed to manage the relationship
- The trust between the stakeholders in order to form a single value proposition that focuses on the customer

Telecoms have tons of different products, service delivery processes, and associated departments. In offering integrated telecommunication services, the various parts of the organization are highly interdependent. Many departments are involved in installing triple play. The operations departments in the back office need to program the infrastructure, and usually multiple services and service companies are involved, for the basic connection, for ADSLs (asymmetric digital subscriber lines), and for additional telecommunication equipment. This is typically not a single process.

Often every department has its own planning process. This makes it hard to coordinate a single installation, since there is a specific order of how an installation needs to take place. The order fulfillment time is negatively affected by such a process. What further complicates the service is that equipment is often sent by yet another department or comes from the hardware vendor of choice, by mail. If the wrong material is sent, or incomplete material has been sent, the service company has to return on another date. The call center needs to be called again for a next appointment. If there is a problem with the installation, each division has its own help desk. This makes taking ownership of a problem (Internet doesn't work) very hard, help desks start referring to each other. For a complete installation, customers have to fill out different forms. In addition to that, there are different billing systems; however, sometimes there is an integrated billing system, overlaying the various product-specific billing systems. All the coordination required makes a triple-play installation very error prone.

Often, when confronted with suboptimal overall results, divisions or departments invest in a more added-value relationship with each other. This translates in, for instance, internal account management offering internal customers a single person to coordinate horizontal alignment. Although this will help fix problems, it doesn't solve the issue of a fundamentally disconnected process. It will help further to connect processes by, for instance, swapping planning data between systems. However, there are still multiple systems in place. Service will still not be fast, right, easy, and cheap. The process also doesn't drive growth, optimize profit, lead to a positive customer opinion, or build trust.

Building the Performance Network

The only real solution for telecoms to offer good customer service is to define an internal performance network based on joint-value relationships. Within joint-value relationships, there are no internal customers or internal suppliers, just colleagues sharing the same goals and objectives geared toward customer service and needs, instead of their own service level agreements. Colleagues each contribute unique skills and resources to service joint customers.

The joint-value relationship defines success in terms of results for the consumer of the service. Within the joint-value relationship, there most likely still are departments and divisions, but they do not each own a part of the process. The involved departments act more as a resource pool in a process-oriented organization. The planning, fulfillment, and billing systems are not connected to the department, but to a certain product group or set of services. Where work needs to be handed over from one department to the next for the process to continue, there should be a focus on the business interface metrics as well. However, most performance indicators should be focused on the results for the joint customers, the consumers. These performance indicators should also be co-owned by the involved departments.

Table 15.1 shows an overview of reciprocal performance indicators between divisions of a telecom. The table lists which performance indicators are needed to drive and evaluate the different types of relationships. In the performance networks for insurance and retail, the types of relationships are descriptive. They are all good, as long as the choice for a certain relationship is made explicit. In managing internal relationships within the telecom industry (and other divisionally organized companies), the relationship style is normative. Transactional relationships lead to dysfunctional behavior and local optimizations; a joint-value relationship is needed to optimize the overall process. This is also the reason why the added-value relationship is missing in Table 15.1. The performance indicators in a joint-value relationship are co-owned between the two departments that are interfacing.

Table 15.1

Reciprocal Performance Metrics in the Telecom Performance Network

	Transactional Relationship	Joint-Value Relationship
Receiving Department Requirements		
Fast	• Average time per process within department • Turnaround time for queries and cross-domain processes	• Time order-to-fulfillment customer process • Average waiting time between departments • Time to market • Time to decision-making process
Right	• Internal service level agreement • Data quality	• % right first time overall products and services (external) • % perfect handover (internal) • Days-sales-outstanding
Cheap	• TCO department benchmark • On budget	• Overall process TCO • Competitive comparison • Cost from a customer perspective
Easy	• Function points per departmental process	• Function points for overall customer process • Crossover resources (capital, staff, material, use of facilities, information exchange)
Supplying Department Requirements		
Profit	• Positive result internal charging ± cost budget	• Joint profit, based on sales to consumers
Growth	• Growth of department • Growth of budget	• Revenue growth of integrated products and services
Opinion	• Annual internal customer satisfaction survey	• External customer satisfaction • Continuous internal feedback
Trust	• Not measured	• # customer referrals • Growth triple play (#, $) • Brand trust, brand preference

TCO = total cost of ownership

The table lists stakeholder contributions and requirements based on the performance prism (discussed in Chapter 12), connecting both internal and outsourced functions involved in the triple-play installation process.

In transactional internal relationships, internal coordination, or horizontal alignment, is usually done using service level agreements (SLAs). SLAs often trigger transactional behavior, and tend to focus on costs. Cost savings on a departmental and divisional level are usually achieved by optimizing economies of scale in one's own process, instead of alignment of the overall process. Also, SLAs tend to be defined in terms of the department's own processes, or the "internal customer's" processes, instead of the real customer's (the consumer's) results.

Information exchange is often very transactional of nature, such as planning details or many kinds of internal charging. Although the results for each department may look acceptable or even good, the results in terms of customer satisfaction may not be good. In general, performance indicators should not focus on department processes, but on customer processes, such as concept-to-market, lead-to-cash, and trouble-to-resolve processes.

To measure the speed of the processes ("fast"), performance indicators should shift from optimizing the planning for their own department to overall installation speed. Optimization per department leads to large batches of repetitive work or single activities, to get efficiencies of scale. This means, however, that each individual installation must wait until a complete activity batch is finished, before the installation moves to the next process step. The average time from order to fulfillment will be much longer than needed, due to long waiting times between steps. On the managerial and coordination level, speed on a transactional basis is measured by the turnaround time for every query that comes in. As important as it is, success comes from a more strategic perspective: a shorter time-to-market, and swift cross-domain decision-making processes.

On the transactional level, quality is measured based on the output of the department. Service level agreements are put in place to provide transparency to other departments. Process data quality is important to create valid reports. Within a joint-value relationship, all this is of secondary importance. The key metric is which percentage of installations is done "right first time," sometimes also referred to as the "once and done rate." No errors, no need to come back.

Internally, the coordination between departments can be improved by tracking the quality of handover moments, how many mistakes are made handing over work from one department to the other. A very tangible way of measuring the result of high (or low) quality, is tracking the days-sales-outstanding, the amount of time it takes the customer to pay the invoice. If mistakes are made or processes take too long, the customer will not (and should not be forced to) pay. This information is not only vital for the finance department, but for all departments involved in the process, including planning.

To manage cost within a transactional relationship, the only thing you can do is manage departmental budgets. And once in a while the specific process undergoes an external benchmark. Within a more collaborative, joint-value process, cost-effectiveness is measured by an overall total cost of owner ship (TCO). A competitive comparison on cost, price, and margin (estimated if there is no precise public information) has more meaning than in internal budget variance analysis.

The bottom line, however, is cost from the customer perspective. Local optimizations may lead to various service organizations visiting customers, each performing their own installation process for a specific product or service. However, the customer must be home multiple times, and may even be faced with multiple charges for at-home visits. Although this represents revenue for each product division, the key question is if this revenue is "healthy," as it represents unneeded costs for the customer. An operationally excellent triple-play installation process minimizes the customer cost.

Function-point analysis is a technique used in IT application development as well as in the automotive industry. Every activity (programming in IT, or assembly in automotive) is evaluated on its complexity and is tagged with a number of function points. The higher the complexity, the more points. Telecoms would do good to perform such analysis on complex installation processes as well, to better manage the ease of doing business. It helps to identify local optimizations, and design overall processes with lower complexity. On the managerial level, in joint-value relationships, the ease of collaboration could be measured by tracking to which extent resources such as capital, staff, materials, facilities, and information are shared and reallocated dynamically between the various departments.

In many organizations, finance professionals frown on double counting outcomes. However, in a joint-value relationship, all involved parties should be recognized for the results that are being generated, such as revenue, profit, and growth. With even a single party missing in the process, the results wouldn't be what they are. Even if it is possible to break down revenue or profit by department, division or function, this should not be attempted. Departments should be recognized for the full result that was achieved by all parties involved, in order to drive the right behavior, which is seeking ways to optimize the overall process. When outcomes are broken down by department, the usual suboptimization will start to appear again.

In transactional relationships, customer satisfaction surveys are often a once-in-a-while activity, typically reactive after informal feedback becomes hard to ignore. Projects are started to improve satisfaction, and business returns to normal. However, a transactional focus on managing the department doesn't invite managers to continuously mind customer satisfaction. Yet, this information should be continuous and driven down to the people on the work floor who interact with customers every day. External customer satisfaction surveys should be a continuous process. Within internal joint-value relationships, an internal customer satisfaction survey is not even needed. As the management teams between divisions collaborate all the time, there is a continuous stream of feedback.

Trust is usually not even relevant in transactional relationships; there is a focus on doing transactions only, not on recurring business within the organization. This is hard to understand, as departments need to work with each other every single day. However, with vertical alignment, only reporting up, there is simply not much horizontal dialogue. Trust by customers is bound to be not very high if all departments work in isolation and cannot commit to a certain customer result. The best way of measuring trust, and providing that feedback to all departments, is to measure customer referrals. If customers are happy with the service, then they feel comfortable endorsing the company to their friends (the so-called net-promoter score); this is the true measure of success

In order to reach flawless execution in a complex and fast-moving environment, joint-value relationships are required. Performance indicators focus on external results and on internal collaboration. In order to build trust, right first time, order to fulfillment time, and customer

Figure 15.2

Key Performance Indicators for Triple-Play Installations in Telecom

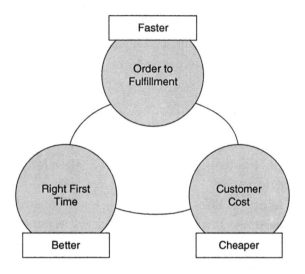

cost are crucial and key differentiators in a hypercompetitive market (see Figure 15.2).

Within the three performance indicators in Figure 15.2, the most important driver of trust is the right-first-time percentage, how many installations succeed without any mistakes. Although each department may independently achieve its service level of, say 95 percent, a combination of that service level across five departments leads to an overall score of not more than 77 percent (0.95 to the power of 5). And if only one department scores 60 percent for one month, the overall result immediately drops dramatically to 48 percent. This leads to more rework and more delays, negatively affecting the second crucial performance indicator: order fulfillment time. This is the time that it takes between a customer ordering the service and its being operational at the customer's address. Also, the need for several service people drives the cost of the service up. Every set of balanced performance indicators tracks cost, quality, and time, and a disconnected process makes a telecom score bad on all three.

CLOSING THOUGHTS

Performance comes from Venus, but management from Mars.

Before you started reading this book, performance management probably looked like a straightforward, top-down process: make sure everyone understands the corporate objectives, put plans in place, measure outcomes, and adjust where needed. And then this book discusses the next level, performance leadership, introducing among other things business interfaces, performance networks, expanding the focus to include all stakeholders, and dealing with conflicting requirements. That's a tall order. It's a great idea, but is it only for the distant future? Is it wonderful only for that handful of organizations at the bleeding edge? Probably not. The principles of performance leadership are for everyone.

One of the lessons of the book is that copying best practices gets you only so far. We all know that from our personal lives too. Have you ever asked an older brother or sister to do your homework for you? And how well did you do on the test afterward? Dr. Stephen Covey, on whose lessons this book heavily relies, teaches us that we all have a choice and a responsibility for those choices. He also teaches us how to increase our circle of influence, our own performance network. Covey teaches us to think for ourselves. There are no typical "12 steps to success." There is no magic recipe for successful personal relationship or personal development. I have closely examined the best practices, sometimes defied conventional wisdom, and constructed a set of tools that allow us to think for ourselves. To grow to performance leadership means that the journey *itself* is the destination.

But the most important lesson from the book is that performance management is highly connected to behaviors of people. In many ways measurement drives behavior, so we need to understand those behaviors. Behaviors trigger actions, and actions lead to business performance (or not). People's behaviors, what we find important, and how we define performance, are highly related to their culture. In other words, *performance* comes from Venus; it is based on emotion, drive, and passion. But *management* comes from Mars, focusing on control, ratio, and obeying strict marching orders. Seen this way, performance management is a contradiction in terms.

In this book I referenced an industrial conglomerate with factories in France, the United States, and The Netherlands. The American business culture is all about contract and who you work for. The French business culture is about background, honor, and to which group you belong. The Dutch business culture focuses on consensus, where many business decisions are openly discussed and debated. While writing this book, and particularly this section on values, I all of a sudden realized that perhaps some of my conclusions and trains of thought might be driven by my own cultural background.

In the Dutch culture, performance indicators are there to debate. And, as I have pointed out repeatedly, that is exactly the point of performance management. Would that not work in the United States? I talked about business interface metrics that drive cross-domain collaboration. In The Netherlands, people are usually quick with providing advice, invited or uninvited, on someone else's activities, and we don't hold back. Would that work in France, where one group's "interfering" impacts on the feeling of honor of the other group?

Yet, I stick to my guns, because I like to think that you've just read a book about *relationships*. And, although how to deal with relationships may not be universally exactly the same, building relationships bridges many cultures. Moreover, it is something most of us have a lot of experience with. Many of the lessons in personal development directly relate to performance management.

In many of our performance management initiatives we think that we can manage our relationship with a partner or a client with a service level agreement. Would that work in our personal lives? Will we live happily ever after with our spouse or partner if we have clear targets and objectives as to whose task it is to clean out the dishwasher, do the laundry, clean the bathroom, take out the garbage, sweep the driveway, and paint the woodwork once in a while? Will we have a better relationship if we outsource all that work? I like to think it doesn't work that way. Granted, it does work the other way around. If there is no agreement as to who does which household tasks, it becomes a constant source of annoyance.

A happy relationship allows both partners to be *interdependent*, where each of the partners respects the other's values and views, but where both partners choose to share those with each other. In a happy relationship each of the partners is balanced and chooses to be aligned with the other. You do that by discussing your day over dinner or your dreams about the future while drinking a nice glass of wine in front of the fireplace. It's about sharing feelings and querying your partner about his or her emotions, trying to help each other to build a clear picture about yourself, your partner, and your relationship. We provide feedback to keep each other on a straight path; we honestly and deeply enjoy cleaning the courtyard or driveway because our partner will say "thank you" and smile. We give to get. The result is a mutually beneficial relationship. We add value to the relationship, instead of extracting it from the relationship.

Compare and contrast this to how we work with our partners in business. We set objectives, targets, and have service level agreements. We say "the numbers speak for themselves." In my view, numbers never speak for themselves; there is always a story behind them. The *most important purpose* of performance indicators is to trigger discussion between coworkers, inside and outside the organization, in order to create alignment. Alignment between the mind and the heart, between what people do within the organization and what people tell the outside world, between how the organization is being perceived by the different stakeholders, and how the organization perceives itself.

The performance network creates that alignment between the various stakeholders. It doesn't always mean that they have the same objectives or the same set of values, but building the performance network will make you discover the differences. In a true performance network, we are interdependent. In order to be successful, we need to make each other successful. Contrast this to the common best practice of focusing on shareholder value.

So, dear reader, my advice to you is to apply the lessons from your private life and how you deal with relationships in the business world. Do this by building alignment between all stakeholders in your company's performance network, instead of maximizing shareholder value. Make sure you are all on the same page. Visit www.performance-leadership-book.com and share your own experiences, for others to learn from. And start off your own journey toward performance leadership by giving a copy of this book to all the people you work with. My shareholders thank you.

NOTES

Chapter 1

1. There are subtle differences in the definition of a measure, a metric, and a key performance indicator (KPI), although there are no standard and commonly agreed-upon definitions. In general, a measure is a piece of gathered business data, such as "total." A metric is often presented in the form of a ratio, relating multiple measures, such as "average sales per employee." A KPI is a metric that is deemed of strategic importance to an organization. For practical purposes, I will use these terms interchangeably throughout this book.

2. Neely, A. (1998), *Measuring Business Performance: Why, What and How*, Economist Books, London.

3. McGee, J.V. (1992), *What Is Strategic Performance Measurement?* Ernst & Young Center for Business Innovation, Boston.

4. Gartner Inc. (2006), "Understand Performance Management to Better Manage Your Business," available at www.gartner.com.

5. Robbins, S.R. (1993), *Organizational Behavior*, Prentice Hall, Englewood Cliffs. N.J.

6. PEST analysis (also known as STEP analysis) stands for "Political, Economic, Social, and Technological analysis" and describes a framework of macroenvironmental factors used in environmental scanning. (Source: wikipedia.org, March 2006.)

7. Riel, C.B.M. van (1995), *Principles of Corporate Communication*, Prentice Hall, London.

Chapter 2

1. In this chapter, I provide a very short overview of performance management methodologies in order to create a baseline understanding. For more detailed information, visit www.performance-leadership-book.com,

2. Waal, A.A. de (2002), *Minder is Meer* (in Dutch), Holland Business Publication, Haarlem.

3. Accenture (2001), "Driving Value through Strategic Planning and Budgeting: A Research Report from the Cranfield School of Management and Accenture."

4. Hope, J.; Fraser, R. (2003), *Beyond Budgeting: How Managers Can Break Free from the Annual Performance Trap*, Harvard Business School Press, Boston.

5. Atrill, P. (2003), *Financial Management for Non-Specialists*, Prentice Hall, London.

6. Hansen, S.C.; Torok, R.G. (2004), *The Closed Loop: Implementing Activity Based Planning and Budgeting*, CAM-I and Bookman Publishing, Fort Worth.

7. This paragraph is largely based on the www.wikipedia.org entry on "Six Sigma."

8. http://www.dmreview.com/glossary/s.html

9. The majority of the text on CSF is based on Bullen, C.V., Rockart, J.F. (1981), *A Primer on Critical Success Factors*, Sloan School of Management, Cambridge, MA.; and Daniel, D.R. (Sep.–Oct. 1961), "Management Information Crisis," *Harvard Business Review*.

10. The text of EFQM is largely based on the paper called "EFQM: Introducing Excellence," 2003, www.efqm.org.

11. Kaplan, R.S.; Norton, D.P. (1996), *Balanced Scorecard: Translating Strategy into Action*, Harvard Business Press, Boston.

12. Brignall, T.J.S. (2002), "The Unbalanced Scorecard: A Social and Environmental Critique," *Performance Measurement and Management: Research and Action*, Performance Measurement Association, UK.; Nørreklit, H. (2000, No.11), "The Balance on the Balanced Scorecard—A Critical Analysis of Some of Its Assumptions, *Management Accounting Research*.

13. Maltz, A.C.; Shenhar, A.J.; Reilly, R.R. (2003, no. 36) "Beyond the Balanced Scorecard: Refining the Search for Organizational Success Measures," *Long Range Planning*.

14. Kaplan, R.S.; Norton, D.P. (2000), *The Strategy-Focused Organization: How Balanced Scorecard Companies Thrive in the New Business Environment*, Harvard Business School Press, Boston.

15. Neely, A.; Kennerley, M.; Martinez, V. (2004), "Does the Balanced Scorecard Work: An Empirical Investigation," Cranfield School of Management, PMA 2004 Conference, Edinburgh.

16. Argyris, C.; Schon, D. (1978), *Organizational Learning: A Theory of Action Perspective*, Addison-Wesley, Reading, MA.

17. Tiggelaar, B. (2006), *Dromen, Durven, Doen* (in Dutch), Spectrum, Utrecht.

Chapter 3

1. Marr, B. (2006), *Strategic Performance Management, Leveraging and Measuring Your Intangible Value Drivers*, Butterworth-Heinemann, Oxford.

2. Robbins, S.R. (1993), *Organizational Behavior*, Prentice Hall, Englewood Cliffs.

3. Academics do not agree on the validity of the Hawthorne effect. However, the Hawthorne principle is taught in every university and business school as an important principle in the social sciences, and teaches an important lesson. The Hawthorne effect describes "an experimental effect in the direction expected but not for the reason expected; i.e., a significant positive effect that turns out to have no causal basis in the theoretical motivation for the intervention, but is *apparently due to the effect on the participants of knowing themselves to be studied in connection with the outcomes measured*." See http://www.psy.gla.ac.uk/~steve/hawth.html#Hawthorne%20overall.

4. Ridgway, V.F. (1956), "Dysfunctional Consequences of Performance Measurement," *Administative Science Quarterly*.

5. Bititci, U., et al. (2004), "The Interplay Between Performance Measurement, Organizational Culture and Management Styles," *Performance Measurement and Management: Public and Private*, Performance Measurement Association, Edinburgh.

6. Ridgway, V.F. (1956).

7. Smith, M. (1995, Vol.18 No. 2/3)," On the Unintended Consequences of Publishing Performance Data in the Public Sector," *International Journal of Public Administration.*; Jackson, A. (2005, Vol.31 No. 1), "Falling from a Great Height: Principles of Good Practice in Performance Measurement and the Perils of Top Down Determination of Performance Indicators," *Local Government Studies*; Radnor, Z.J. (2005), "Developing a Typology of Organisational Gaming," European Group of Public Administration (EGPA) Conference, Bern, Switzerland.

8 Waal, A.A. de (2001), *Power of Performance Management. How Leading Companies Create Sustained Value*, John Wiley and Sons, New York.

9. Buytendijk, F.A.; Slaghuis-Brinkhuis, J. (2000), *Balanced Scorecard: Van Meten Naar Managen* (in Dutch), Wolters-Kluwer, Amsterdam.

10. Kerr, S. (1995), "On the Folly of Rewarding A, While Hoping for B," *Academy of Management Executives.*

Chapter 4

1. Geus, A. De (2002), *The Living Organization*, Harvard Business Press, Boston.

2. Collins, J.; Porras, J.I. (2004), *Built to Last: Successful Habits of Visionary Companies*, HarperCollins, New York.

3. Covey, S. (1989), *The Seven Habits of Highly Effective People*, Simon and Schuster, New York.

4. Covey, S. (2004), *The 8th Habit: From Effectiveness to Greatness*, Free Press, New York.

5. Kotter, J.P.; Heskett, J.L. (1992), *Corporate Culture and Performance*, Free Press, New York.

Chapter 5

1. Malone, T.W. (2004), *The Future of Work: How the New Order of Business Will Shape Your Organization, Your Management Style, and Your Life*, Harvard Business Press, Boston.

2. Schwartz, P. (1991), *The Art of the Long View: Planning for the Future in an Uncertain World*, Random House, New York.

Chapter 6

1. Buytendijk, F.A. (2007), "The Myth of the One Version of the Truth," White paper for software company Hyperion Solutions.

Chapter 7

1. Author interview with the former finance manager of Heineken, Cok van Boheemen (2006).

Chapter 8

1. COSO—Committee of Sponsoring Organizations of the Treadway Commission (2004), "Enterprise Risk Management—Integrated Framework Executive Summary," available at www.coso.org.

2. Basel Committee on Banking Supervision (2001), "Working Paper on the Regulatory Treatment of Operational Risk," available at www.bis.org.

3. www.wikipedia.org, "Financial risk management."

4. Eccles, R.G; Newquist, S.C.; Schatz, R. (Feb. 2007), "Reputation and Its Risks," *Harvard Business Review.*

5. According to wikipedia, Islamic banking refers to a system of banking or banking activity that is consistent with Islamic principles and guided by *Islamic economics*. For instance, in an Islamic *mortgage* transaction, instead of lending the buyer money to purchase the item, a bank might buy the

item itself from the seller, and resell it to the buyer at a profit, while allowing the buyer to pay the bank in installments.

Chapter 9

1. Idea taken from Trompenaars, F. (2003), *Did the Pedestrian Die?* Capstone, Oxford.

2. Loosely based on Rokeach, M. (1973), *The Nature of Human Values*, Free Press, New York.

3. Trompenaars, F. (1997), *Riding the Waves of Culture: Understanding Cultural Diversity in Business*, Nicholas Brealey Publishing, London.

4. Robbins, S.R. (1993), *Organizational Behavior*, Prentice Hall, Englewood Cliffs, NJ.

5. Ouchi, W.G. (1980, 25), "Markets, Bureaucracy and Clans," *Administative Science Quarterly*.

6. Collins, J. (Summer 1996), "Aligning Action and Values," *Leader to Leader*.

7. D'Iribarne, P. (1989), *Eer, Contract en Consensus* (in Dutch), Uitgeverij Nieuwezijds, Amsterdam.

8. Trompenaars, F. (1997), *Riding the Waves of Culture: Understanding Cultural Diversity in Business*, Nicholas Brealey Publishing, London; Hofstede, G. (2004), *Cultures and Organizations: Software of the Mind*, McGraw-Hill, London; Kluckhohn, F. Strodtbeck, F.L. (1961), *Variations in Value Orientations*, Row Peterson, Evanston, IL.

9. McGregor, D. (1960), *The Human Side of Enterprise*, McGraw-Hill, New York.

10. Riel, C.B.M. van (1995), *Principles of Corporate Communication*, Prentice Hall, London.

11. Olins, W. (1989), *Corporate Identity: Making Business Strategy Visible Through Design*, Thames & Hudson, London.

12. Ford, R.P. (Sep.-Oct. 1987), "The Importance of Image," *The Bankers Magazine*.

13. Although the terms *corporate identity/personality* and *corporate image* are more business-like than *self-perception* and *external perception*, I prefer the latter, as identity and image are terms very much connected with corporate communication.

14. www.ikea.com.

15. Kling, K.; Goteman, I. (2003, Vol 17, No. 1), "IKEA CEO Anders Dahlvig on International Growth and IKEA's Unique Corporate Culture and Brand Identity," *Academy of Management Executives*.

16. Edvardsson, B.; Enquist, B. (2002, Vol 22, No. 4), "The IKEA Saga: How Service Culture Drives Service Strategy," *Service Industries Journal.*

Chapter 10

1. GDP was compared with Net Revenue using http://www.indexmundi.com/g/r.aspx?t=100&v=65 (CIA Factbook) for the GDP of all countries on January 1, 2007, and http://money.cnn.com/magazines/fortune/fortune500/2007/full_list/index.html (Fortune 500) for the net revenue of the largest corporations per April 30, 2007.

2. Cook, C. (Jan. 22, 2005), "The Good Company: A Survey of Corporate Social Responsibility," *The Economist.*

3. ISO (2002), "Strategic Advisory Group on Corporate Social Responsibility: Preliminary Working Definition of Organizational Social Responsibility," International Organisation for Standardisation, Switzerland.

4. Commission Green Paper (2001), Promoting a European Framework for Corporate Social Responsibility, COM 2001 366 final, http://ec.europa.eu/employment_social/soc-dial/csr/greenpaper_en.pdf,

5. Friedman, M. (1962), *Capitalism and Freedom,* University of Chicago Press, Chicago.

6. Kaplan, R.S.; Norton D.P. (2004), *Strategy Maps: Converting Intangible Assets into Tangible Outcomes,* Harvard Business Press, Boston.

7. Drucker, P.F. (1977); *People and Performance: The Best of Peter Drucker on Management,* Butterworth-Heinemann, New York.

8. Porter, M.E.; Kramer, M.R (December 2006), "Strategy & Society: The Link between Competitive Advantage and Corporate Social Responsibility," *Harvard Business Review.*

9. Mintzberg, H. (1983, 4), "The Case for Corporate Social Responsibility," *The Journal of Business Strategy.*

10. Zadek, S. (December 2004), "The Path to Corporate Responsibility," *Harvard Business Review.*

11. www.nikeresponsibility.com.

12. Porter, Kramer (2006)

13. Prahalad, C.K.; Hart, S.L. (2002, Issue 26), "The Fortune at the Bottom of the Pyramid," *Strategy + Business.*

14. Bieker, T.; Gminder, C., (2001), *Towards a Sustainability Balanced Scorecard, Environmental Management & Policy and Related Aspects of Sustainability,* University of St. Gallen. Also: Figge, F.; Hahn, H.;

Schaltegger, S.; Wagner, M. (2002), "The Sustainability Balanced Scorecard—Theory and Application of a Tool for Value-Based Sustainability Management," Greening of Industry Network Conference on Corporate Social Responsibility—Governance for Sustainability, Gothenburg.

15. *Fortune* (Nov. 2007), "The 2007 Accountability Ranking."

16. *Manager Magazin* (2007, 2), Good Company Ranking, Germany.

17. Prahalad, C.K.; Hamel, G. (1994), *Competing for the Future*, Harvard Business Press, Boston.

18. Zadek, S. (November 12, 2007), "Inconvenient but True: Good Isn't Always Profitable, *Fortune*.

19. January 29, 2003, press release, "Europe's Largest Pension Fund Buys a Minority Stake in SRI Research Firm," available at http://www.socialfunds.com/news/article.cgi/1020.html.

20. Bissacco, I.; Spinelli, C.; Maccarrone, P. (2006), "The Measurement of the Degree of Corporate Social Responsibility of a Firm," *Performance Measurement and Management: Public and Private*.

21. Global Reporting Initiative (2002), "Sustainability Reporting Guidelines," available at www.globalreporting.org.

22. Author interview with Jani Rautiainen, manager, corporate reporting systems (October 2007); also, Metso's "Sustainability Report" (2006), available at www.metso.com.

23. Rabobank (2005), "Annual Sustainability Report," available at www.rabobankgroup.com, Netherlands.

Chapter 11

1. Mintzberg, H. (1983), *Power in and Around Organizations*, Prentice-Hall, Englewood Cliffs, NJ.

2. Smith, M.; Heady, R.B.; Carson (Phillips), P.; Carson, K.D. (2001, 6), "Do Missions Accomplish Their Mission? An Exploratory Analysis of Mission Statements and Organizational Longevity," *Journal of Applied Management and Entrepreneurship*.

3. www.bain.com.

4. Ahn, H. (2004), "Developing Individualized Balanced Scorecards: Status Quo and MCDM Approach," *Performance Measurement and Management: Public and Private*, Performance Measurement Association, Edinburgh.

5. Bart, C.K.; Bontis, N.; Taggar, S. (2001, 39/1), "A Model of the Impact of Mission Statements on Firm Performance," *Management Decision*.

6. Baetz, M.C.; Bart, C.K. (August 1996, Vol. 29), "Developing Mission Statements Which Work," *Long Range Planning*.

7. I have visited many different corporate Web sites, but drew a significant portion of the analysis from http://manonamission.blogspot.com/.

8. Collins, J. (Summer 1996), "Aligning Action and Values," *Leader to Leader*.

Chapter 12

1. Cohen, L.; Young, A. (2006), *Multisourcing: Moving Beyond Outsourcing to Achieve Growth and Agility*, Harvard Business Press, Boston.

2. Tapscott, D.; Ticol, D. (2003), *The Naked Corporation: How the Age of Transparency Will Revolutionize Business*, Free Press, New York.

3. Allee, V. (2002), *The Future of Knowledge: Increasing Prosperity through Value Networks*, Butterworth-Heinemann, Boston.

4. Douma, S.; Schreuder, H. (2002), *Economic Approaches to Organizations*, Pearson Education, London.

5. Hopwood, A.G. (1996, Vol. 21, No. 6), "Looking Across Rather Than Up and Down: On the Need to Explore the Lateral Processing of Information," *Accounting, Organizations and Society*.

6. Dyer, J. (1997, Vol. 18, No. 7), "Effective Interfirm Collaborations: How Firms Minimize Transaction Costs and Maximize Transaction Value," *Strategic Management Journal*.

7. Summary based on Barringer, B.R.; Harrison, J.S. (2000, Vol. 26, No. 3), "Walking a Tightrope: Creating Value through Interorganizational Relationships," *Journal of Management*.

8. Neely, A.; Adams, C.; Kennerley, M. (2002), *The Performance Prism: The Scorecard for Measuring and Managing Business Success*, Prentice Hall, London.

9. Although the case study is real, I have changed the name of the company and the industry in which it operates. However, the dynamics of the generic car parts industry are the same as in the original case.

10. Sako, M. (1992), *Prices, Quality and Trust: Inter-firm Relationships in Britain and Japan*, Cambridge University Press, Cambridge, UK.

11. Vosselman, E.G.J.; van der Meer-Kooistra, J. (2006, Vol. 19, No. 3), "Changing the Boundaries of the Firm: Adopting and Designing Efficient Management Control Structures," *Journal of Organizational Change Management*.

12. Yang, K.; Holzer, M. (Jan.-Feb. 2006), "The Performance-Trust Link: Implications for Performance Measurement," *Public Administration Review*.

BIBLIOGRAPHY

Accenture (2001), "Driving Value through Strategic Planning and Budgeting." Research report from Cranfield School of Management and Accenture, UK.

Ahn, H. (2004), "Developing Individualized Balanced Scorecards: Status Quo and MCDM Approach," paper presented at Performance Measurement and Management: Public and Private Conference, Performance Measurement Association, UK.

Allee, V. (2002), *The Future of Knowledge: Increasing Prosperity through Value Networks*, Butterworth-Heinemann, UK.

Argyris, C.; Schon, D. (1978), *Organizational Learning: A Theory of Action Perspective*, Addison-Wesley.

Atkinson, A.A.; Waterhouse, J.H.; Wells, R.B. (1997, Spring), "A Stakeholder Approach to Strategic Performance Measurement," *Sloan Management Review*.

Atrill, P. (2003), *Financial Management for Non-Specialists*, Prentice Hall, UK.

Baetz, M.C.; Bart, C.K. (1996, Vol. 29, August), "Developing Mission Statements Which Work," *Long Range Planning*.

Barringer, B.R.; Harrison, J.S. (2000, Vol. 26, No. 3), "Walking a Tightrope: Creating Value through Interorganizational Relationships," *Journal of Management*.

Bart, C.K.; Bontis, N.; Taggar, S. (2001, 39/1), "A Model of the Impact of Mission Statements on Firm Performance," *Management Decision*.

Basel Committee on Banking Supervision (2001), "Working Paper on the Regulatory Treatment of Operational Risk," available at www.bis.org

Bieker, T.; Gminder, C. (2001), "Towards a Sustainability Balanced Scorecard," paper presented at Environmental Management & Policy and

Related Aspects of Sustainability Conference, Switzerland. Available at www.oikosstiftung.unisg.ch/academy2001/Paper_Bieker_Gminder.pdf.

Bissacco, I.; Spinelli, C.; Maccarrone, P. (2006), "The Measurement of the Degree of Corporate Social Responsibility of a Firm," paper presented at Performance Measurement and Management: Public and Private Conference, Performance Measurement Association, UK.

Bititci, U.; et al. (2004), The Interplay Between Performance Measurement, Organizational Culture and Management Styles," paper presented at Performance Measurement and Management: Public and Private conference, Performance Measurement Association, UK.

Brignall, T.J.S. (2002), "The Unbalanced Scorecard: A Social and Environmental Critique," paper presented at Performance Measurement and Management: Research and Action conference, Performance Measurement Association, UK.

Bullen, C.V.; Rockart, J.F. (1981), *A Primer on Critical Success Factors*, Sloan School of Management.

Buytendijk, F.A. (2007), *The Myth Of The One Version of the Truth*, Hyperion Solutions.

Buytendijk, F.A.; Slaghuis-Brinkhuis, J. (2000), *Balanced Scorecard: Van Meten Naar Managen*, Wolters-Kluwer, Netherlands. (In Dutch.)

CFO Magazine (1998, Jan.), "Tis the Gift to Be Simple: Dupont's Framework for Financial Analysis," *CFO Magazine*.

Cohen, L.; Young, A. (2006), *Multisourcing: Moving Beyond Outsourcing to Achieve Growth and Agility*, Harvard Business Press.

Collins, J. (1996, Summer), "Aligning Action and Values," *Leader to Leader*.

Collins, J.; Porras, J.I. (2004), *Built to Last: Successful Habits of Visionary Companies*, HarperCollins.

Cook, C. (Jan. 22, 2005), "The Good Company: A Survey of Corporate Social Responsibility," *The Economist*.

Committee of Sponsoring Organizations of the Treadway Commission (2004), "Enterprise Risk Management—Integrated Framework Executive Summary," report available at www.coso.org.

Covey, S. (1989), *The Seven Habits of Highly Effective People*, Simon and Schuster.

Covey, S. (2004), *The Eighth Habit: From Effectiveness to Greatness*, Free Press.

Daniel, D.R. (1961, Sep.–Oct.), "Management Information Crisis," *Harvard Business Review*.

Deloitte (2007), "In the Dark II: What Many Boards and Executives STILL Don't Know About The Health of Their Business." Follow-up survey report available at www.deloitte.com.

D'Iribarne, P. (1989); Eer, *Contract en Consensus*, Uitgeverij Nieuwezijds, Netherlands. In Dutch.

Douma, S.; Schreuder, H. (2002), *Economic Approaches to Organizations*, Pearson Education, UK.

Drucker, P.F. (1977), *People and Performance: The Best of Peter Drucker on Management*, Butterworth-Heinemann, UK.

Dyer, J. (1997, Vol. 18, No. 7), "Effective Interfirm Collaborations: How Firms Minimize Transaction Costs and Maximize Transaction Value," *Strategic Management Journal*.

Eccles, R.G.; Newquist, S.C.; Schatz, R. (2007, Feb.), "Reputation and Its Risks," *Harvard Business Review*.

Edvardsson, B.; Enquist, B. (2002, Vol. 22, No. 4), "The IKEA Saga: How Service Culture Drives Service Strategy," *Service Industries Journal*.

Figge, F.; Hahn, H.; Schaltegger, S.; Wagner, M. (2002), "The Sustainability Balanced Scorecard—Theory and Application of a Tool for Value-Based Sustainability Management," Greening of Industry Network Conference Corporate Social Responsibility—Governance for Sustainability.

Ford, R.P. (1987, Sep.–Oct.), "The Importance of Image," *The Bankers Magazine*.

Fortune (2007, Nov.), "The 2007 Accountability Ranking," *Fortune Magazine*.

Friedman, M. (1962), *Capitalism and Freedom*, University of Chicago Press

Gartner Inc. (2006), "Understand Performance Management to Better Manage Your Business," available at www.gartner.com.

Geus, A. De (2002), *The Living Organization*, Harvard Business School Press.

Global Reporting Initiative (2002), "Sustainability Reporting Guidelines," available at www.globalreporting.org.

Hansen, S.C.; Torok, R.G. (2004), *The Closed Loop: Implementing Activity Based Planning and Budgeting*, CAM-I and Bookman Publishing.

Hofstede, G. (2004), *Cultures and Organizations: Software of the Mind*, McGraw-Hill.

Hope, J.; Fraser, R. (2003), *Beyond Budgeting: How Managers Can Break Free from the Annual Performance Trap*, Harvard Business School Press.

Hopwood, A.G. (1996, Vol. 21, No. 6), "Looking Across Rather Than Up and Down: On the Need to Explore the Lateral Processing of Information," *Accounting, Organizations and Society*.

ISO (2002), "Strategic Advisory Group on Corporate Social Responsibility: Preliminary Working Definition of Organizational Social Responsibility," Report prepared by the International Organisation for Standardisation, Switzerland.

Itner, C.D.; Larcker, D.F. (2003, Nov.), "Coming Up Short on Nonfinancial Performance Measurement," *Harvard Business Review*.

Jackson, A. (2005, Vol. 31, No. 1), "Falling from a Great Height: Principles of Good Practice in Performance Measurement and the Perils of Top Down Determination of Performance Indicators," *Local Government Studies*.

Kaplan, R.S.; Norton, D.P. (1996), *Balanced Scorecard: Translating Strategy into Action*, Harvard Business Press.

Kaplan, R.S.; Norton, D.P. (1996, Jan.-Feb.), "Using the Balanced Scorecard as a Strategic Management System," *Harvard Business Review*.

Kaplan, R.S.; Norton, D.P. (2000), *The Strategy-Focused Organization: How Balanced Scorecard Companies Thrive in the New Business Environment*, Harvard Business School Press.

Kaplan, R.S.; Norton, D.P. (2004), *Strategy Maps: Converting Intangible Assets into Tangible Outcomes*, Harvard Business Press.

Kerr, S. (1995, Feb.), "On the Folly of Rewarding A, While Hoping for B," *Academy of Management Journal*.

Kim, W.C.; Mauborgne, R. (2005), *Blue Ocean Strategy: How to Create Uncontested Market Space and Make Competition Irrelevant*, Harvard Business Press.

Kling, K.; Goteman, I. (2003, Vol. 17, No. 1), "IKEA CEO Anders Dahlvig on International Growth and IKEA's Unique Corporate Culture and Brand Identity," *Academy of Management Journal*.

Kluckhohn, F.; Strodtbeck, F.L. (1961), *Variations in Value Orientations*, Row Peterson.

Kotter, J.P.; Heskett, J.L. (1992), *Corporate Culture and Performance*, Free Press.

Malone, T.W. (2004), *The Future of Work: How the New Order of Business Will Shape Your Organization, Your Management Style, and Your Life*, Harvard Business Press.

Maltz, A.C.; Shenhar, A.J.; Reilly, R.R. (2003, No. 36), "Beyond the Balanced Scorecard: Refining the Search for Organizational Success Measures," *Long Range Planning*, UK.

Manager Magazin. (2007, 2), "Good Company Ranking," *Manager Magazin*, Germany. (In German.)

Marr, B. (2006), *Strategic Performance Management, Leveraging and Measuring Your Intangible Value Drivers*, Butterworth-Heinemann, UK.

McGee, J.V. (1992), *What Is Strategic Performance Measurement?* Ernst & Young Center for Business Innovation.

McGregor, D. (1960), *The Human Side of Enterprise*, McGraw-Hill.

Minton, S. (2007), "IT Market Outlook 2008: The Information Explosion," available at www.idc.com,

Mintzberg, H. (1983), *Power in and around Organizations*, Prentice-Hall.

Mintzberg, H. (1983, 4), "The Case for Corporate Social Responsibility," *The Journal of Business Strategy*.

Neely, A. (1998), *Measuring Business Performance: Why, What, and How*, Economist Books, UK.

Neely, A.; Adams, C.; Kennerley, M., (2002), *The Performance Prism: The Scorecard for Measuring and Managing Business Success*, Prentice Hall, UK.

Neely, A.; Kennerley, M.; Martinez, V. (2004), *Does the Balanced Scorecard Work: An Empirical Investigation*, Cranfield School of Management, UK.

Nørreklit, H. (2000, No.11), "The Balance on the Balanced Scorecard—A Critical Analysis of Some of Its Assumptions," *Management Accounting Research*.

Olins, W. (1989), *Corporate Identity: Making Business Strategy Visible through Design*, Thames & Hudson.

Ouchi, W.G. (1980, 25), "Markets, Bureaucracy, and Clans," *Administative Science Quarterly*.

Porter, M.E; Kramer, M.R. (2006, December), "Strategy and Society: The Link between Competitive Advantage and Corporate Social Responsibility," *Harvard Business Review*.

Prahalad, C.K.; Hamel, G. (1994), *Competing for the Future*, Harvard Business Press.

Prahalad, C.K.; Hart, S.L. (2002, Issue 26), "The Fortune at the Bottom of the Pyramid," *Strategy + Business*.

Rabobank (2005), "Annual Sustainability Report," available at www.rabobankgroup.com.

Radnor, Z.J. (2005), "Developing a Typology of Organisational Gaming," presented at the European Group of Public Administration (EGPA) Conference, Bern, Switzerland.

Ridgway, V.F. (1956), "Dysfunctional Consequences of Performance Measurement," *Administrative Science Quarterly.*

Riel, C.B.M. van (1995), *Principles of Corporate Communication*, Prentice Hall, UK.

Robbins, S.R. (1993), *Organizational Behavior*, Prentice Hall International, UK.

Rokeach, M. (1973), *The Nature of Human Values*, Free Press.

Sako, M. (1992), *Prices, Quality, and Trust: Inter-Firm Relationships in Britain and Japan*, Cambridge University Press, UK.

Schwartz, P. (1991), *The Art of the Long View: Planning for the Future in an Uncertain World*, Random House.

Smith, M; Heady, R. B.; Carson (Phillips), P.; Carson, K. D., (2001, 6), "Do Missions Accomplish Their Mission? An Exploratory Analysis of Mission Statements and Organizational Longevity," *Journal of Applied Management and Entrepreneurship.*

Smith, M., (1995, Vol. 18, No. 2/3), "On the Unintended Consequences of Publishing Performance Data in the Public Sector, *International Journal of Public Administration.*

Smith, M., (1998, Vol. 76), "Measuring Organizational Effectiveness," *Management Accounting CIMA.*

Stewart, G.B. (1990), *The Quest for Value: The EVA ™ Management Guide*, HarperBusiness.

Tapscott, D.; Ticol, D. (2003), *The Naked Corporation: How the Age of Transparency Will Revolutionize Business*, Free Press.

Tiggelaar, B. (2006), *Dromen, Durven, Doen*, Spectrum, Netherlands. In Dutch.

Trompenaars, F. (1997), *Riding the Waves of Culture: Understanding Cultural Diversity in Business*, Nicholas Brealey Publishing, UK.

Trompenaars, F. (2003), *Did the Pedestrian Die?* Capstone.

Vosselman, E.G.J.; van der Meer-Kooistra, J. (2006, Vol. 19, No. 3), Changing the Boundaries of the Firm: Adopting and Designing Efficient Management Control Structures, *Journal of Organizational Change Management.*

Waal, A. de; Counet, H. (2006), *Lessons Learned from the Balanced Scorecard, Performance Measurement and Management: Public and Private*, Performance Measurement Association, UK.

Waal, A.A. de (2001), *Power of Performance Management: How Leading Companies Create Sustained Value*, John Wiley and Sons.

Waal, A.A. de (2002), *Minder Is Meer*, Holland Business Publication, Netherlands. (In Dutch.)

Yang, K.; Holzer, M. (2006, Jan.–Feb. 2006), "The Performance-Trust Link: Implications for Performance Measurement," *Public Administration Review*.

Zadek, S. (2007, Nov. 12), "Inconvenient but True: Good Isn't Always Profitable," *Fortune Magazine*.

Zadek, S. (2004, Dec.), "The Path to Corporate Responsibility," *Harvard Business Review*.

INDEX

CPSIA information can be obtained at www.ICGtesting.com
Printed in the USA
LVOW10*2035050214

372537LV00003B/8/P